Goldwork Embroidery
DESIGNS AND PROJECTS

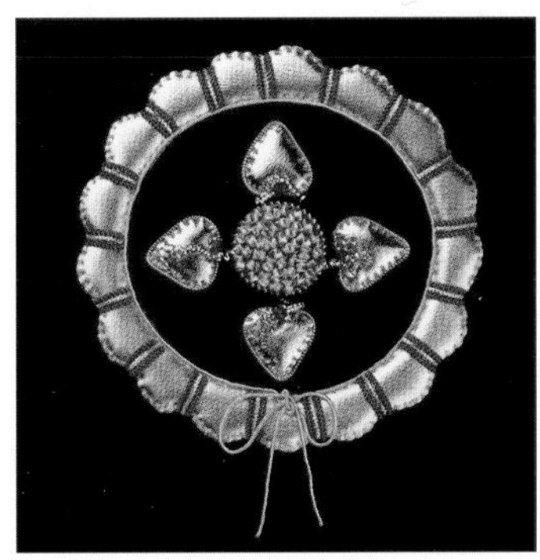

MARY BROWN

In memory of my mother, Elizabeth Sawyer

First published in 2007 by
Sally Milner Publishing Pty Ltd
734 Woodville Road
Binda NSW 2583
AUSTRALIA

Design: Anna Warren, Warren Ventures Pty Ltd
Editing: Anne Savage
Photography: Tim Connolly
Illustrations: Wendy Gorton

Printed in China

National Library of Australia Cataloguing-in-Publication data:

Brown, Mary Elizabeth, 1947- .
Goldwork embroidery : designs and projects.

Bibliography.
ISBN 9781863513661.

1. Gold embroidery. I. Title. (Series : Milner craft series).

746.44

10 9 8 7 6 5 4 3 2 1

Disclaimer

The information in this instruction book is presented in good faith. However, no warranty is given, nor results guaranteed, nor is freedom from any patent to be inferred. Since we have no control over the use of information contained in this book, the publisher and the author disclaim liability for untoward results.

Acknowledgements

In 2000–2001, I undertook the Certificated Course at the Royal School of Needlework. I am indebted to this institution and its tutors for being in the position today of writing a book on goldwork embroidery. My initial thanks must go to Elizabeth Elvin, Gill Holdsworth and my tutors at the Royal School of Needlework.

My profound thanks are now due to several people, my precious husband Philip being the first. He accompanied me when I went overseas for five months to research this book, and on our return he assumed my responsibilities in the home, without neglecting his own, so that I could devote my entire time and energy to writing, designing and embroidering. Two other wonderful people have gone beyond the call of duty to accommodate me—Althea Mackenzie, both Curator of the Wade Collection at Berrington Hall and Curator of Costumes and Textiles at Hereford Museum and Art Gallery, and Richard Blakey, who is responsible for so many of the beautiful photographs of historical items. William Kentish Barnes and his wife Diana are also two very special people. I have called upon William's expertise so many times and he has been more than prepared to assist me in gathering and clarifying the technical information on the metal threads. My two dear friends, Pam and Stan Zeal, ferried me to the Museum of Welsh Life in Cardiff and to Abergavenny and Skenfrith. Margaret Hall-Townley, Barbara Dawson and Janice Rawlinson very graciously allowed me into their homes to talk about their work, and Anthea Godfrey invited me to spend time in her home viewing her mother, Margaret Nicholson's, work. Anthea was also more than happy to photograph Margaret's work for the book. Alistair Macleod, Frances Sinclair and Carne Griffiths of Hand & Lock, the embroidery firm in London, have been particularly supportive. Toni McCrohan gave me a week of her time to work on the samples, to dress frames and to proofread the instructions for the projects. Karen Torrisi likewise helped with the samples, dressed many frames and totally worked two of my designs—Horus Eye and White Poppy. Helen Parsons very graciously accepted the task of pre-editing the historical section, and spent a couple of days with me to complete the task of proofreading the instructions for the projects. To all of you, your contribution has been significant and invaluable.

I am also very appreciative of the help given by Phyllis Magidson and Faye Haun at the

Museum of the City of New York; Edwina Erhman and Beth Thomas at the Museum of London; Deanna Cross at the Metropolitan Museum of Art, New York; Elaine Morris at the Victoria & Albert Museum, London; Lowri Jenkins and Catherine Bevan at the Museum of Welsh Life, Cardiff; Jeremy Farrell at Nottingham Museum, and Sarah Wood, Dorothy Tucker and Lynn Szygenda at the Embroiderers' Guild, Hampton Court Palace.

Lastly, an enormous thank-you to my two sons Nicolas and Reuben, and to my daughter-in-law Sian Evans; along with Philip, they have made the path to creating this book smooth and easy in so many ways.

Contents

Introduction

Goldwork is a hold-all term referring to the technique of embroidering with metal threads, not just gold threads. Goldwork embroidery has very ancient roots, having originated some two thousand years ago in the Middle East and moving west to become firmly established in European embroidery practice by the seventh century AD.

Traditionally, in Britain and Europe, goldwork embroidery appeared on ecclesiastical vestments and church furnishings, on ceremonial dress and accoutrements, and on court costumes and domestic furnishings destined for royal and aristocratic households. It was an ostentatious display of power and wealth. With metal threads being very expensive, at times even attracting sumptuary laws because of their scarcity, and with the techniques for their use requiring a long apprenticeship, for centuries thereafter this form of embroidery remained for the most part out of the reach of embroiderers not in the service of church or court.

In the mid-20th century, however, embroiderers and workers in many other disciplines in the arts begin experimenting with traditional techniques. Artists with very little knowledge of embroidery techniques were exploiting fabrics and threads as a means of expression. With the period's increasing focus on the representation of ideas rather than technical expertise, embroidered works became expressive and conceptual and came to be deemed art objects rather than craft objects. In the modern context, metal thread, above all other threads, had potential as a fine art medium because of its conceptual and historical associations and sensual properties. In the 1960s the picture panel and the wall hanging replaced costume as the preferred secular vehicle for the artist embroiderer. Some of the more progressive clergy commissioned artist embroiderers, especially those who worked with metal threads, to do ecclesiastical work. Thus the conceptual content of ecclesiastical embroidery and the format of church vestments remain amenable to the artist embroiderer after many hundreds of years.

As cheaper versions of the traditional metal threads became available in the latter half of the 20th century, lay embroiderers fascinated with their scintillating effects could feel less inhibited about using them to create their own sumptuous works. One can now say that goldwork embroidery has rightfully been democratised.

Section I covers the background and techniques of goldwork embroidery. Because it is impossible to cover its entire history in the Western world, let alone the East, in a book that is primarily a project book, in the first chapter I focus on the history of goldwork embroidery in Britain, in a brief overview mentioning embroidery generated in European countries only if it had a bearing on the British scene or made a contribution that could not be overlooked.

Chapter 2 briefly explores the technology of metal thread production.

Chapter 3 covers the materials, equipment and preparation process required to set up a project, while chapter 4 covers goldwork techniques. The methods I describe reflect my training at the Royal School of Needlework. Acquaint yourself with the various techniques before embarking on a project. In the instructions for the projects I have not repetitively described the most frequently used techniques, therefore you will need to refer back to this chapter quite frequently. Any technique out of the ordinary is described and illustrated within the instructions for that project.

In section II many of the projects reference the techniques and designs seen in the gold-embroidered costumes and textiles which I examined in the United Kingdom and the United States in 2005–2006. Having emphasised techniques rather than style or content in chapter 1, in the hope that this will lead the goldwork embroiderer into exploring the techniques of the past in their own work, in the same way, I would like to see my projects used as a platform for acquiring new skills for original work.

I would like to think that this book will be the catalyst for many of you to be able to create wondrous and original works in this field of embroidery.

MARY BROWN, 2007

SECTION I:

BACKGROUND AND TECHNIQUES

1. A Brief History of Goldwork Embroidery

There is no absolute evidence of gold embroidery in the British Isles before the 7th century AD; by contrast there is much written evidence of a rich tradition of gold embroidery embellishing costumes and furnishings in Mesopotamia and the Levant before the birth of Christ. When the Roman emperor Constantine founded an Eastern imperial city in Byzantium, the Western empire was able to access the opulent textiles and embroideries being produced there, as well as those in the Middle East. The importance of this contact with the East on the development of Western European textiles and embroidery is inestimable.

Literary references to royal and noble English gold embroiderers date back to the 7th century. The earliest mention is of St Etheldreda, who founded a convent on the Isle of Ely in East Anglia in 673 and gifted ecclesiastical vestments which she had embroidered herself with gold thread and precious stones to St Cuthbert.

The earliest extant examples of English embroidery featuring goldwork are the much deteriorated 'Maaseik fragments' in Belgium, dated late 8th to early 9th century. The fragments feature gold threads surface-couched on a background embroidered in split and stem stitch with coloured silk threads. The pure gold threads were flattened and wound onto a single strand of animal hair.

The most renowned pre-Norman Conquest examples of English embroidery are the beautifully preserved St Cuthbert Stole and Maniple, now on display in the library of Durham Cathedral. Inscriptions on the reverse of both pieces tell us they were made at the behest of Queen Aelfflaed (died 916) to give to Fridestan, Bishop of Winchester from 901 to 931. The figures of Old Testament prophets, popes and attendants, foliage and lettering on these two pieces are embroidered in split stitch using very fine silk threads, with stem-stitched outlines in a heavier silk. The background is covered entirely with gold laid work running vertically and surface-couched with red silk. The laid-work threads are of pure gold flattened and wound around a core of red silk. The gold threads within the haloes are laid horizontally and couched in various diaper patterns. Gold threads are used to define the folds of the garments, the hillocks and the veins of the acanthus leaves.

Medieval goldwork: 12th to 15th centuries

A history of goldwork embroidery in the West usually unfolds with the *opus anglicanum* (English work) period, the term referring to the ecclesiastical embroideries made in England from the 12th to the 15th century. The embroiderers of *opus anglicanum*, which reached its peak between 1250 and 1350, the period when England was building its great Gothic cathedrals, were highly respected and their work much sought after on the Continent, with the result that a large proportion of surviving examples are to be found in the cathedral treasuries and the museums of Europe. The 13th and 14th century popes particularly prized English ecclesiastical vestments. A Vatican inventory of 1295 listed 113 *opus anglicanum* embroideries, far exceeding in number any other form in their collection.

The most significant technique used in *opus anglicanum* is underside couching. In this method the couching thread, which is silk or linen, is brought up through the fabric, passed across the metal thread, returned through the same hole it came up in and pulled firmly to take a small loop of the metal thread through to the back of the background fabric. The couching thread actually runs through these loops of metal thread at the back. Intricate diaper patterns can still be created on the surface of underside couching, but they are more discreet than they are in surface couching because it is the little depressions created by pulling the metal thread down into the fabric, which creates the pattern and not the actual couching stitches. This way of working with metal threads allowed the garment to flow and move, whereas surface couching made the garment rigid.

When and how did underside couching supersede surface couching in English embroidery? This form of couching does not appear on extant 13th and 14th Byzantine embroideries so it is unlikely that it came from this source, but it is known that the Muslim Fatamid rulers introduced new silk weaving and embroidery techniques into Spain and Sicily when they occupied this region of the Mediterranean in the 7th century.

The Normans conquered Sicily in 1077 (the famous Norman invasion of England occurred in 1066). During the Norman occupation, the Norman rulers embraced the Fatamids' magnificent lifestyle, which kept the island's textile industries flourishing. In the 11th and 12th centuries, the royal workshops at Palermo became famous for their ecclesiastical and court embroidery, including the 'Coronation' Mantle and Dalmatic of the Norman ruler, Roger II, which are now on display in the Schatzkammer Museum, Vienna. Both are decorated with stylised Arabic motifs, which have been worked in gold using the underside couching technique. Muslim artisans made these two costumes, so one could rightly assume that there was a tradition of using this form of couching in the Middle East.

When did underside couching appear in England? A chasuble in a set of vestments, believed to have been used by St Thomas of Canterbury when he was exiled in 1164, in the treasury of Sens Cathedral in France is of great interest because the embroidery which appears on its neck is embroidered with underside-couched gold and the pattern of scrolling stems is typical of English work at this time. A pair of late 12th century episcopal sandals and buskins (bishop's long stockings), discovered in the tomb of Archbishop Walter at Canterbury, are embroidered with gold and silver in underside couching on a silk background. It can therefore be assumed that embroiderers in the train of the Norman conquerors introduced the technique into England, probably towards the end of the 11th century, and if not then certainly sometime during the 12th.

The great period of *opus anglicanum* embroidery lasted from the mid-13th to the mid-14th century. Many well-preserved ecclesiastical vestments, mostly copes and chasubles, have survived from what is considered the period of highest achievement in the history of Western European embroidery. The cope is a semi-circular shape with a radius of almost 150 cm (5 feet), open at the front. The chasuble is slipped over the head.

Gold threads were used lavishly in *opus anglicanum*. If the ground fabric was linen, the entire background was worked in gold and the figures worked in silk (although the renowned Syon Cope in the Victoria & Albert Museum in London is embroidered in the reverse way). If the ground fabric was silk or velvet, only the figures were worked in gold.

Silk threads are used in a split stitch so fine and dense that the stitches coalesce, which explains why *opus anglicanum* embroidery was also described as *acu pictura*, the Latin term for 'painting with a needle'.

At the time the St Cuthbert Stole and Maniple were made, the metal wound around the silk cores for embroidery was pure gold. By the *opus anglicanum* period the metal was silver-gilt, silver plated with gold. The floss-silk threads, imported from the Levant, came in varying thicknesses, the finest being used for faces and hands. *Opus anglicanum* embroideries were sometimes further embellished with pearls, semi-precious stones and gold and silver ornaments.

The embroidery was worked on linen or silk twill or, towards the end of the period, lustrous velvet. Linen grounds were used when the intention was to cover the background entirely with stitching, and two layers were required: a fine linen on top, a coarser one underneath. Silk grounds were usually lined with linen unless the fabric was very heavy. By the 1330s velvet, a sumptuous material in its own right, offered an alternative, but the pile made it difficult to embroider directly onto it. Thus the velvet ground was given an overlay of fine linen or silk as well as a lining of linen, and the embroidery worked through all layers. On completion, the exposed parts of the overlay were cut away.

The cartoons (designs) for *opus anglicanum* ecclesiastical embroidery may well have been drawn by artists who designed manuscript illuminations, for the two art forms have much in common. The finest age of *opus anglicanum* fell within the Gothic period, when there was a renewed interest in the natural world, and figures became more naturalistic and animated, conveying profound human emotions through facial expressions and gestures. A medieval cope presented a very large and difficult semi-circular format, and the numerous biblical narrative scenes and images of saints had to be united within some form of framework, a problem resolved by referencing contemporary architecture. We see frameworks such as concentric rows of interlocking quatrefoils being employed, as in the Syon Cope, or rows of Gothic arcading, as in the Pienza Cope, on display in the Diocesan Museum of Pienza in Italy.

Chichester-Constable chasuble, 14th century, English. Back view of the chasuble. By kind permission of the Metropolitan Museum of Art, Fletcher Fund 1927.

The Chichester-Constable chasuble in the Metropolitan Museum of Art in New York, an example of later *opus anglicanum*, has been dated 1330–1350. It has been cut down from a cope, as indicated by the truncated figures on the side of the chasuble.

The sacred scenes on this chasuble are depicted under ogee arches supported by intertwined leafy oak stems decorated with lion masks. There are angels holding stars in the spandrels. Three scenes are arranged hierarchically, with the most important, the Virgin's coronation, at the top; directly beneath is the Adoration of the Kings and below that the Annunciation.

Besides underside couching and split stitching, the Chichester-Constable chasuble features raised work to indicate the veins on the oak leaves, laid silk work with surface-couched trellis stitch using silver-gilt threads on the Virgin's throne and on the decorative borders of the garments, and satin stitch using silver-gilt and silver threads, mainly to embroider the angels' wing feathers. Interesting textures are created with underside couching. For example, the metal threads on the acanthus leaves have been couched to create the illusion that they were laid in pairs. The couching also created a brick pattern on the leaves. The metal threads on the architectural tracing have been couched and bricked as single threads.

Gold embroidery was also employed on royal and aristocratic costumes and domestic furnishings during the medieval period. Countless examples appear in 14th century English and French royal accounts. Two gloriously extravagant and light-hearted concoctions were created for a very wealthy young man, Roger Mortimer, 4th Earl of March, for the Christmas and New Year festivities of 1393–94:

> a white satin doublet embroidered in gold with orange trees on which hung one hundred silver-gilt oranges, and a 'hancelyn', also of white satin, which was embroidered with leeches, water and rocks, and amongst which were placed fifteen silver-gilt mussels and fifteen silver-gilt whelks.[1]

1 Kay Staniland, *Medieval Craftsmen Embroiderers*. British Museum Press: 1991, p 148

Chichester-Constable chasuble, 14th century, English. Detail of the Adoration of the Magi on the centre back of the chasuble. By kind permission from the Metropolitan Museum of Art, Fletcher Fund 1927.

Needlework historians Mary Symonds and Louisa Preece noted:

> The inventory of Thomas Woodstock, Earl of Gloucester, made in 1397 lists his embroidered beds. He owned a large bed of blue baudekyn (silk woven with threads of gold for royalty, nobility and the church) embroidered with silver owls and fleurs-de-lys ... a large bed of white satin embroidered with his arms and helm in Cyprus gold ...[2]

By the mid-13th century, so many orders were coming in from home and abroad for *opus anglicanum* work that merchants set up professional embroidery workshops, mainly in London, to meet the demand.

English ecclesiastical embroidery changed dramatically after the mid-14th century. We see the reappearance of surface couching, a less demanding and painstaking technique than underside couching. The delicate split stitch was replaced with stem stitch, brick stitch, satin stitch and long-and-short stitch using thicker floss-silk threads. The adoption of quicker and cheaper methods of stitching may have been necessary to fill the numerous orders more quickly.

By the late 14th century, church robes were being made in sumptuous woven silks and velvets, and the only parts to carry the characteristic dense embroidery of *opus anglicanum* were the decorative bands called 'orphreys', usually in the form of a cross for the back of a chasuble and a pillar for the front, and the shield-like hood on the back of a cope. Orphreys were also used along the entire straight edge of copes. The orphreys and the hoods were embroidered on linen and then appliquéd onto the vestments.

At the same time there was a shift from the linear and delicate *opus anglicanum* style to a more weighty and sculptural style, possibly influenced by contemporaneous European, especially German, ecclesiastical embroidery, which was worked in padded relief. By the 15th century, raised work was very much a feature of English ecclesiastical embroidery, mostly in the form of string padding under silver-gilt threads to create diaper patterns across backgrounds, but also used on figures and architectural elements. Surface couching enabled the embroiderers to undertake the raised sculptural work not possible with underside couching.

Embroiderers were not totally reliant on this more corporeal means of realism; they also used foreshortening to create the illusion of depth, following developments in contemporary painting. The flat and whimsical Gothic tracery of the arches which had previously framed biblical narratives was replaced by solid exterior architectural settings. The saints stand in entrances which lead into interior spaces and the foreshortened sides of the entrances create at least a shallow sense of depth.

The biblical scene most favoured for the orphrey cross is the Crucifixion, with angels at either end of the arms of the cross holding chalices to collect the flowing blood of Christ. Two representations of the Virgin Mary also appear on 15th century copes: the Virgin nursing her child on her knee was usually the designated scene for the hood and the Assumption featured on the centre back.

These central subjects were surrounded by

2 Mary Symonds and Louisa Preece, *Needlework Through the Ages*, quoted in Rozsika Parker, *The Subversive Stitch: Embroidery and the Making of the Feminine*. The Women's Press, p 41

The back view of the cross orphrey and powder motifs on the early 16th century, English red velvet chasuble in the Catholic Church of Our Lady and St Michael, Abergavenny, Wales. By kind permission of Father Thomas Regan. Photography by Richard Blakey.

isolated decorative motifs which are referred to as 'powderings' because they are sprinkled across the expanse of velvet. The most common were six-winged seraphim-on-wheels, double-headed eagles, Tudor roses, thistles and fleurs-de-lys (a stylisation of the lilies known as 'Mary's flowers' in the medieval period), mass produced in workshops as appliqués. Once they were attached, an arrangement of lines and spangles was added to soften the contrast between the gold appliqués and the dark background. These powderings and rays were peculiar to English embroidery, right up to the Reformation in the 16th century.

Good examples of pre-Reformation English vestments can be seen at Skenfrith and Abergavenny in South Wales. The red velvet Skenfrith Cope complete with orphrey and hood, in the Church of St Bridget, has been fully extended into its semi-circular shape and is displayed behind glass which is covered at all times by a curtain. It is, unfortunately, in a sadly worn condition. There is still a considerable amount of silver-gilt thread on the Virgin's mantle, laid vertically and surface-couched with cream floss silk. Her gown was worked in yellow and green floss-silk threads in long-and-short stitch.

Appliqués of six-winged seraphim-on-wheels, double-headed eagles, fleurs-de-lys and other floral motifs are powdered over the rest of the velvet ground. On some of them the linen grounds are still well covered with surface-couched metal threads and floss-silk threads.

Detail of a seraphim on the early 16th century, English red velvet chasuble in the Catholic Church of Our Lady and St Michael, Abergavenny, Wales. By kind permission from Father Thomas Regan. Photography by Richard Blakey.

Detail of a fleur-de-lys on the early 16th century, English red velvet chasuble in the Catholic Church of Our Lady and St Michael, Abergavenny, Wales. By kind permission from Father Thomas Regan. Photography by Richard Blakey.

On the hood there are mere vestiges of silver-gilt threads on the Virgin's mantle but substantial areas of silk laid work remain on the canopy above her. The once brilliant yellow floss-silk threads are laid vertically and anchored with horizontal parallel lines of silk threads in the same colour.

At Abergavenny, the Catholic Church of our Lady and St Michael hosts a collection of wonderful pre-Reformation vestments. I have chosen to describe an original red velvet chasuble and the Wharton chasuble pillar and cross orphreys, which have been remounted on cream silk in recent times.

It has been proposed that this red velvet chasuble came from the same workshop as the Skenfrith Cope, but there are so many technical and stylistic differences between the powder motifs on the two that these elements at least were surely made in different workshops. The embroidery on the Skenfrith cope's orphrey and hood is too threadbare to make a comparison with the well-preserved orphrey on the Abergavenny chasuble, so it remains possible that these parts came out of the same workshop. Seraphim-on-wheels and fleurs-de-lys have been appliquéd on both, the colour scheme is the same and much use has been made of spangles, but that is where the similarity ends.

The seraphim on the Abergavenny chasuble feature more padded relief and the metal threads are laid more closely and couched with greater care than those on the Skenfrith cope. The

The 16th century Wharton pillar orphrey remounted on a cream silk damask chasuble in the Catholic Church of Our Lady and St Michael, Abergavenny, Wales. By kind permission of Father Thomas Regan. Photography by Richard Blakey.

Left: The 16th century Wharton cross orphrey remounted on a cream silk damask chasuble in the Catholic Church of Our Lady and St Michael, Abergavenny, Wales. By kind permission of Father Thomas Regan. Photography by Richard Blakey.

appliqués on the Abergavenny chasuble are outlined in blue or yellow floss-silk thread and couched with the same colour, whereas those on the Skenfrith cope are outlined with metal threads and couched in blue and yellow.

The iconography of the cross orphreys on the Wharton and red velvet Abergavenny chasubles is the same but the embroidery on the Wharton orphrey is technically far more proficient.

The backgrounds of the Crucifixion scenes of both orphreys are embroidered with metal threads couched over string padding to create diaper patterns. On the red velvet chasuble, a

Detail of the Crucifixion scene on the cross orphrey on the early 16th century, English red velvet chasuble in the Catholic Church of Our Lady and St Michael, Abergavenny, Wales. By kind permission from Father Thomas Regan. Photography by Richard Blakey.

Detail of the Crucifixion scene on the 16th century Wharton cross orphrey in the Catholic Church of Our Lady and St Michael, Abergavenny, Wales. By kind permission from Father Thomas Regan. Photography by Richard Blakey.

single metal thread is worked vertically over the string padding. Christ, the angels and their chalices were worked separately and appliquéd onto the already embroidered background. The angel on Christ's left (right side of the crucifixion scene), worked by a more skilful embroiderer than the one who worked its background, is completely intact. The doubled metal threads running vertically through the angel, ignoring the figure's contours, are laid very closely and the couching stitches very precisely placed to create a brick pattern. The outlines and contours are defined with a vivid blue floss-silk thread couched with the same colour. The angel on Christ's right (left side of the crucifixion scene) is worked in a vastly different style, in which the embroidery models the form.

The panels featuring the saints on the red velvet chasuble are predominantly embroidered with floss-silk threads. The yellow, blue and green are still very vivid but the red has faded to a subtle terracotta. This polychromatic scheme is used for the medieval architecture in all panels. The exterior elements are embroidered in long-and-short stitch except for the windows, which are filled in with laid work superimposed with trellis filling stitch in a contrasting colour. Raised

Detail of the left side of the Crucifixion scene on the early 16th century red velvet chasuble in the Catholic Church of Our Lady and St Michael, Abergavenny, Wales. By kind permission of Father Thomas Regan. Photography by Richard Blakey.

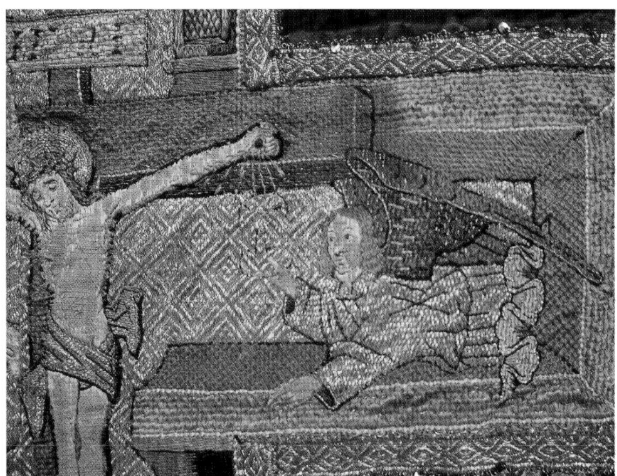

Detail of the right side of the Crucifixion scene on the early 16th century red velvet chasuble in the Catholic Church of Our Lady and St Michael, Abergavenny, Wales. By kind permission of Father Thomas Regan. Photography by Richard Blakey.

Panel of Saint Peter on the early 16th century red velvet chasuble in the Catholic Church of Our Lady and St Michael, Abergavenny, Wales. By kind permission of Father Thomas Regan. Photography by Richard Blakey.

Detail of the Bishop beneath his rebus on the 16th century Wharton pillar orphrey in the Catholic Church of Our Lady and St Michael, Abergavenny, Wales. By kind permission of Father Thomas Regan. Photography by Richard Blakey.

goldwork embroidery is confined mainly for the interior space and saints' mantles.

The Wharton orphreys, in comparison, are extravagantly worked, with more use of raised metal thread embroidery and a greater diversity of patterns and textures in the laid goldwork. A very fine basket-weave pattern is used for the borders, and a very high padding raises the porticos framing the saints. The metal threads are laid and couched so expertly and close to each other over the string padding that this looks like repoussé work rather than embroidery.

These vestments were the end-product of a glorious period for English ecclesiastical embroidery. When Henry VIII split from the Roman Catholic Church a wholesale destruction of ecclesiastical vestments took place. The metals from the embroidery were retrieved from the ashes and reconstituted for use in secular articles. Some vestments did survive this and later persecutions, however, because brave Catholic families continued to have masses said in the privacy of their homes and hid vestments for this purpose. (This is how the vestments at Abergavenny survived.) Many vestments were also taken onto the Continent.

While English medieval *opus anglicanum* ecclesiastical embroidery was sought after on the Continent, equally magnificent examples were made there in the 14th and 15th centuries, but by the time the English work was on the decline, French and Flemish embroiderers were surpassing English accomplishments.

The royal inventories from the period of Charles V (1338–1380) and Charles VI (1368–1422) of France describe the most glorious of vestments, very few of which have survived. An important piece on permanent display in the Musée de Cluny in Paris gives an indication of what they were like. It is a mitre from the Sainte-Chapelle, made between 1330 and 1370. The narratives on both sides, relating to Christ's birth, are embroidered on cream silk with silk, silver-gilt and silver threads. Tiny pearls are also used. The figures are very highly padded, with lines worked in black silk threads defining the contours of the garments. The metal threads are laid in pairs between the contours, with cream silk couching stitches spaced 2 millimetres (1⁄10 in) apart and bricked.

The highly padded Gothic architectural elements, the acanthus leaves and the heart-shaped leaves are embroidered in satin stitch using a very fine silver-gilt thread. We see the tentative beginnings of *or nué* (shaded gold) work, used for the garden settings on both sides of the mitre. Here, silk threads in tones of green are couched over horizontal rows of gold threads to give a sense of spatial depth.

In the middle of the 15th century, or nué began to eclipse other techniques in gold embroidery all over Europe. The exception was Protestant England, where there was no opportunity for embroiderers to embrace a technique only really appropriate for the ecclesiastical vestments and church furnishings that were now banned.

The Renaissance artists in Italy and the Low Countries were responsible for a new realism in the arts. With a new and greater understanding of the moving body, they evolved the technique of chiaroscuro (the modelling of forms in light and shade) to make figures appear more corporeal. They also understood the principles of perspective, allowing them to situate their figures in settings which gave a very real sense of depth. Artists were employed by professional embroidery workshops to provide cartoons in the new realistic style for embroiderers to follow.

Embroiderers began experimenting with effects to accurately interpret the artists' intentions. Up to this point they had laid their metal and silk threads directionally to follow architectural lines and create the illusion of a third dimension. From one angle, the different tones created by the play of light on the gold laid work could suggest the correct perspective, but change the angle and the image could become difficult to 'read'. The *or nué* technique, in which the gold threads are laid in straight horizontal lines so that the play of light remains constant, was to resolve this problem. Usually two gold threads were laid at one time and vertically couched with silk threads, with modelling effects achieved by tonal gradations of the coloured silks and variable spacing of the stitching. *Or nué* is one of the most labour-intensive gold embroidery techniques that has ever been created, but it gave embroidered pictures a more realistic three-dimensional quality than any other technique before or since.

The finest surviving examples of *or nué* work are the set of vestments for the Order of the Golden Fleece, founded by Philip the Good of Burgundy in 1429, which can now be viewed at the Schatzkammer (Treasury) in the Hofburg in Vienna. This set includes three copes of similar design which take their names from the subject featured on the hood—the copes of Mary, John the Baptist, and God the Father. The embroidery, which completely covers the linen background, is exquisite. On the hood of the Cope of Mary the Virgin is dressed in a simple green robe and voluminous blue mantle, each embellished with an edging of pearls. She is seated on a throne under a canopy in the unadorned classical style of the Renaissance, its green curtains edged with pearls. Almost the entire hood is worked in *or nué*. The Virgin's face and hands are so finely modelled as to appear painted, but are embroidered in split stitch. The golden threads for her long hair cascade over the *or nué* work of her mantle.

The borders around the hexagons on the body of the cope are a series of bands, the first a wide band of laid gold silk superimposed with a trellis of metal thread; then a red velvet band decorated with two straight lines, and a scalloped line worked in chain stitch using a metal thread. Enclosing the red velvet is a band of laid metal thread surface-couched over string padding to create a basket-weave pattern. At every junction there is a circle outlined with pearls; within this is a six-petalled flower outlined in chain stitch with a metal thread and filled in with tiny pearls. Every hexagon frames a saint dressed in Renaissance costume and set into a contemporary interior. The costumes and the floor tiles are worked in horizontal *or nué* and the wall panels on either side of the saint in vertical *or nué*. The architectural tracery of the arches was worked separately in satin stitch using metal threads, then appliquéd.

Tudor, Elizabethan and Stuart goldwork: 16th and 17th centuries

Following the Reformation, secular embroidery replaced ecclesiastical embroidery in the professional workshops of England. During the reign of Henry VIII professional embroiderers were needed to provide larger furnishings, such as bed valances, for noble houses and to meet the increased demand for ceremonial work. The professionals also travelled throughout England and Scotland to tutor the noblewomen of affluent households in embroidery techniques and to provide them with designs.

There are very few extant examples of English metal thread embroidery on clothing from the 16th century. Most of our knowledge of the goldwork on the more spectacular costumes worn by Henry VIII (1491–1547) and Elizabeth I (1533–1603) has been acquired from contemporary paintings, wardrobe accounts and inventories. Sumptuous clothing embroidered with metal threads and embellished with pearls and precious stones was particularly vulnerable to destruction—for example, it was recorded in 1517 that approximately 450 ounces of gold and 850 pearls were removed from one of Henry's robes to be re-used, we presume, for a new garment. When Elizabeth died at the age of 70 she left over 1000 dresses in the Great Wardrobe. Many of her magnificent clothes were subsequently altered for Anne of Denmark, wife of King James I.

Portraits of Henry show his garments laden with gold embroidery and jewels. The accounts of his royal wardrobe list many velvet and satin garments embroidered with 'Venice gold', with an occasional mention of 'damask gold'. Both are flat metal threads wound around a silk core which have to be couched onto a background fabric. The gold embroidery in his portraits appears to be of this type. There is no indication of raised work.

The designs for the embroidery are pure abstractions, referred to as 'arabesque' because they derived from Arab Islamic art. The textiles from Asia Minor and Turkey imported in this period featured this type of ornamentation, which was soon adopted by European textile makers and was the preferred form during Henry's reign. Arabesque designs are formally symmetrical and composed of the interlaced lines and arcs so suited to the couching techniques, of goldwork. This form of ornament also came to be known as strapwork.

The embellishment of textiles during Elizabeth's reign became even more extravagant. Portraits show Elizabeth dressed in rich silk and velvet garments completely covered with embroidery. Goldwork seemed to be the most desirable form of embroidery, as represented in these portraits, but other forms with entirely different aesthetics have been paired with goldwork in a few cases. The magnificent effect was made possible because a noblewoman's costume in the Elizabethan period was composed of several detachable and interchangeable parts: sleeves, stomacher, petticoat and gown, and perhaps a cloak.

Possibly two items from Elizabeth's wardrobe have survived. One is a piece of petticoat reputedly given by the queen to Blanche Parry, the keeper of her books and jewels which is on display in a church in Bacton, England. The other is a bodice known as the 'Devereux heirloom' (now in the Kyoto Costume Institute, Japan), said to be a gift to the queen from the Countess of Leicester. Its linen foundation fabric is entirely covered with surface-couched silver thread. Superimposed over this is the much-loved Elizabethan pattern of curling tendrils supporting all manner of flowers and fruits and interspersed with caterpillars and butterflies. The tendrils are raised on the background in the form of a chain created with silver-gilt check purls. The flowers were worked separately as 'slips', mostly in the form of canvas work in silk using tent stitch. Lizerine outlines the various parts of the slips. Some of the leaves and petals on the slips have wires around the edges to allow them to stand away from their bases. This rare survival does much to confirm that the artists who painted Elizabeth in those extravagant costumes did have the most fabulous confections to work from.

There is another extant white satin petticoat

panel, embroidered in polychrome silks and metal threads, and dated c.1600, which is in the Victoria & Albert Museum. Its exotic and fantastic images are also comparable to the painted and written evidence we have of Elizabeth's dresses.

Venice gold and silver appear regularly in the inventories of Elizabeth's wardrobe, as do gold twist, plate and purls. The Elizabethan embroiderers raised cut purls over high padding, giving a more bejewelled effect than provided by flat goldwork. The beautiful portrait known as the 'Phoenix Portrait' shows the queen wearing a black velvet gown decorated with an allover design of acorn leaves within a trellis pattern. The artist clearly shows the leaves filled in with purls raised over padding and outlined with what seems to be lizerine.

An early 17th century painting shows one Margaret Laton wearing a bodice that has survived to the present. The bodice, dated c.1620, and the painting are on display side by side in the Victoria & Albert Museum, a perfect demonstration of artistic accuracy at the time. Here we see surface-stitched curling tendrils, always worked with a metal thread, linking and enclosing a great variety of flowers, leaves, fruits, birds and insects also worked in surface stitches, but using polychrome silk threads. This is the first appearance in English embroidery of surface stitching with metal threads, made possible because wire-drawers now possessed the technology to draw out wires to hair-like fineness. Wound onto a core of yellow silk, they produced an extremely pliable passing thread, which could be taken through the fabric in a needle rather than having to be couched on the surface.

Two late Elizabethan panels for coifs dated 1600–1625, the earliest pieces in their collection, are held in the Embroiderers' Guild Museum at Hampton Court Palace. Coifs were informal women's headwear; while very common, they rarely appear in contemporary portraits.

The panel illustrated here has a more idiosyncratic design than the usual Elizabethan coiling stem pattern, being a staggered repeat of a twisted stem on the diagonal with a single leaf and a bunch of red berries, beautiful in its severity and simplicity. The colour palette is limited to red and green floss-silk threads plus a silver-gilt passing thread. Each twisted stem is embroidered in plaited braid stitch using the silver-gilt passing thread, with a row of open chain stitch in green floss-silk thread on either side. Open chain stitch is used for the leaf outlines, but the veins, featuring rosettes, are worked in Cretan stitch in green silk. The stems holding the berries are also worked in Cretan stitch, the red berries in trellis stitch. Horizontal laid work with double rows of passing threads couched with green floss-silk thread in a brick pattern fills some leaves; others are filled with 'rosettes' or threaded crosses, a simple form of woven wheel using silver-gilt passing, arranged along the veins.

The Costume and Textile Department of the Nottingham City Museums and Galleries has on permanent loan a very important collection of 17th century embroidered costumes belonging to Lord Middleton. The earliest costume in this collection is a very fine cream linen bodice, dated c.1610–20, lined with red silk which has faded to a subtle pink. It has an allover pattern of leaf-like shapes curling into scrolls which are outlined with silver-gilt and silver threads in a form of Pekinese stitch. On this bodice a silver-gilt or a silver thread is laid down and couched approximately every 4 mm with a black floss-silk

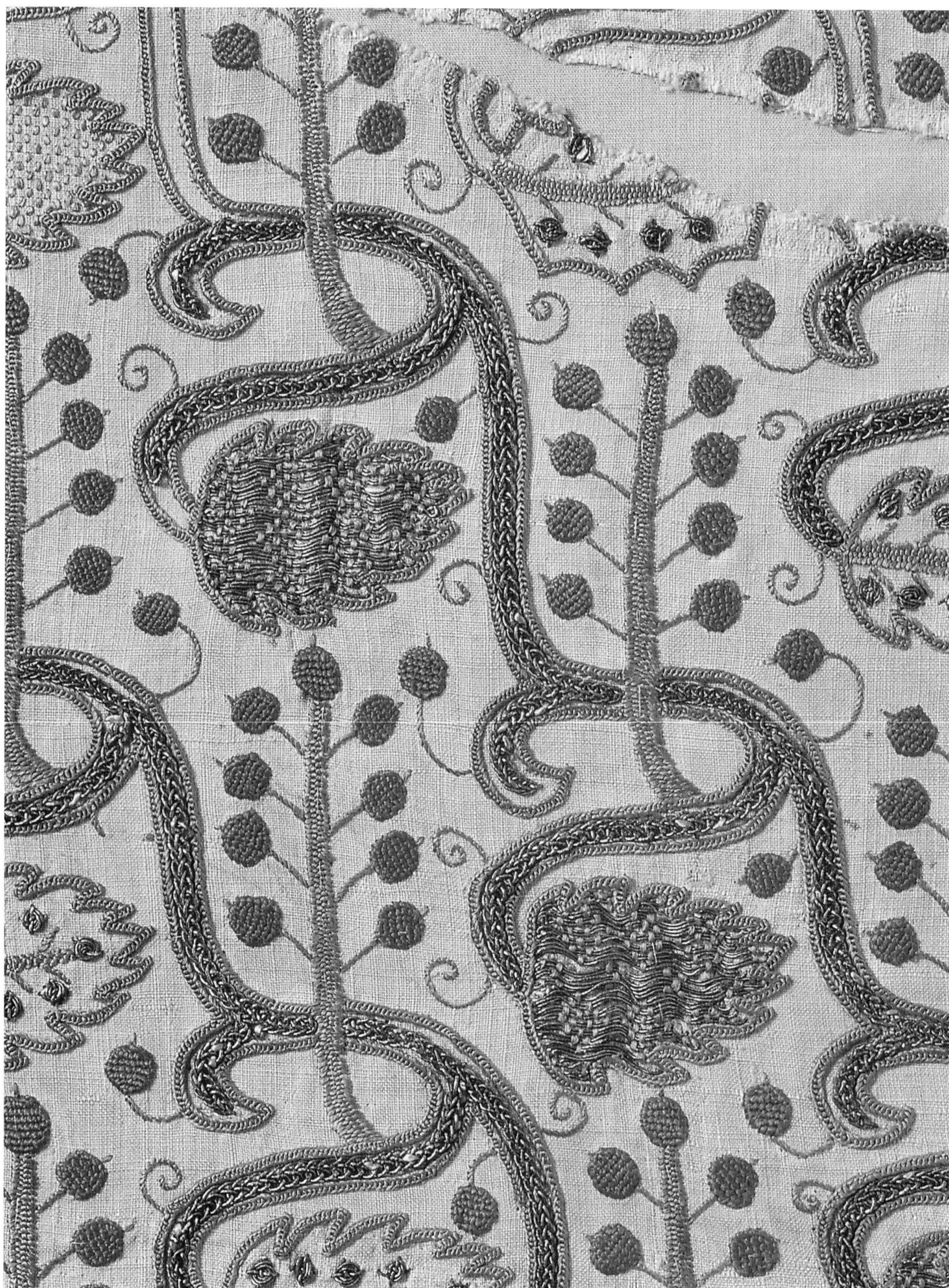

Detail of the embroidery on a British coif, 1600–1625, from the Embroiderers' Guild (UK) Museum Collection. Photography by Stephen Brayne.

thread. Where silver-gilt thread is used for the foundation, silver is used for the lacing, and vice versa. Silver spangles caught with little black beads are scattered between the leaves.

Also in the Costume and Textile Department of the Nottingham City Museums and Galleries, but not part of the Middleton Collection, is a pair of metal-embroidered linen sleeves dated c.1610–20, on which the coiling stem pattern includes roses, carnations, honeysuckle, pea pods, butterflies and birds, all worked with surface stitches using silver-gilt and silver threads. No silk threads are used. The stems in silver-gilt are created with a detached buttonhole stitch used extensively throughout the design. Contrast is provided by always juxtaposing silver with the silver-gilt threads. The Tudor roses are of particular interest, the very centre being a silver-gilt woven wheel which is surrounded by five silver woven wheels. The silver-gilt petals are worked in detached buttonhole and the silver turnover is filled in with ladder stitch. The small silver leaves between the petals are worked in plaited braid stitch.

Between 1625 and 1660 (the period of Civil War and Puritan Reformation in England) the very lavish forms of embroidery disappeared, as the layering of variously embroidered garments for women went out of fashion, to be replaced with simple but elegant gowns in lustrous silk taffetas and satins. Where embroidery was used, it was in the form of very delicate silver or gold work. Embroidery now served the costume, not the other way around.

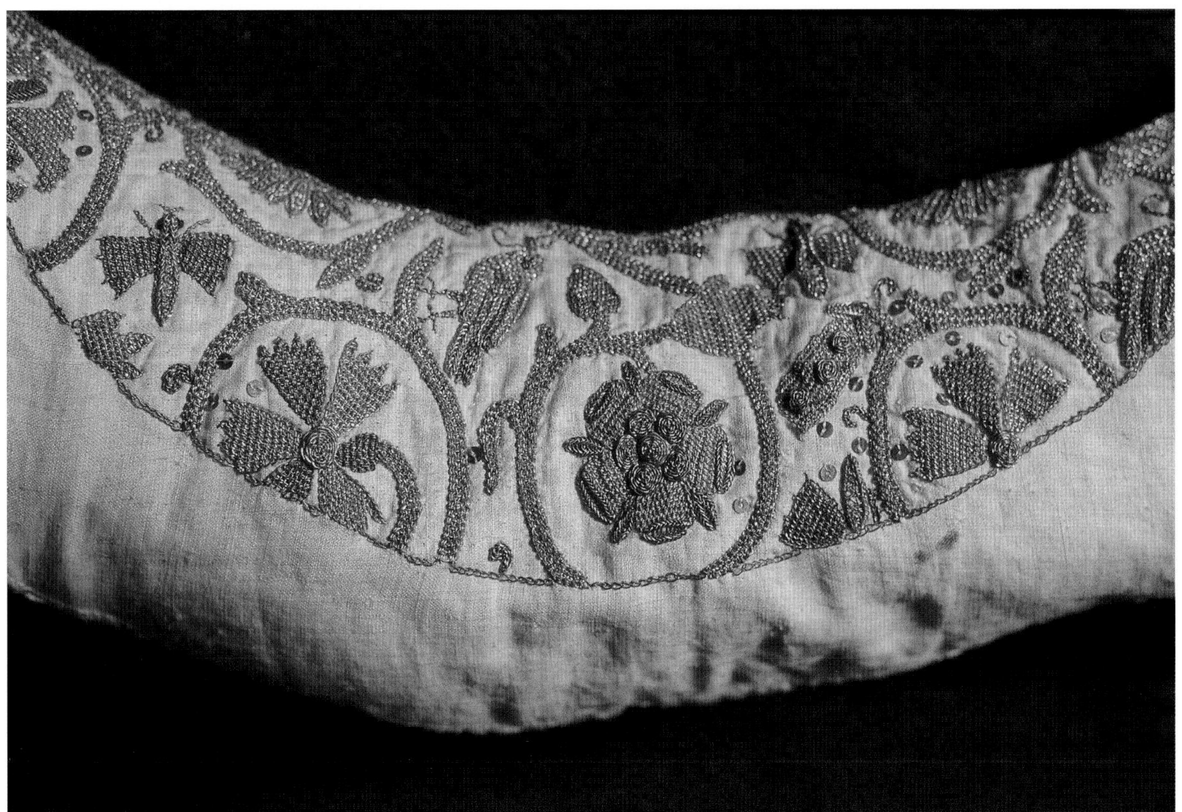

Early 17th century linen sleeve from the Wharton Collection held in the Costume and Textile Department of the Nottingham City Museums and Galleries, England. By kind permission of Mrs Pauline Bayles.

Late 17th century metal-embroidered bodice from the Middleton Collection held in the Costume and Textile Department of the Nottingham City Museums and Galleries, England. By kind permission of the Hon. Michael C.J.Willoughby.

With the restoration of the monarchy in 1660, a heavier and coarser form of embroidery appeared. A tight-fitting bodice made from a heavy corded black silk held in the Middleton Collection dated c.1670–90 features this kind of work. It is divided into three panels front and back, elaborately embroidered with large, stylised floral and foliate patterns in silver-gilt and silver threads. The embroidery on both centre panels is in extremely high relief, but on the side panels and over the shoulders is totally flat. The little cap sleeves are edged with a band of flat silver-gilt and silver embroidery. The silver-gilt threads used for the raised embroidery are laid lengthwise and very closely over the padding. These metal threads look as if they pass through the background fabric, as in satin stitch, but along the edges of the padding, silk thread backstitches hold them in place as they turn back on themselves. For the most part these backstitches are hidden by the thick silver cord which outlines all the shapes. The technique of passing metal threads back and forth across the padding without taking them through the background fabric is known as guimped embroidery; couching stitches are not put in along the lengths of the metal threads as in laid work. Gilt purls fill the small, flat petal-like shapes around some of the highly padded scroll-like forms worked in silver and are used to fill spaces within the design on the centre panels.

The flat embroidery on the side panels used very different techniques. Here all the petals and scroll-like leaves are filled in with laid work, using silver-gilt and silver passing threads in threes and couched with a cream floss-silk thread in a brick pattern. A few small areas are filled with a trellis pattern. All the shapes on the side panels are also outlined with a thick silver cord.

The other garment in the Middleton Collection to feature this bravura type of embroidery is a bright blue satin petticoat (which has been unpicked). It has been dated c.1670–1700, when a fashionable skirt consisted of a petticoat and a robe (the robe being a combination of bodice and overskirt). The centre of this piece is entirely embroidered from waist to hem, using silver-gilt and silver smooth and wavy passing threads. The high padding of the petals of the large exotic flowers is covered with a single layer of satin stitch in cream floss-silk threads, with silver-gilt and silver passing threads guimped over the satin stitch. The cream or yellow silk backstitches at the edges of the padding are hidden beneath the thick silver-gilt cord which outlines every part of the flowers, the leaves and the scrolls. The centres of the flowers are also highly padded and surmounted with a basket-weave pattern in which four metal threads have been couched as one with silk threads. Other parts of the flowers are filled in

Detail of late 17th century metal-embroidered bodice from the Middleton Collection held in the Costume and Textile Department of the Nottingham City Museums and Galleries, England. By kind permission of the Hon. Michael C.J.Willoughby.

Detail of the metal-thread embroidery on a 17th century skirt (petticoat) from the Middleton Collection held in the Costume and Textile Department of the Nottingham City Museums and Galleries, England. By kind permission of the Hon. Michael C.J.Willoughby.

with a trellis pattern using silver-gilt threads, worked directly over the satin.

The scrolls are worked with what appears to be pairs of silver-gilt passing thread loosely twisted and couched. The leaves attached to the flowers are embroidered in the same way in silver passing. The leaves springing from the scrolls are in laid work, using the textured passing thread we know as wavy passing. Woven wheels appear in the design, and there is a notable absence of purls and spangles.

Before leaving the 17th century, it is worth mentioning the small three-dimensional pictures that were worked mostly by girls or young unmarried women in aristocratic circles and framed to hang on walls or mounted on household objects such as caskets. They were named stumpwork pictures in the 19th century because parts of the embroidery were highly raised with blocks (stumps) of wood or stuffing. Subjects were mostly biblical and classical but dress and settings were contemporary. New metal threads had appeared on the embroidery scene and the young embroiderers used them with great ingenuity to create textures in their work.

In one of the Stuart stumpwork pictures

The biblical stories of Noah and Lot in a 17th century Stuart stumpwork embroidery in the Costume and Textile Collection of the Hereford Museum and Art Gallery. Photography by Richard Blakey.

from the Hereford Museum and Art Gallery's textile collection, dated 1650–75, the young embroiderer was particularly inventive with the new metal threads. Illustrating the stories of Noah's ark and Lot, this picture falls into the category of naïve art. The background fabric of white satin silk is not completely covered with embroidery, as was usually the case. For the top half of the design, the embroiderer worked a random selection of late Elizabethan flower motifs, and added the sun and the moon, a simply outlined image of a cat with a mouse, and a unicorn, all placed without regard for scale. The entrance to a great estate dominates the centre of the lower half. A female figure stands in the entrance dressed in contemporary costume. Her hair is loose, signifying an unmarried girl, perhaps the embroiderer herself. The arch above this figure becomes the cave where Lot's daughters make their father drunk in order to seduce him. Lot's wife, who was turned into a pillar of salt, surmounts the arch. Noah's ark is on the right with several animals making their way to the vessel. The sea beneath the ark features a delightful mermaid and fish. On the left is a patchwork-like square which, oddly, represents a river. Small schematically drawn figures walk across the bridge which spans it.

As in the majority of stumpwork pictures, silk embroidery was juxtaposed with metal thread embroidery. Of great interest is the use of silk-covered purl threads, created in the 17th century. The wire for this thread was spun evenly with silk and purled up. This thread can be couched in the same way as lizerine or pearl purl and is used in this manner to outline the centre arch. Several colours in this thread are featured in this picture: dark red, yellow, dark and light blue and apricot. The patches representing the river are filled with loops of silk-covered purl in a single colour. For contrast, patches worked with loops of silver-gilt wire check purls or silver-gilt rough purls are interspersed throughout the patches of silk-covered purl. Silk threads loosely spun with silver-gilt wires are used, jumbled and couched, in the bottom row of patches. Two blue threads wound with wire have been twisted and couched for much of the outlining. Silk-covered purls, this time overstretched and jumbled to form a ball, appear as raised balls on the bridge, on the bodies of the rams above the centre arch supporting the pillar of salt, and on the right column. There are also balls built up with layers of silk threads and overlaid with silver-gilt wire check purls on which very little of the metal thread remains. This highly idiosyncratic style of embroidered picture was not revived until the later 20th century.

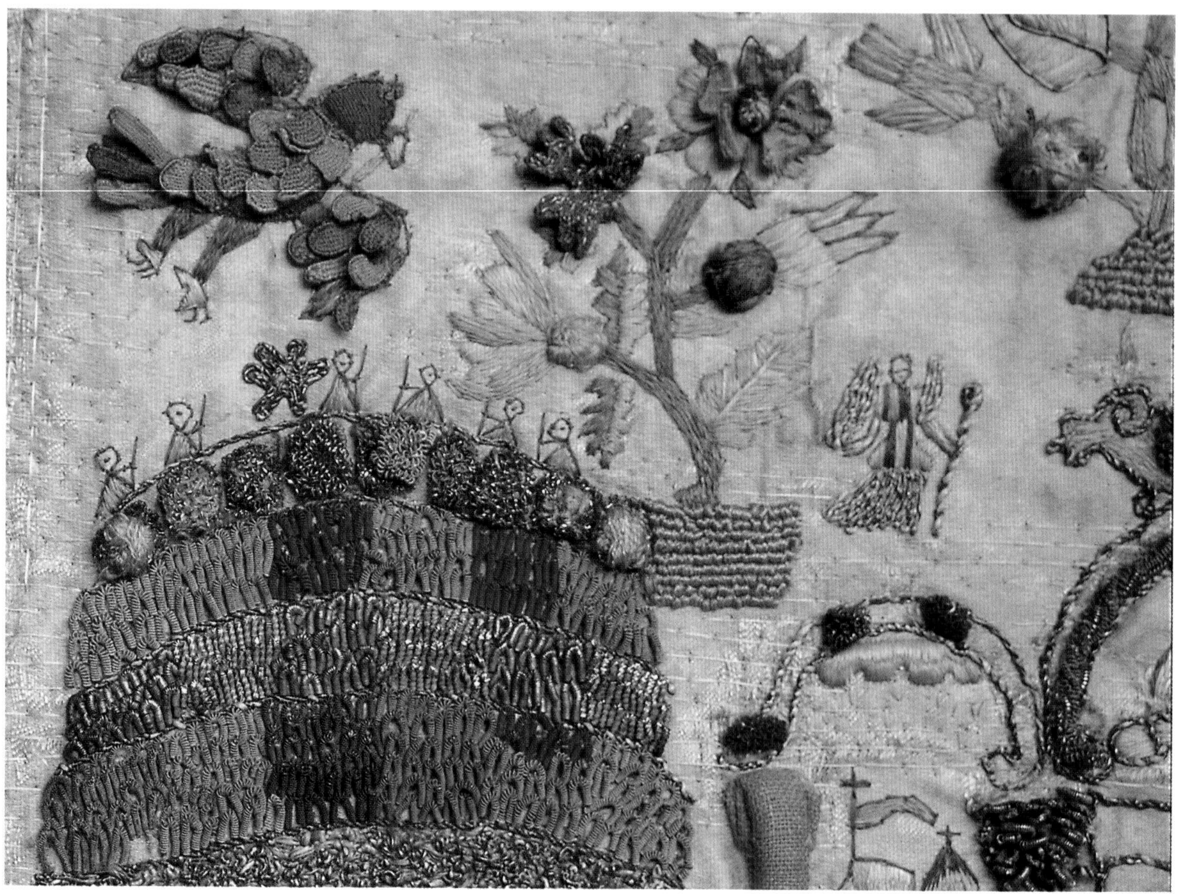

Detail of the 'river' in the story of Noah and Lot in a 17th century Stuart stumpwork embroidery in the Costume and Textile Collection of the Hereford Museum and Art Gallery. Photography by Richard Blakey.

Rococo and Regency/Directoire goldwork: 18th and 19th centuries

Secular costumes

Eighteenth century embroidery designs were largely inspired by the designs on the woven silk textiles produced in Lyon in France and Spitalfields, London. The silk manufacturers changed the designs for their fabrics every year and embroidery designers were obliged to follow their lead. Thus trees and large naturalistic blooms might be in fashion one year, chinoiserie flora and architectural motifs the next.

In the 18th century women's court costumes became as splendid as the men's, but the embroidery was now more artistic and refined. In English embroidery the flora was more naturalistic than in French embroidery, where the fantastic chinoiserie flowers were preferred, but both reflected the influence of chinoiserie in their asymmetric compositions. The scrolls, shells, rocaille (a stylised rock formation inspired by the fashionable artificial grottoes of the period) and the small asymmetrical cartouches, filled in with trellis patterns, that frame or support the floral arrangements are the fantasies of chinoiserie. It was a light-hearted and lyrical style which became known as Rococo. French and Italian gold embroidery was generally held to be of superior quality and design to the work produced in England at the time.

Eighteenth century court petticoat and mantua. By kind permission of the National Museums and Galleries of Wales.

Charles Germain de Saint Aubin (1721–1786), draughtsman and embroidery designer to King Louis XV of France, in *L'Art du Brodeur* (The Art of the Embroiderer)[1], described and illustrated the different techniques of metal thread embroidery in use at the time. They included *or nué* (although Saint-Aubin stated that it was rarely used), *satine* (metal threads placed close to each other on the surface which are taken through and carried across the back of the work), *guipure* or *guipe* (metal threads worked parallel to each other over vellum or some other form of padding and not passed through to the back of the work, and including what we know as guimped embroidery), *frisure guipe* (plate work and the working of cut lengths of purl threads over padding), *couchure* (couched work), *gaufrure* (couched metal threads over string padding to

1 *The Art of the Embroiderer Charles Germain de Saint-Aubin Designer to the King 1770*, translated by Nikki Scheuer, notes and commentary by Edward Maeder, reprinted by permission of David R. Godine, Publisher

Detail of the silver embroidery on an 18th century court petticoat and mantua. By kind permission of the National Museums and Galleries of Wales.

create patterns such as waffle or basket weave), and embroidery in *paillettes* (spangles). He gave a very detailed description of *rapport* embroidery, embroidered motifs or borders worked on taffeta, toile or yellow paper in little frames. When the motif was completed, the underside was glued and the base material cut away, it was ready to be appliquéd onto a costume or an item such as a horse trapping by stitching through the little loops of the *pratique* (gold chain braid) outlining the design.

A court mantua with narrow train and matching petticoat (the mantua is an open robe with a train which required a stomacher and petticoat) is held in the Museum of Welsh Life in Cardiff. Dated c.1732–35, they are made in bright blue damask satin silk embroidered in silver. On the mantua the embroidery is confined to wide borders on the two fronts and on the cuffs of the sleeves; the petticoat is wholly embroidered.

The silver metal *filé* (the French equivalent to tambour), *frisé* (a textured, crinkled thread like check thread) and purl threads are all couched in white floss-silk threads in a design that could be classified as floral chinoiserie. Most of the motifs are worked with couched silver filé and frisé. Filé is used for the diagonal satin stitching of narrow stems and flower petals worked directly onto the silk background. A flame-like flower padded with vellum is guimped. Wide borders, circles, groups of large pendulous leaves, shell shapes and exotic 'fruits' are string-padded and couched in a variety of patterns (*gaufrure*); by couching only on one side of the padding, the most beautiful rippling effect

Eighteenth century Queen Anne apron from the Embroiderers' Guild (UK) Museum Collection. Photography by Stephen Brayne.

is created across the surface of the embroidery. Flat couching (*couchure*) directly onto the background is used for scrolls, serpentine ribbons and outlines. Loops of purls are used judiciously, mainly for the centres of small flowers and in the more open patterns formed by rows of arcading which give relief to the more densely embroidered areas of the design. The embroidery is in remarkable condition.

During the 18th century women in aristocratic and even royal circles in England donned beautifully embroidered aprons for the serving of tea, which had become very fashionable early in the century. A significant number, worked in chinoiserie designs, have survived. They are known as Queen Anne aprons after the last Stuart queen, who possessed several. The apron is characteristically short, and made of yellow or cream silk taffeta, fine lawn or muslin.

The Embroiderers' Guild (UK) Museum Collection includes a superb example of a gold-embroidered cream silk Queen Anne apron. The scalloped border typical of the garment features two cherries on stalks at the junctions of the main scallops (each large scallop is divided up into smaller scallops on the outside edge), with two leaves on stems worked in the middle of each large scallop. The remaining spaces are filled with a vermicelli pattern. The body of the apron is embroidered with a symmetrical design of trailing stems with chinoiserie flowers and leaves.

The embroidery is worked entirely in couching. The silver-gilt threads include filé, frisé and flatworm. The heads of the two protea-like flowers at the top are string-padded, and six filé threads have been couched as one over this padding to create a basket-weave pattern. The leaves are outlined with a double row of frisé and filled in with a vermicelli pattern using the same doubled thread, or string-padded with V's to represent the veins, with a pair of filé threads taken continuously around the leaf shape and couched with yellow floss-silk thread. The bracts of the flowers are given the same alternative treatments. The cherries are worked with a spiral of doubled filé thread begun in the centre, with yellow floss-silk couching creating an additional pattern. This apron was embroidered entirely with metal threads, although quite often metal embroidery was combined with silk embroidery.

Men's court costumes were also extravagantly embroidered. In the 1730s a typical suit, *un habit à la française*, consisted of fitted coat, long waistcoat and breeches. A white shirt, jabot frill and silk stockings completed the outfit. The velvet or wool jacket and breeches were usually matching, the waistcoat invariably made in a contrasting silk. The jacket fronts curved away so the waistcoat could be seen, and the two garments embroidered to match with metal threads, silk threads and spangles.

The Wade Collection at Berrington Hall near Hereford in England includes a great number of 18th century costumes and accessories. On a 1750–55 red velvet waistcoat, a heavy pattern of a wide ribbon sprigged with chinoiserie flowers and leaves winds its way in a wave-like motion down the front edges, over the three point pocket flaps and the entire skirt fronts. Embroidered with silver-gilt threads, it is entirely *broderie de rapport*, worked over what appears to be a fine cream silk fabric. The rapport embroidery is attached to the velvet with small stitches of pink silk, and outlined with a double row of couched silver-gilt rippled thread similar to a fine rococo. The wide ribbon shape is divided into two rows of diagonal satin stitch using filé, separated with *clinquant* (plate)

Detail of the rapport gold embroidery on an 18th century red velvet waistcoat from the Wade Collection at Berrington Hall, England. By kind permission of the National Trust. Photography by Richard Blakey.

held down with purls spaced no more than 2 mm (1/10 in) apart. The scalloped edges are worked in diagonal satin stitch with filé, as are the stems, leaves and petals of the chinoiserie floral motifs. Flower heads are filled in with silver-gilt spangles anchored with a cross of filé and loop of purl. The spaces between the spangles are filled in with loops of purl or satin stitch in dark pink floss silk.

Hereford Museum and Art Gallery has a number of 18th century costumes in their collection, including a fabulous white satin waistcoat dated late 1770s and decorated with silver-gilt embroidery, unusually profuse and heavy for the period. The border pattern is particularly dense, and the remainder of the waistcoat fronts are crossed with rambling branches carrying acorns and heavy flower heads similar in appearance to a protea or waratah. A beautiful serpentine decoration, made to resemble gilt lace, weaves in and out through the oak tree branches of the border. The scalloped edges of the border are created with two couched frisé threads. Within each scallop is an additional straight length of purl inside a circle of purl. Perpendicular lines of single filé threads are laid between the scalloped edges of this decoration, with purls laid in pairs across them in a form of burden stitch. This modification creates a lacy effect, an exquisite counterbalance to the predominance of solid guipure work (in the form of guimped embroidery) on the waistcoat. Filé threads are guimped in pairs, frisé singly. The branches and the acorn cups are guimped with frise; the oak leaves, acorns, bracts of the protea-like flowers and petals of the gigantic sunflower-

Detail of the gold embroidery on a late 18th century white satin waistcoat in the Costume and Textile Collection of the Hereford Museum and Art Gallery. Photography by Richard Blakey.

like flowers with filé. Flat laid work using frisé is used for the smaller branches, and for the spaces between the guimped edges of the waistcoat, the border of intertwined oak branches and the lacy serpentine decoration. The flower heads of the 'proteas' are formed with rows of looped purls filled with straight purls. The 'sunflower' centres are filled with approximately 3 mm (3⁄20 in) lengths of purls surrounded by larger bullions. A single thread of couched frisé meanders around the centre of each flower. The smallest branches carry large gilt spangles anchored from the centre with three small lengths of purl and surrounded with a circle of purls. The texture of the purl embroidery is a beautiful contrast to the smooth guimped embroidery.

By the late 18th century, English and French men's court outfits, usually of striped velvet, were being embellished with a very effeminate style of embroidery featuring naturalistic and semi-naturalistic flowers and grasses. The waistcoat, usually of cream silk, was embroidered to match the coat. Most of the embroidery was executed in coloured floss-silk and chenille threads, bright but not garish because the intention was to remain as faithful as possible to nature, and worked mainly in satin stitch and long-and-short stitch. Stem and chain stitches were used for stems and grasses, and French and bullion knots to suggest the texture of the centres of flowers.

Silk embroidery, silver-gilt and silver threads, spangles in several sizes and sequins, coloured foil shapes, smooth and check purls and glass paste 'jewels' were also used. Single spangles were scattered quite prolifically over the silk waistcoats, usually held down with three silk stitches or a loop of purl. Larger, convex sequins with holes around their edges were attached with small pieces of purl. Rows of spangles or sequins among the silk embroidered grasses were attached with purls creating a line over the spangles.

Informal dress waistcoats worn with suits of plain cloth also became fashionable. These waistcoats were embroidered with neoclassical designs inspired by the Roman wall paintings unearthed at Herculaneum and Pompeii, and characterised by festoons, bows and tassels worked with purls and spangles in highly inventive ways among the silk-embroidered flowers. Spangles tinted in metallic colours, such as pink and green, and coloured foils held in place with purls, were very popular.

On a dress waistcoat from the Wade Collection, many of the lines and little flowers in

Detail of the gold and silk embroidery on a silver lamé waistcoat from the Wade Collection at Berrington Hall, England. By kind permission of the National Trust. Photography by Richard Blakey.

the design were created with doubled spangles anchored with little loops of purl. The bottom spangles are gold and the top spangles, deliberately bent to expose the gold ones beneath, are a metallic pink.

The beginning of the 19th century saw the disappearance of the full rococo dress with its corsets and panniers. In its place the high-waisted or Empire-line cotton or muslin dress become ultra-fashionable in England and France (until Napoleon decreed that men and women were to wear silk at public ceremonies and at court). In England, however, women were still expected to wear hooped dresses and trains at formal court occasions. The *Lady's Magazine* gave a full description of the dress Princess Charlotte of Wales wore for her formal introduction into society at a Drawing Room held by her grandmother Queen Charlotte in June 1814:

> The Princess Charlotte of Wales –An elegant petticoat of rich white satin, with a superb border of the same, and a wreath of silver laurel leaves tastefully intermixed with white roses; draperies of rich embroidered patent lace, in silver lama, with superb borders formed in festoons, and ornamented in an elegant style with wreaths of silver laurel leaves and white roses, with rich silver cord and tassels; train of rich striped and fringed silver tissue, tastefully trimmed with silver lama border and rich silver blond lace, and ornamented with beautiful diamonds.[2]

Silver lama embroidery was a permissible

2 Quoted in Kay Staniland, *In Royal Fashion: The Clothes of Princess Charlotte and Queen Victoria 1796—1901*. The Museum of London, London: 1997, p 45

contemporary touch to this ornate gown. (Lama is a narrow strip of metal which passed easily through the loosely woven muslin when cut into a point.)

The description of Charlotte's dress for her next Drawing Room in April 1815 indicates that it is a little less ornate but still hooped:

> Her dress on this occasion was exquisitely beautiful. Gold Lama and white draperies over a petticoat of rich white satin; beneath the draperies a trimming of superb blond lace, headed with a wreath of white satin and gold twisted trimming; train of rich figured white satin, body elegantly trimmed with rich gold and blond lace ...[3]

While these two whimsical concoctions have not survived, part of Princess Charlotte's 1816 Empire-line wedding gown is now in the London Museum collection. The contemporary fashion magazine *La Belle Assemblée* gave this description:

> silver lama on net, over a silver tissue slip, embroidered at the bottom with silver lama in shells and flowers. Body and sleeves to correspond, elegantly trimmed with point Brussels lace. The manteau was of silver tissue lined with white satin, with a border of embroidery to answer that on the dress, and fastened in front with a splendid ornament.[4]

An Empire-line gown dated c.1820 in the London Museum has wonderfully novel embroidery, very modern for the period. The dress is made of plain machine-made net with a silk shift underneath. The embroidery is a combination of manipulated mauve chiffon with

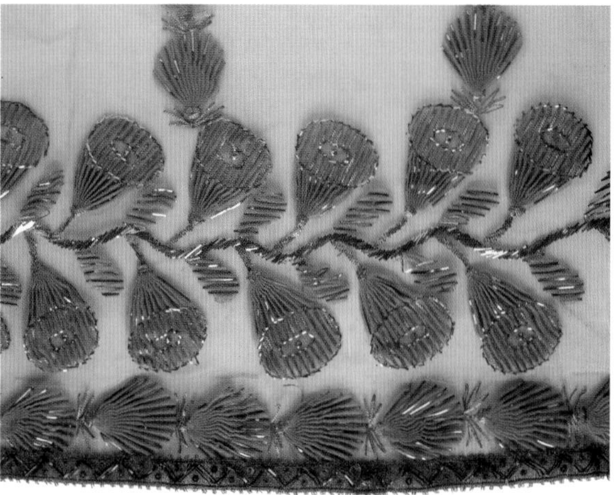

Detail of the lama embroidery on the hem of an early 19th century Empire-line gown. By kind permission of the Museum of London.

silver-gilt smooth and embossed lama. An undulating stem carrying buds and bell-shaped flowers forms a border at the hemline and below this is a row of shell scallops. Rows of scallops, increasing in size, run from below the bodice down to the border. Scallops decorate the little puff sleeves. The mauve chiffon has been concertinaed into accordion pleats to create the bell and scallop shapes and a length of lama sits in each valley. The flat metal thread has also been taken continuously through the net to create a diagonal satin stitch for the undulating stem. The lama has also been ingeniously worked to look like stem stitch for outlines.

Embroidery in haute couture

The father of haute couture, Charles Frederick Worth, did more to raise embroidery to the status of an art, with the help of the House of Michonet in Paris, than anyone before him. Lama embroidery had virtually disappeared, but purls, filé, frisé, *soutache* (gilt braids) and gilt twists

3 ibid p 49
4 ibid p 57

Detail of the embroidery on an 1885 persimmon silk velvet visite designed by Worth. Gift of Mrs George S. Amory. By kind permission of the Museum of the City of New York.

resurfaced and were now used with bead and sequin embroidery.

The Museum of the City of New York has a large collection of gowns by the haute couture designers of the late 19th and early 20th centuries. Of special note is a c.1885 *visite* by Worth. The visite was a type of coat or cape with a split at the back to accommodate the bustle, the back of the visite elaborately decorated to draw attention to the bustle.

Worth's visites were always intricately and fabulously embellished and this one was no exception. It is made in persimmon silk velvet and embroidered with silver soutache, silver twist, crystals and beads, in a design which seems to be inspired by Kashmiri designs or filigree lace patterns. There is certainly no reference to the natural world. The soutache is laid flat and couched invisibly to enclose rows of cut beads (now milky with age) which define the borders of lacy patterning that follow all edges of the front and back of the visite, and the arcades across the front and back of the garment. The technique of using soutache upright (*debout*), that is, on its side, is extensively employed to outline the abstract patterns and to encapsulate crystals and cut beads within the borders and arcades. A fine silver twist has been used for a knotted surface stitch which has been used to fill the remaining spaces in the pattern to create the effect of lace. The twist has also been teamed with beads to create a pretty edge along the soutache borders.

Ecclesiastical vestments

Saint-Aubin remarked in his treatise on 18th century embroidery that in the Middle Ages and the 16th century the making-up of vestments had been in the hands of members of the Guild of Chasubliers (vestment finishers), but in his

Late 18th century French chasuble in the Embroiderers' Guild (UK) Museum Collection. Photography by Stephen Brayne.

Detail from the back of the late 18th century French chasuble in the Embroiderers' Guild (UK) Museum Collection. Photography by Stephen Brayne.

century this work had passed over to the Brodeurs (embroiderers who used gold or silk threads on an already woven fabric). He scathingly commented of the work produced by the chasubliers: 'I believe it is only necessary to look at Pl. 6 of the illustrations to get an idea of the frugality with which these vestments are trimmed.'[5] Plate 6 was devoted to the layout of a set of 16th century vestments, on which only the orphreys were decorated, with acanthus leaves and sprays of flowers. Under the brodeurs in the 18th century, the decorations broke from their traditional boundaries and flowed over the entire vestment, but were still given over largely to the floral patterns that appeared on secular costumes. Large naturalistic blooms, worked in brilliantly coloured floss-silk threads using the painterly long-and-short stitch, were supported and framed by baroque strapwork and elements of rococo chinoiserie worked in silver-gilt and silver threads.

An 18th century French chasuble of this type in the Embroiderers' Guild (UK) Museum Collection is made of cream silk which has been interwoven with silver threads. While the silk background is not in good condition, the embroidery is in an excellent state. The designs on the back and the front are symmetrical, that on the back more prominent.

The gold-embroidered cartouches and C

5 *The Art of the Embroiderer Charles Germain de Saint-Aubin Designer to the King 1770*, translated by Nikki Scheuer, notes and commentary by Edward Maeder , reprinted by permission of David R. Godine, Publisher, p 66

Detail from the back of the late 18th century French chasuble in the Embroiderers' Guild (UK) Museum Collection. Photography by Stephen Brayne.

scrolls are padded with vellum and guimped with silver-gilt filé threads taken back and forth in pairs, slightly raising these elements above the other gold embroidery. Two cartouches on the back frame a shield-like motif worked in low relief with filé threads. Rows of textured frisé couched around the smooth padded shield separate it from the equally smooth guimped cartouche. Filé and frisé threads are couched in a variety of patterns. The frisé threads are laid in pairs; three filé threads are laid and couched over as one. The guipure and couchure work is so finely done that it looks remarkably like gold repoussé work.

A beautiful trellis pattern fills in the other two cartouches on the back. Four threads of frisé laid down for the intersecting diagonal lines are anchored with tiny stitches of single filé. Four very small circles, worked with gilt plate, fill each diamond shape so created. Plate work is used as little scintillating accents throughout the gold and silk embroidered areas and interspersed through areas of couched work. The series of spots or tear-drop shapes that follow the contours of the guimped scrolls are executed in plate work.

Church vestments had not been produced in England since the Reformation, despite two attempts to revive the use of liturgical dress. In the 1830s, however, three developments were instrumental in the revival of ecclesiastical embroidery: the right to practice Roman Catholicism was legalised; a group of clergymen at Oxford pushed to return the Church of England to its period of greatness, which in their opinion was the 14th century, the period of *opus anglicanum*; and a number of prominent architects became involved in the Gothic revival movement, which resulted in the construction of numerous churches. These architects believed in designing not only the building but also all the furnishings within it, including vestments.

Their early designs did not reference 14th century *opus anglicanum* vestments, although this was the form they wished to revive. This was hardly surprising, for most surviving examples were in Europe. The loss or disuse of some *opus anglicanum* techniques was also a contributing factor. Late 15th and early 16th century pre-Reformation vestments were more accessible as models, and their applied motifs of seraphim-on-wheels, fleurs-de-lys, pomegranates and Tudor roses were easier to reproduce than the graceful figures of *opus anglicanum* work. The characteristic powder motifs of pre-Reformation vestment embroidery dominated Gothic revival designs for some decades.

An increased use of gold threads followed the introduction of Japanese gold into England about 1870, while the figures that began to appear in designs for vestments, altar frontals and banners were as naturalistic and as finely worked as those on the 16th century Flemish and Italian vestments from which they were derived. The perfect rendering of facial features in silk embroidery, and the meticulously couched and raised laid work mostly carried out in Japanese gold threads, became hallmarks of High Victorian ecclesiastical embroidery. This style continued to be employed for church commissions until World War II.

Ceremonial gold embroidery

This section encompasses the execution of gold embroidery on military and civil uniforms, and a 19th century Lord Chancellor's burse.

The purpose of a burse, actually a large flat drawstring purse, was to hold the monarch's

Nineteenth century Lord Chancellor's burse from the reign of George III or George IV in the Costume and Textile Collection of the Hereford Museum and Art Gallery. Photography by Richard Blakey.

Great Seal. Few are known to survive. The burse in the Hereford Museum can be dated to the reign of either George III (1801–1820) or George IV (1820–1830) because the coat of arms on the shield in the centre was theirs. The embroidery on this burse encompasses an enormous variety of silver-gilt and silver threads and techniques. The preponderance of metal is enlivened with colour provided by the rich red velvet background, the pink and blue silk appliqués and the green silk satin stitching. Cabochons, pearls, spangles and 'found objects' such as the chain on the unicorn were added to the mix.

Most parts are worked in extremely high relief. The round shield carrying the coat of arms, and the crown above it, were embroidered separately as flat pieces on heavy canvas, then shaped and stiffened with glue to stand proud of

Detail of the embroidery on the 19th century Lord Chancellor's burse from the reign of George III or George IV in the Costume and Textile Collection of the Hereford Museum and Art Gallery. Photography by Richard Blakey.

the background. The Scottish quarter and one field of the Hanoverian escutcheon are embroidered in silver laid work, the yellow silk couching stitches creating a pattern of parallel diagonal lines. The lions passant gardant and the harp are embroidered as satin stitch using silver rough purls without padding, and the single lions rampant in satin stitch with a gold silk thread. The harp strings are worked with plate in a singular technique—the plate is laid flat, and couched perpendicularly approximately 3 mm (3⁄16 in) in from the beginning of its length, then folded directly back on itself and couched again about 1 mm (1⁄16 in) back from the fold, the folding back and forth repeated along its length. The plate work has been flattened, probably with a mellor. Unflattened plate couched in an open zigzag fashion appears on the cheeks of the heraldic lion, and coils of plate in curious little baskets are dotted around the heraldic beasts. The quarters on the shield, and the three fields on the escutcheon, are separated with long lengths of silver bright check bullion between two couched silver passing threads.

The large crown above the coat of arms is raised above the surface; embroidery work is visible under its frame. The lowest part of the band of the crown is worked in laid work using silver passing thread, with white silk couching stitches creating a brick pattern; above this, yellow silk couching stitches form a chevron pattern. The top part of the band features cross

Detail of the embroidery on the 19th century Lord Chancellor's burse from the reign of George III or George IV in the Costume and Textile Collection of the Hereford Museum and Art Gallery. Photography by Richard Blakey.

pattées and fleurs-de-lys worked with silver purls over padding and outlined with silver lizerine. The three levels are separated with lengths of bright check bullion. The arches surmounting the band and meeting in the centre above the red velvet are also worked in silver laid work with yellow silk stitches creating a chevron pattern. Band and arches are further embellished with pearls. This frame was worked on the flat, and shaped and stiffened with glue to stand well proud of the surface. Rows of silver purls create a brick pattern over the red velvet.

The heraldic lion is worked entirely with silver-gilt threads and the unicorn with silver threads, although its mane is silver-gilt; both are fine examples of relief gold embroidery using the rapport technique. Their heads and bodies are padded quite substantially, the thickness gradually reducing down the top hind leg, and entirely covered with close rows of lizerine running down and invisibly couched. The mane and the other three legs of each beast are rapport pieces that have been added to the padded bodies. The legs are embroidered with close rows of lizerine, while the manes are made up of massive bright bullions interspersed with bright check bullions, all as long lengths. The lion's mane is particularly impressive. A mass of bullions has also been added to the hind legs of the lion to suggest longer tufts of hair. The lion's cabochon-eyed face is grotesque, the red-painted wooden tongue protruding rudely from a grimacing mouth outlined with bright bullions.

The heads of the eight cherubim in the borders are in such high relief that the embroidery must be covering wooden moulds. The short, wiry, mop hairstyles are their most interesting feature: short rows of overstretched metal threads on the surface, with a tangle of metal threads that somewhat resembles steel wool underneath. Laid work in silver wavy passing covers their faces, and their features are detailed with silk embroidery. The embroiderers had a little fun with the cherubim—they have laughter lines around their bulbous eyes, crease lines around their little pink mouths, and the most definitive eyebrows. Far from pretty, but delightful.

Many other intriguing three-dimensional symbols on this burse, if space permitted, could be described, such as the two little coffers on which each heraldic beast rests a foot, and the cornucopias, roses and thistles in the borders. Any remaining background is filled in with little rapport embroideries of naked angels, flowers and leaves, and spangles and loops of purls.

Designs on military and civil uniforms in the 18th and 19th centuries are spare of the detail on the Lord Chancellor's burse. Military officers' coats were richly embroidered with gold embroidery and by the 1770s could be worn to the English court at St James, although the French *habit habillé* was still worn for Drawing Rooms and marriages.

By the 19th century, patterns inspired by the austere and more masculine 18th century neoclassical style had been standardised for British regimental dress uniforms. Classical motifs of acorns, oak leaves and palm clusters became ubiquitous on both military and civil uniforms. All three appeared on the dress version of the 'Windsor Uniform' designed by George III.

Two long-established London embroidery companies specialising in ceremonial embroidery merged in 2001 to become Hand & Lock. Carne Griffiths, the company's young designer draftsman, showed me archival material dating back to 1790 and described the techniques and terms specific to ceremonial gold embroidery for the last 200 years. The archival drawers were full of card cuttings which are stencils for patterns on dress uniforms. Card cuttings are carefully stored away to be used repeatedly. When using a card cutting as a stencil, it is laid on top of what is now acid-free standard card. The cut cards are called card raisings and they give a very clear definition to the pattern to be embroidered. Hand & Lock glue them to the heavy woollen cloths used for uniforms with wallpaper glue. The woollen cloth is then pasted onto a heavy open-weave Holland cloth mounted in the embroidery frame. Raising threads and raising cloths give further height to the elements in the design, while carpet felt is used for very high relief.

Most of the shapes are worked as cutwork over padding. As the padding is quite high, the cutwork does not need to be outlined with a metal thread, although lizerine is sometimes used for lettering because it gives a more defined edge. Size 8 rough purls are mostly used for the cutwork, occasionally size 9 for very fine work. As an alternative to cutwork, no. 5 or no. 6 smooth and wavy passing thread are worked as satin stitch over the padding. In many designs the oak leaves are worked with purls on one side and passing on the other side. S-ing is used for delicate stems and tendrils; broader stems are worked as satin stitch using rough purls, or with spangles anchored with purls using the backstitch technique. Plate work is reserved for acorns.

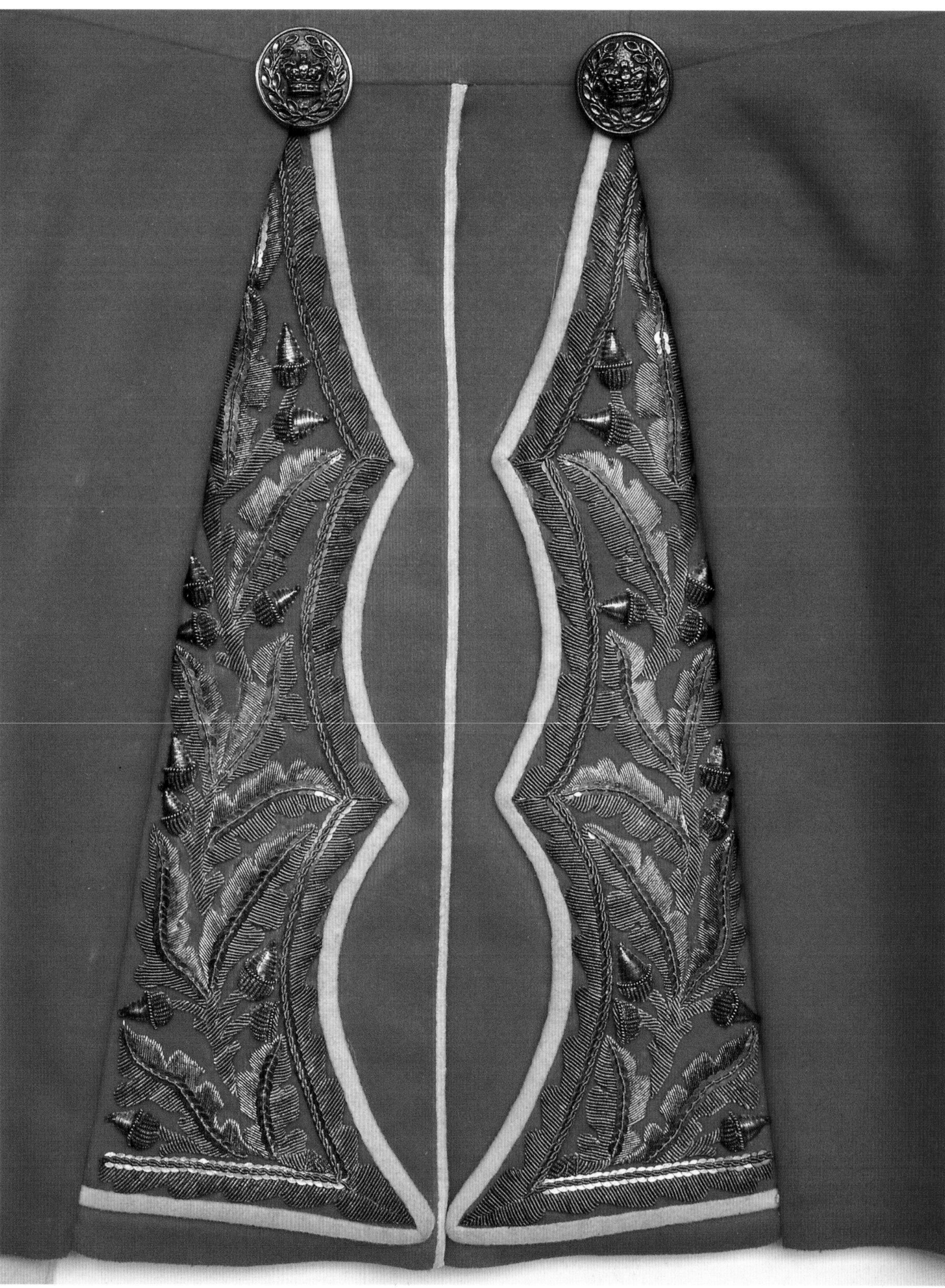

Detail of the gold embroidery on a 19th century dress uniform jacket for a Deputy Lieutenant of Herefordshire, in the Costume and Textile Collection of the Hereford Museum and Art Gallery. Photography by Richard Blakey

Hereford Museum and Art Gallery has a number of 19th century dress uniforms in their costume and textile collection. The red woollen dress uniform jacket of a Deputy Lieutenant of Herefordshire has a black stand-up collar and black cuffs embroidered with silver rough purls, passing threads, plate and spangles. The vents at the back of the jacket each feature a three-point bordered panel embroidered with the same silver threads. All embroidered areas are decorated with oak leaves and acorns and have the wavy edging signifying a first-class civilian uniform. The collar bears two gold Tudor roses, which may well be examples of the 'cut clean-outs' which Hand & Lock still make. Cut clean-outs, similar to French rapport embroideries, are edged with pearl purl. The silver oak leaves on the collar are not outlined, but the roses are outlined with pearl purl, as are their segments. Pearl purl separates the wire check cutwork on the cups from the plate work on the acorns. The plate work that covers the four outer petals of the roses has been worked over very high padding and would have needed shaping with a mellor.

Twentieth century goldwork

Haute couture gold embroidery: 1900-1960

At the turn of the century there were two streams evident in haute couture fashion: the conservative and the avant-garde. I saw an exciting example of the former in the Victoria & Albert Museum's exhibition, *Style and Splendour: the Wardrobe of Queen Maud of Norway 1896–1938*. Queen Maud's Coronation gown (1906), given pre-eminence, was made in a shimmering gold lamé in the princess style made fashionable by Queen Alexandra, her mother. The style gave uninterrupted passage to the trails of ribbons, curlicues and flowers that tumble down the front and back of the gown. The hemline is all swags, garlands and bows. Gilt filé thread is couched to render the ribbons and to outline the flowers and leaves, gold-coloured sequins, artificial pearls and diamantes are added to dazzling effect, but for all that, it is still in the conservative Rococo revival style of the turn of the century.

A few days before I had seen a turn-of-the-century Paquin gown embroidered by Michonet in the Museum of the City of New York. Michonet was an embroiderer extraordinaire who was prepared to be experimental, even if the end result was a hotch-potch of techniques and the embroidery lost in an accumulation of lace and tulle and gigantic chiffon and satin roses—a criticism which certainly applies to the bodice of this gown. Medallions of silver iridescent lama work are interspersed throughout the mix. The leaves are worked in copper lama and edged with ombre ribbon. This more radical form of embroidery represented the avant-garde.

There is a sublimely beautiful wedding gown dated c.1910 in the Hereford Museum and Art Gallery's costume and textile collection, again representing the conservative. The skirt is profusely decorated with large Baroque blooms, bell-shaped flowers, petite flowers and masses of leaves and stems, all their parts outlined with a single couched silver passing thread. The meandering fine stems are worked with double rows of silver passing thread. The large leaves with many pointed lobes are filled in with laid work using silk and metal threads similar to today's no. 20 couching threads. Some of these leaves feature a white silk thread wound with a gilt metal thread, others a yellow silk thread wound with a gilt metal thread, the threads taken

Detail of the embroidery on a c.1910 white satin wedding gown in the Costume and Textile Collection of the Hereford Museum and Art Gallery. Photography by Richard Blakey.

back and forth diagonally across each side of the leaf. The couching stitches are invisible. Little loops of silver bright check held down with silver smooth purls are arranged on either side of the central vein, and appear along the stems. Much of the embroidery on this gown is cutwork over a high padding which appears to have been built up with crossed layers of white floss-silk. There are petals and small leaves in silver bright check and other petals in silver smooth purls. The cutwork on the thicker stems is a combination of two silver bright check purls to one silver smooth purl. The bellflowers and the outer petals of the large blooms are filled in with rows of floss-silk French knots in bright and pale pink, golden yellow and a very light turquoise, surrounded by loops of silver smooth purl. A trellis pattern fills the centres of the large blooms, long lengths of silver bright check forming the grid and small lengths of silver smooth purl anchoring the intersections. The raised cutwork makes the gown appear to be ornamented with pieces of jewellery.

By the second decade of the 20th century, women's dresses were no longer three-dimensional constructions, but 'flat' and made of soft and flimsy fabrics. Sequins, beads and gold and silver filé threads couched or worked as satin stitch became the only appropriate materials of embellishment because they adhered to the flat plane of the dress. These *robes-chemises*, as the French called them, persisted through the twenties.

On 14 October 1929 the New York Stock

Detail of the gold embroidery on a midnight blue wool coat designed by Schiaparelli for Mrs James A. Thomas. By kind permission of the Museum of the City of New York.

Exchange crashed, plunging the Western world into the Great Depression. It was disastrous for the whole haute couture industry, with thousands of workers being laid off, and for four years no hand embroidery appeared on evening dresses.

In 1935 embroidery made a sudden reappearance, largely due to the arrival of Elsa Schiaparelli on the French fashion scene, and this time it was of the bravura kind. The embroidery firm of Lesage et Cie in Paris was on the verge of closing its doors in 1934 when the Italian designer who had become known for her sportswear made contact with Albert Lesage and asked for embroidered belts.

Schiaparelli had a trial run with the belts, progressed to *trompe l'oeil* collars, and soon thereafter launched into jackets, coats, boleros, gowns and capes embroidered in a grand theatrical style. She referenced ecclesiastic and military ornamentation in her designs but also produced thematic collections based on the zodiac, music and the circus. Obviously struck by the beauty of goldwork, she made great use of purl, smooth, textured and coloured plate and sequins. Other innovative materials used in Lesage's embroideries for Schiaparelli included porcelain flowers, mirrors, and imitations of hard stones such as lapis lazuli and jade, which were often set within gold embroidery. Many of her designs required the embroidery to be in very deep relief.

The Museum of the City of New York holds a 1929 Schiaparelli midnight blue, full-length woollen evening coat with a Baroque design in gold embroidery worked on midnight blue silk velvet diagonal panels which increase in width down the front of the coat. The panels are bordered with a foliated decoration worked with 'bumble-bee cord' (gold thread wrapped around a cotton core) couched with the same gold thread. Within these ornate borders, two rows of large lozenge shapes, very highly padded and covered with smooth gilt lama, create a vermicelli-like pattern across the panel. The embroidery on this coat harks back to that on the 17th century corded black silk bodice in the Middleton Collection, for the embroidery on both garments was planned for spectacular effect. This bravura form was adopted by other couturiers using Lesage, such as Balenciaga and Lelong, mainly to keep in step with Schiaparelli, during the years leading up to World War II.

After World War II, women wanted a more romantic and feminine look, which Balenciaga and Dior gave them. Their dresses, for evening especially, emphasised the bust, made the waist even tinier, and rounded the hips. Full skirts flaring over the hips provided a vast canvas for embroidery. The bold embroidery of the pre-war years did not suit the romantic look, however. Embroidery became more precious in style, but was still wonderfully lavish. A more polychromatic colour scheme was favoured, and when metal threads were brought into the mix it was to provide sparkle. Such was the embroidery on the Coronation gown designed by couturier Norman Hartnell in 1953 for Elizabeth II.

By the beginning of the 1960s, materials never destined for embroidery were being integrated with traditional materials. Balenciaga, for example, asked François Lesage (the son of Albert) to combine plastics with other embroidery materials, which is precisely what was done on a cream gazar gown now held in the Victoria & Albert Museum, on which bunches of plastic threads are juxtaposed with silver leaves. By the end of the 1970s, metal threads had virtually disappeared from haute couture embroidery.

New directions: 1950–2006

In the post-war years in England the ever-larger wall hanging became the most popular vehicle for embroidery. In this form embroidery became of interest to artists. Rebecca Crompton and Elizabeth Grace Thomson, working before World War II, had paved the way to the 'new form of embroidery'. Their abstract, stylised designs were original, expressing the feeling of the age, showed an awareness of developments such as collage in modern painting, and their use of appliqué and free surface and machine stitching was appropriate to their works.

Post war, embroiderers built on Crompton and Thompson's innovations. Figurative work dominated at first, but by the end of the 1950s non-representational Abstract Expressionism began to make an impact. Some embroidery designs were now worked as pure abstractions, with texture and colour to appeal to the senses or express deep feeling. Mixed media and fabric collage were the choice of many embroiderers. Interesting threads were used to create vibrant line-patterns superimposed on areas of appliqué.

By 1961 the contemporising of ecclesiastical work had begun, and the use of gold and silver kid leather was becoming more popular in both secular and ecclesiastical work. Embroidery students began to design and work embroideries for ecclesiastical purposes. In a review of an embroidery exhibition in October 1964, Joan Skinner wrote:

> Each panel represents months of experiment and research following the choice of central theme. With the exception of the cats—all are biblical. The Crucifixion, the Burning Bush, St. Veronica ... the Crown of Thorns—all are examination pieces from students taking their National Diploma in Design at the Goldsmiths' College of the School of Art in London. They have studied colour, design and pure drawing, and learnt what they may demand of the many textured materials used in their appliqués ... some find their way into churches as centrepieces for altar frontals ...[1]

The photographs accompanying the review revealed the same stylistic and technical changes that had already occurred in secular embroidery.

England's Beryl Dean did more than anyone to show that good new design and technical perfection went hand in hand. When she was commissioned to create five small religious pieces she became determined to move church embroidery into the 20th century, teaching her first course in ecclesiastical embroidery in the mid-1950s.

Dean designed for her medium: 'gold work is characteristic of ecclesiastical embroidery' and 'the nature of Japanese gold and the metal and wire threads must be fully appreciated and their application understood, as each has its own particular technique'.[2] She advises the designer to consider the play of light upon the direction taken by the gold and this direction should always be planned before stitching, 'in order that the flow of the threads may enhance or make more understandable the subject of the design'.[3] She explains the various methods of treating gold to produce textures which can break up the surface, such as basket stitch, and suggests using the more textured crinkled or check threads to contribute another kind of texture against the smooth gleam of the Japanese gold, and to use those threads that are not commonly used in ecclesiastical work such as the purls. She also recognised that thick gold cords and braids were sometimes more appropriate for a contemporary design than rows and rows of meticulously couched Japanese gold. Most of the goldwork techniques explained and illustrated in her book Ecclesiastical Embroidery were used in Byzantine and medieval English embroidery; she used them with absolute precision in her own work but employed in such a way as to have affinity with her modern designs. Her hard-edge abstract figurative designs make a powerful statement, and are completely harmonious in their whole when seen from a distance; when viewed closely the sum is made up of the most intricate patterns, mostly created with a wide range of goldwork techniques.

In May 1968, Dean mounted an exhibition of over 200 pieces of ecclesiastical embroidery in the crypt of St Paul's Cathedral in London, of which a journalist wrote:

> It must come something as a shock to the moderns to find that the designs on altar cloths, copes and mitres, worked out by artists whose field is non-

---

1 From an article in the collection of material belonging to Barbara Dawson which is now held in the Constance Howard Resource and Research Centre in Textiles, London. Author unknown.

2 Beryl Dean, *Ecclesiastical Embroidery*. B.T. Batsford, London: 1960, p 96

3 Ibid p 97

Back of the Dean's cope designed and worked by Barbara Dawson. By kind permission of Reverend Peter Judd, Dean of Chelmsford Cathedral. Photo taken by author.

Detail of the Dean's cope designed and worked by Barbara Dawson. By kind permission of Reverend Peter Judd, Dean of Chelmsford Cathedral. Photo taken by author.

> representational, still make definite statements in terms of religious symbolism. The straight line is seen as an arm of the Eternal Cross; the circle as an emblem of the Trinity …[4]

Barbara Dawson had some pieces in this exhibition, which were very much in step with the contemporary non-representational Abstract Expressionist movement. In particular, her cope for the Dean of Chelmsford Cathedral created a great deal of interest with its design inspired by modern architectural trends for churches and cathedrals. All the interest is on the back. The background fabric is white and the additional colours to the gold metal threads and the cloth of gold tissue, are brilliant sun colours—oranges and yellows. On a central band running the entire depth of the fabric are arranged three crosses surrounded by circles to represent the Trinity. The cross at the top is complex and laden with gold and silk threads. The middle cross is not as significant and, according to Dawson, 'the third, at the hem, is freely composed, symbolizing the freedom of present-day ideas, and is worked with least detail as it is least noticeable'. She adds: 'The design is wider at the hem, than the top, and gold lines emanate from the centre in a circular manner giving an impression of the movement of a pendulum … and suggests a feeling of time and the enduring quality of faith'.[5]

Much use is made of appliqué. The large abstract and geometrical shapes and lines uniting the design, as well as the three crosses and circles, are appliqués. Yellow and gold silk appliqués predominate, with the most intense orange silk used as an accent throughout. In the top cross, metal and yellow and orange floss-silk threads are embroidered over the appliqués. Purls are laid loosely over cords, pearl purl and Japanese gold threads, with much variation in length and spacing; in areas where purls are massed, they are not contained and ordered as in traditional work. Many parts of the design are worked on the horizontal and vertical, especially the floss-silk laid work. The yellow and orange silk threads are anchored with strips of gold kid, purls or pearl purl. The gold kid discs in the segments formed by the crosses and the circles framing the crosses, the dynamic elements of the design, are textured with purls laid in patterns and edged with a mixture of radiating purls. Lines of couched Japanese gold threads whirl around the discs in the top cross, the paths of the orbs or spheres. Yellow and orange silk thread lines in a darning stitch spiral dynamically around the crosses.

Margaret Hall-Townley, the Curator of the Material Collection in the Constance Howard Resource and Research Textile Centre, was a student of Dawson's in the 1960s. Hall-Townley's embroidered low-relief sculpture *Goldfishers* was worked for an exhibition in 1986 at the Royal Institute of British Architects to a brief requiring exhibitors to design a work of one metre square or more to become an integral part of a building. *Goldfishers* was designed for a dark corner of a newly renovated Norman castle, hence its semi-circular format, with metal thread embroidery as the medium because it shows up particularly well in dark confined places. The play of light and movement in this work were far

4 From an article in the collection of material belonging to Barbara Dawson which is now held in the Constance Howard Resource and Research Centre in Textiles, London. Author unknown.

5 Barbara Dawson, *Metal Thread Embroidery*, B.T. Batsford, London: 1976, p 100

Detail of Margaret Hall-Townley's Goldfishers. *Photo provided by Margaret Hall-Townley.*

more important to the artist than the figures. Garlanded figures fly in towards the centre of the design, while goldfish are submerged into layers of various papers on the marine-ply base.

A pink silk and wool fabric was secured on a calico base and overlaid with sheer fabrics in a large quilter's frame. All the areas to be padded were backstitched with strong cotton to reinforce the edges of the shapes to allow for solid padding. Margaret used the traditional trapunto technique of padding where slits were cut into the calico at the back of the work and kapok was packed very firmly into the shapes.

The passing threads for *Goldfishers* were specially twisted, two hues of bronze and one of copper making the fiery colour required. Several threads are bunched to work the strands of hair. The figures, arms and bodies are embroidered in laid work, single passing threads alternating with twisted passing threads, each thread couched separately with a rich brown cotton perle. Single passing threads alternated with the twisted passing threads are taken horizontally across the background. The laid work sets up the most wonderful rhythmic patterns over the entire work. To complete the embroidery part the ribbon garlands were filled in with satin stitch using a single fibre of a rayon machine thread.

The embroidery was cut away from the base fabric and attached to a paper ground in the form of an arch built up with gold paper from tea packets. White tissue paper, painted, was also applied. The paper ground was given a final coat of polyurethane. The embroidery and paper ground were mounted on a semi-circular marine-ply board, also covered with layers of gold paper and tissue paper, painted with poster paint and varnished. The board has a deep lip around its edges to resemble the relief-sculptured tympanums above the entranceways to Romanesque churches.

As this monumental work resonates with me, so too do the relatively diminutive works of Janice Rawlinson in Sydney, Australia. Rawlinson developed a deep love for gold threads and used them exclusively when her ideas needed to be expressed in stitch. The play of light on metallic surfaces intrigued Rawlinson; to her, goldwork is akin to jewellery and sculpture. She tends to favour creating a body of work on a theme, which collectively show a fascination with fragments, the patterns and forms from ancient civilizations and exotic cultures.

Rawlinson's *Enduring Forms I* and *II*, created in 1992 for a multi-media exhibition in Christchurch, New Zealand, were inspired by an exhibition at the Powerhouse Museum in Sydney in the early 1990s of fibre arts from around the world. Rough black pen sketches of a few of the pieces in this exhibition were transposed to *Enduring Forms I* and *II* in a print medium while maintaining their original character. These two works are primarily works on paper with the gold embroidery worked separately on a frame

Enduring Forms II *by Janice Rawlinson.*

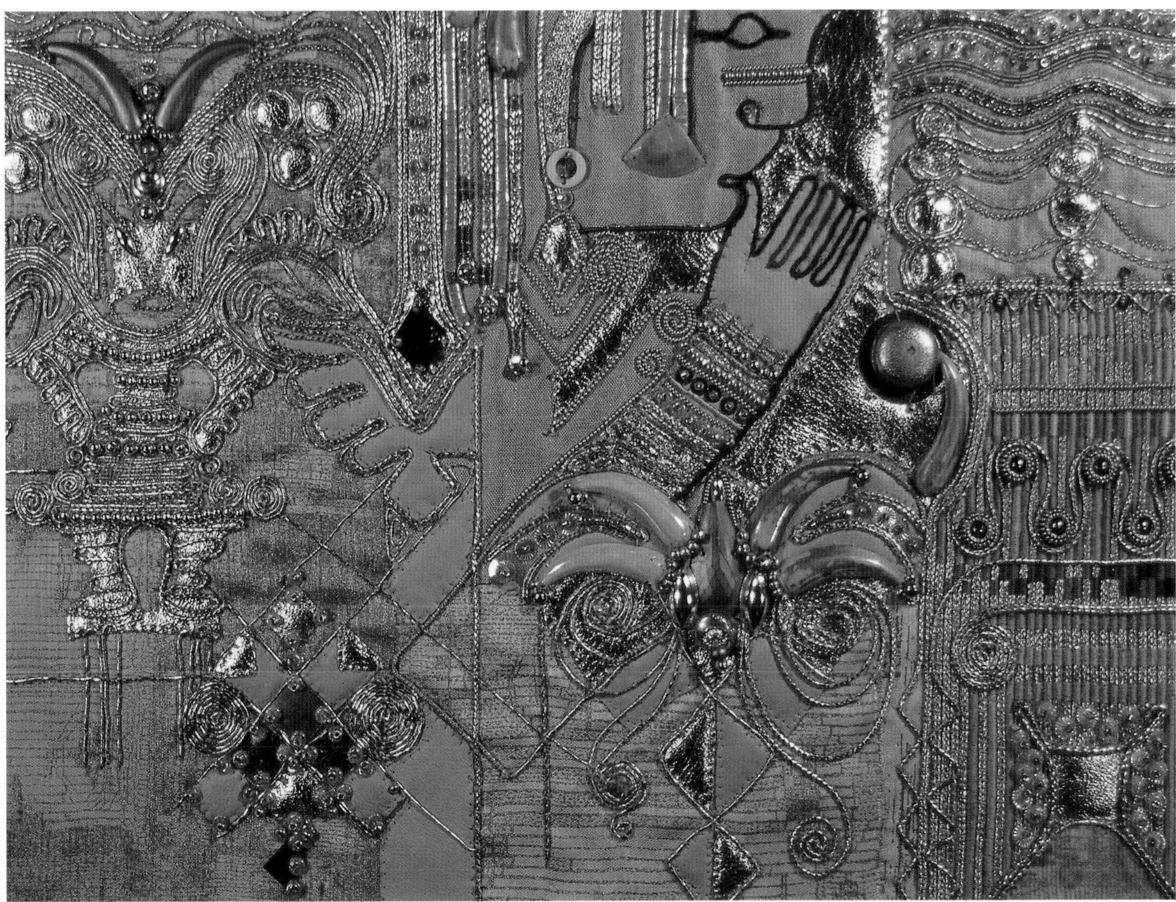

Detail of Margaret Nicholson's Coyolxauqui II *Photo courtesy of Anthea Godfrey.*

and added as a collage piece. Rawlinson shows a preference for metal threads that have to be couched rather than sparkly purls. For *Enduring Forms I* and *II* she embroidered pure abstract shapes on grey fabric with Japanese gold, chosen for its unsurpassed brilliance. She juxtaposed these gleaming threads with physical pieces from nature. In *Enduring Forms I*, she has attached horizontal rows of racemes from a palm tree to create a basket weave pattern. The gold threads were then continued over an unpadded surface around the upper half of the rectangle, only to traverse the racemes once again on the other side. The extremely long tails of metal thread at the beginning and end of each couched row are bunched and partially wrapped in gold tissue fabric, allowing the unwrapped sections to extend far beyond the boundaries of the works.

This story is not complete without a salute to Margaret Nicholson, who was embroidering up to her death in early 2005, aged in her early nineties. Nicholson's passion for goldwork embroidery stemmed from her background, her father being a master gilder. In 1929 she enrolled at Sheffield College of Art to do the five-year Industrial Design course, in the last two years specialising in dress and embroidery and at the same time taking on an additional embroidery course. Both Beryl Dean and Margaret Nicholson successfully married goldwork embroidery with other embroidery techniques in their work.

Nicholson is renowned primarily for her *or nué* embroideries, yet she only came to specialise

One of the works in the series on the four seasons embroidered by Margaret Nicholson. Photo courtesy of Anthea Godfrey.

in the technique in her seventies. Her daughter Anthea Godfrey encouraged her to take up *or nué* seriously after the death of her husband, knowing that such a precious and painstaking technique would be totally absorbing. With a passion for surface stitching and beading from her haute couture experiences, Nicholson married these two forms of embroidery with *or nué* in many of her works. The artist who inspired her was Gustave Klimt, whose paintings have the quality of decorative icons because of their intricate patterns and abundant use of gold leaf. Where his paintings are on a monumental scale, however, most of Nicholson's works are small; but like Klimt, the subjects of many of her works, such as *Coyolxauqui 1* and *2* (an Aztec goddess) and *Circe* (a powerful witch in Greek mythology), pertain to allegory and her designs are highly decorative, and gold of course reigns supreme.

Or nué embroidery in the 15th century was physically a flat technique in which varying the spacing between couching stitches to model the forms created the illusion of a third dimension. Nicholson's designs, however, are so densely composed of patterns that she emphasises the flatness of the surface. She made *or nué* more relevant to the 20th century by couching over a variety of metal threads such as pearl purls, twists and braids, and even strips of kid leather, instead of just over the traditional silver-gilt passings or Japanese gold. She sometimes worked the technique in reverse—that is, laying coloured threads and couching them with a fine gold thread. Invariably metal threads such as pearl purl, twist and braid were couched over the *or nué* embroidery to outline features or to

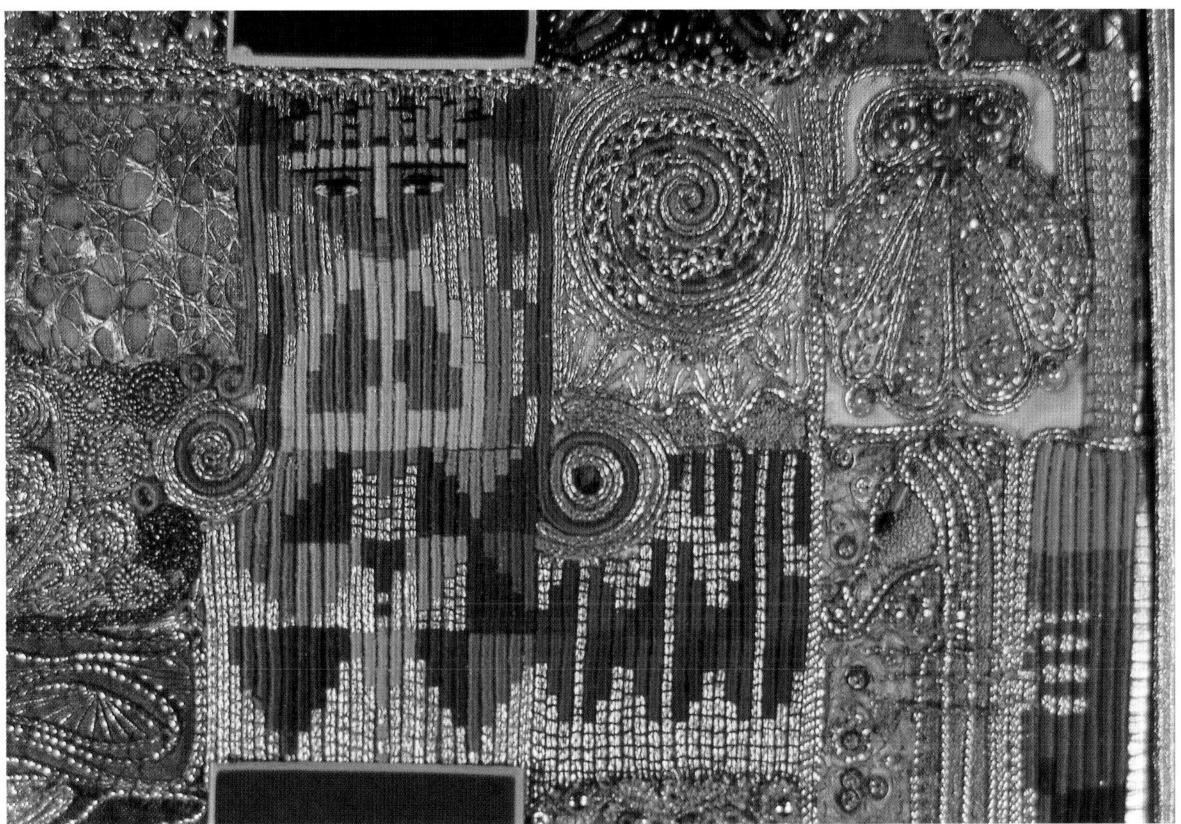

One of the works in the series on the four seasons embroidered by Margaret Nicholson. Photo courtesy of Anthea Godfrey.

create a more dynamic pattern. She always embellished with beads and sometimes incorporated found objects which were intriguing in themselves.

In many of her works Nicholson used *or nué* almost exclusively, but there are just as many where she combined it with other embroidery techniques, as in the design shown here based on Coyolxauqui, the Aztec goddess. The silk background is screen-printed, which allows it to play a significant role, and the figure of the goddess appliquéd with eau de nil silk. Many other parts of the design are appliquéd with gold kid leather. Nicholson did not turn the edges of her appliqués under in the traditional manner, discreetly stab-stitching the cut edges. A variety of gold threads couched into spirals and undulating lines represent Aztec symbols and patterns. Beads, sequins and found objects have been integrated into the embroidery. The only part of this particular work embroidered in *or nué* is a small architectural element in the bottom right-hand corner.

Anthea Godfrey showed me a series of Nicholson's works based on the four seasons. Each small piece is based on a combination of squares and rectangles derived from two squares joined together. There is a positive emphasis on surface effects achieved through the use of *or nué*, couched metal threads, surface stitching with metal threads and encrustations of beads, sequins and purls. Each square is given a different surface treatment. Pure abstract patterns fill some squares, stylised faces and symbols occupy others. One of the pieces has a large rectangular panel on the left featuring a stylised angel appliquéd in gold kid leather and enveloped with ornamental patterns, and worked entirely in different hues of gold. Intense colours of red-orange, burnt orange, violet and blue-purple are used with gold in the rest of the piece. The other works in the series are equally brilliant.

Beryl Dean, Barbara Dawson and Margaret Nicholson were extremely influential in elevating original gold-embroidered works to the status of fine art objects in the latter half of the 20th century. These three embroiderers had the courage to exhibit their work and the vocation to teach in order to pass on their new ideas in this glorious and ceremonious field.

2. Metal Threads: History and Construction

On display in the London Museum are some of the earliest metal threads yet discovered in Europe. In 1999, excavations in East London revealed a section of a 4th century Roman cemetery in which archaeologists discovered a limestone sarcophagus containing a lead coffin and the skeletal remains of a young woman from one of the wealthy classes. In the silt which had collected in the bottom of the coffin, bay leaves, fragments of wool and silk textiles, and gold threads were preserved. The gold threads lay across the torso and just below the pelvis, their arrangement suggesting a pattern of decorative stripes on a garment. There is no evidence for gold embroidery being worked in this period, so it is most likely that the threads were woven into the fabric. The sarcophagus and some examples of the remains in the coffin are now on display in the museum.

A fragment of the lustrous gold thread was analysed and found to be 90 per cent pure. At approximately 0.17 mm diameter, the thread is the finest ever recorded from the Roman period. It is made of a very flat, thin strip or ribbon of gold that had been spun by hand around a fine, strong thread core, most probably silk, possibly cotton or flax. None of the core material remains. The gold strips were spun in the Z direction, indicating that the thread was made in the western part of the Roman Empire. Gold threads found in the eastern Roman Empire were spun in the opposite, S direction.[1]

The technique was to cut thin strips from a metal sheet, and to either twist them around a mandrel (a length of wire) to form a tube ('strip twisting') or twist them on their axis ('block twisting'). The twisted metal strips were made into a seamless round wire by rolling them between two flat surfaces. At some point it was discovered that lapping a strip cut from a hammered sheet of metal around a fibre core, instead of twisting it around a mandrel, produced a round thread malleable enough to be woven into a fabric or used for embroidery, although its structure still necessitated that it be couched to the surface rather than pulled

1 Chris Thomas at the Archaeological Archive and Research Centre, London

through the fabric. This technology continued in use well into the medieval period.

Surviving examples of medieval woven fabrics, dating from the 11th to the 15th centuries, are embellished with gold threads made from strips of gilded membrane spun around a core of thread, a technique which also produced a thread more suitable for weaving than for embroidery. Both membrane gold and wound hammered gold were referred to in medieval inventories as 'Cyprus gold'. 'Venice gold' seems to have superseded Cyprus gold in the 16th century, when it becomes the type most frequently mentioned in the Great Wardrobe Inventories of Elizabeth I.

As demand for wires increased, a more advanced technology of drawing wires through draw-plates to create round wires developed. The first definite record of wire drawing is in a treatise written by Theophilus, a 12th century Benedictine monk and craftsman, in which he described an iron draw-plate with three or four holes of diminishing size through which wires could be drawn.

By the 12th century, there were thus three technologies for making metal filaments for embroidery threads. The gold threads of the Jesse Cope (an early 12th century *opus anglicanum* cope in the Victoria & Albert Museum) have a smooth surface and a sharply rectangular cross-section, typical of threads where metal has been beaten and cut, and wound around a silk core.[2] Two colours of metal thread were used on the Jesse Cope, X-ray fluorescence spectroscopy showing 'the sample taken from the Jesse vine to be a silver-gilt thread and that from the names of the prophets to be a corroded silver thread'.[3] The technology of coating silver ingots with gold before they were beaten into sheets of foil for cutting into narrow strips had been established by the 11th century.

Prior to the 11th century, pure gold or *aurum battutum* had been used for the metal filaments of embroidery threads, like those on the renowned 10th century maniple and stole of Saint Cuthbert. The modern equivalent to *aurum battutum* is Japanese gold. Silver-gilt threads were less expensive but still had the brilliance of pure gold.

The medieval wire-drawer had to rely on his own strength and a pair of heavy pliers, and could only draw wires in short lengths. 'The first "quantum leap" [in the production process] came around the year 1300 when a mechanical wire-drawing machine was invented in Germany. The device was water-powered'[4], and much greater lengths of wire could be produced.

Draw-plates were crude affairs and probably not suited to the manufacture of silver-gilt wires at the time when the Jesse Cope was made, but by the time of Elizabeth I they 'had been developed to a degree of refinement which allowed a composite gold-plated silver wire to be manufactured'.[5]

Producing drawn gold and silver wires with water-powered machinery began in England about the 1560s. Once established, 'this craft was destined to become of considerable importance: in 1740 more than six thousand people, mostly women and children, were employed by the

2 Marion Kite, 'The conservation of the Jesse Cope', *Textile History: The Journal of Textile and Costume History and Conservation*: Autumn 1989, Vol. 20, No. 2

3 ibid.

4 From a draft written by William Kentish Barnes for a series of articles for *Embroidery Magazine*

5 ibid

master wire-drawers of the London parishes of St Giles', Cripplegate and St Luke's'.[6]

Legal standards in 1698 required that the silver rod be 98 per cent sterling silver to 2 per cent copper, the copper eliminating the risk of fracture.[7] The rod was thoroughly cleaned and polished to remove all impurities, then wrapped in gold leaf and rubbed with burnishing stones to ensure that the gold married effectively with the silver, and annealed in a charcoal fire.

The drawing of wires was, and still is, a repetitive process, a gilded rod being drawn through a hundred or more holes before the wire was of gossamer fineness. Today series of tungsten carbide dies is used, then finer diamond dies, and possibly ruby dies for the very finest wires. The wire on exiting the die is mechanically wound around a drum which rotates and it is this action which draws the wire through the die. The wire may then be passed through rollers to be flatted or 'bruised'.

Metal threads such as pearl purl, purls, passing, tambour and rococo are made from flatted wires. Once the desired diameter is achieved, the wire is passed through rollers, which since the mid-18th century have been made of highly polished steel, to be flattened or 'bruised'. This provides a gleam to the wire. The matte metal threads such as rough and wire check purl and gimp are made from round wires.

Many threads are also taken through a spinning or lapping process.

Ingenious pieces of machinery have been invented to speed up the production processes, although much handwork and control are still necessary today, and 'some of the large purls are still made by hand using simple equipment that would be recognizable to a seventeenth-century craftsman.'[8]

Fibre-core metal threads

Silk was used for the cores of expensive metal threads and cotton and flax for threads of lesser quality. Today, cotton and man-made fibres have mostly replaced silk, although silk 'produces a finish that is second to none'.[9] The core consists of many yarns or 'ends' which are spun into a twist before being lapped with a flat metal filament. The thickness of the core partly determines the size of the finished thread.

Passing thread

There are two types of passing thread. *Smooth passing* has a relatively heavy flat metal filament which is lapped around a relatively thick core in the opposite direction to the twist of the core. The non-tarnishable passing thread available today consists of a metallised polyester flat ribbon lapped around a core. Passing threads are traditionally laid in pairs and couched to the surface of the background fabric. There are three standard sizes: 4 (the finest), 5 and 6.

Wavy passing appears textured in comparison to smooth passing, although the flat metal filament is the same. An unevenness of the core gives this thread its 'texture'. A 'rogue end' or loose yarn is deliberately introduced to the core body for wavy passing. It remains separate to the other yarns in the core body, and is loosely spun around the core to take away the evenness. The flat metal filament is lapped in the opposite direction to the spin of the core.

6 Therle Hughes, *English Domestic Needlework 1660—1860*. Abbey Fine Arts, London, p 58

7 ibid.

8 From a draft written by William Kentish Barnes for a series of articles for *Embroidery Magazine*

9 ibid.

Tambour thread

The metal thread classified as tambour thread (French *filé*) has half the diameter of a passing thread, its spun core has finer yarns than the core in passing, and its flat metal filament is lighter. The metal filament is lapped around the fibre core in the opposite direction to the twist of the core. Being a softer thread than passing, tambour thread is ideal for surface stitchery in goldwork embroidery.

Rococo and check threads

The core for these threads is prepared similarly to that for wavy passing: a number of yarns are spun into a twist, then rewound with the thrust in the opposite direction with a number of rogue ends added. Pulled up into the already tightly twisted core, the rogue ends create an even wave-like configuration. If the configuration is tight, the finished thread is known as a *check thread*; if the wave has a more gradual undulation, it is termed a *rococo thread*. Finally, the wavy core is lapped with a flat metal filament. Check and rococo threads are available in a range of sizes and traditionally are laid with smoother threads such as passing.

Imitation Japanese gold

Real Japanese gold is made from narrow ribbons of gilded paper lapped around a core of orange silk. It will never tarnish. It is still available today but is expensive.

Imitation Japanese gold consists of a metallised polyester ribbon lapped around a yellow synthetic core. It is made in the same way as smooth passing, the difference being that the metallised ribbon is much wider than the metal filament used for passing. There are four sizes available, the core determining the size: no. 13 (K1), no. 12 (K2), no. 9 (K3) and no. 8 (K4). No. 8 is the smallest size and the one most frequently used.

Metal threads with spongy fibre cores

The multi-yarns for the cores of such threads as gimps, flatworms and back threads are spun around a tapered needle. To make the core soft and spongy, a tapered needle is located in the spinning pipe with the point protruding just pass the 'point of spin'. The needle prevents the yarns, as they are fed through the pipe, from twisting tightly together.

Flatworms

Flatworm has some of the same components as passing: a multi-end core, untwisted, lapped with a flat metal filament. The spongy core is lapped with a flat metal filament in the usual manner. Finally the thread is passed through a light flatting operation to produce the flatworm appearance, adjustments in pressure producing different widths. This thread is sometimes used as an alternative to plate. *Vellum thread* is very similar to flatworm, except that two round wires rather than a flat metal filament are spun around the core, resulting in a matte appearance. It is an extremely beautiful thread and more expensive than flatworm.

Back threads

Back threads are made in the same way as flatworms except that they are not subjected to the flatting process. There is a large back thread which has a much wider diameter than flatworm and is very lustrous in appearance. Back threads and flatworms can only be couched to the surface of the fabric.

Gimps

Gimps also have a spongy core, around which

three very fine round wires are lapped simultaneously and produce a matte appearance. This thread has to be couched, and on its own makes a beautiful outlining thread. Round-wire gimp can be twisted up as a three-ply or four-ply thread, when it is known as *peak gimp*. Round-wire gimp twisted with a type of back thread known as bright or smooth gimp results in *Grecian gimp*. Peak gimp and Grecian gimp were originally used for the edging on military and naval hat peaks.

Metal-only threads

Purls

Purls (French *canetilles*) are fine wires that are coiled up tightly on a needle spinning at high speed. They form long snake-like coils which the embroiderer cuts into small lengths and attaches like beads. There are four variations of purl: rough, smooth, bright check and wire check.

Rough purl (French *matte*) is a perfectly round wire that has been coiled around the needle and has a matte surface.

Smooth purl (French *brilliante*) is the 'sister' to rough purl. Before spinning a smooth purl, the round wire is passed through rollers to 'bruise' or slightly flatten it, which imparts a smooth, brilliant surface to the finished product.

Wire check purl is a variation of rough purl. The round wire is coiled on a three-cornered needle to achieve a faceted appearance.

Bright check purl is a variation of smooth purl in that the wire is bruised before being coiled on a three-cornered needle.

Rough purl and wire check purl are both available in an extensive range of colours. All four purls are available in sizes from 9 (the smallest diameter) to 4 (the largest). Size 6 is most frequently used.

Another form of purl available today is the *silk-covered purl*, originally used in 17th century stumpwork. It consists of a copper round wire lapped with a silk thread and then purled up.

Bullions

Once the diameter of a purl exceeds size 4, it becomes known as a bullion. Bullions range in size from 1 (the smallest) to 10. *Wire bullion* is made with a round wire and has a matte appearance; *bright bullion* is made from a flat wire and has a shiny surface. *Bright check bullion*, made from a flat wire coiled around a three-cornered needle, has a faceted, shiny appearance.

Bullions are made from larger, heavier wires than purls. As the size of the bullion increases, the diameter of the wire also increases, keeping the finished bullion from being too floppy.

Bullions are still made by hand using a spinning wheel which drives a long needle. The wire is attached to the needle where there is a small notch. As the wheel is turned with the right hand, the left hand guides the wire up the length of the needle, keeping a steady tension. On reaching the end, the wire is cut and, with a deft stroking movement of the forefinger of the left hand, the tension in the purled wire is released, causing it to expand and loosen along the length of the needle. The anchor point is cut and the finished bullion slid from the needle. Before mechanisation all purls and pearl purls were made in this manner.[10]

Pearl purls

While it is not known where pearl purls originated, *lizerine*, a precursor of pearl purl, was

10 ibid.

used in the Elizabethan period to give definition to shapes. In 1882, the *Dictionary of Needlework* listed pearl purl as a 'gold cord of twisted wire resembling a small row of beads strung closely together'.[11]

Lizerine and pearl purl begin as round wires with a diameter between 0.25–0.45 mm (.010–.018 in). They are both flatted into a stout wire ribbon. Lizerine is purled up at this stage, but the flat wire ribbon destined to be pearl purl is passed through a diamond die over the top of a round wire. As the two wires are drawn through the die, the flat ribbon wire curves over the round wire, giving the top side of the ribbon (now referred to as a 'bead') a beautiful convex shape. To separate the bead wire from the round wire, each is wound onto its own spool. The bead wire is then purled up.

While the demand for lizerine is only a fraction of that for pearl purl, it is made in a comparable range of sizes. Pearl purl, which comes in several sizes from 'very fine' through to size 4, is mostly used as an outlining thread and is couched to the surface of the fabric. As a rule it is not used on costumes because it is such a heavy thread—uniforms being the exception.

Plate

Plate is difficult to make correctly. The wire goes through the rollers many times and the difficulty lies in keeping the flatted plate from developing a corkscrew dimension. Plate can be made in a variety of widths, the widest for embroidery being just under 2 mm (1⁄10 in). Plate can be lapped with either a fine wire or fine thread, when is referred to as *whipped plate*. Plate is usually laid by folding it back and forth across a shape, which breaks up its 'gleam'.

Although plate is not easy to make or apply properly it is one of the most stunning products available to goldworkers.[12]

Milliary

This very unusual thread has three components. A heavy wire is purled up, then carefully stretched to a predetermined length to be wound onto a reel and combined with a similar length of passing thread. The two threads are lashed together with a fibre-core thread even finer than tambour thread. Milliary makes a very attractive edging.

11 Quoted in Therle Hughes, *English Domestic Needlework 1660—1860*, Abbey Fine Arts, London, p 64

12 From a draft written by William Kentish Barnes for a series of articles for *Embroidery Magazine*

3. Materials, Equipment and Preparation Techniques

Tool kit

A tool kit for goldwork includes:

- An assortment of crewel needles. Size 10 crewel needles are utilised for most goldwork techniques and threads but the smaller purls, spangles and petite glass beads will need size 12 sharps needles. Size 7 crewel needle is best for Tambour Thread.
- A chenille needle for making a lasso to assist in plunging the tails of metal threads through to the back of the work.
- Curved needles for couching the tails of fibre-core metal threads that have been taken through to the back of the work.
- Sewing threads for couching fibre-core metal threads and pearl purl, and for attaching purls. Gutermann 968 is a popular choice for couching gold metal threads. YLI Silk Thread 078 is a beautiful thread to use for flat laid work.
- A cube, bar or cake of beeswax. Sewing threads need to be waxed to keep them smooth and to protect them against the metal threads.
- A pair of small scissors with sharp points. KAI 5100 have proved to be excellent scissors for goldwork. They give a good clean cut to pearl purl and purls.
- A pair of tweezers for manipulating pearl purl and for creating hooks on plate.
- A mellor and a stiletto. One end of the mellor has a sharp point which can be used as a stiletto to make holes. The point can also be used to assist in turning fibre-core metal threads in laid work. The other end of the mellor is wide and curved which is used to smooth laid work or plate work that has been done over high padding. This end is also used to move metal threads into position. Today's mellors are made from stainless steel and a good mellor will be perfectly smooth. The stiletto is used for making holes to facilitate the plunging of metal threads.
- A velvet board for cutting purls to prevent them jumping as they would on a hard surface. This board can be simply made by covering a square or rectangle of card with velvet, or by covering the inside of a small shallow lid with velvet.

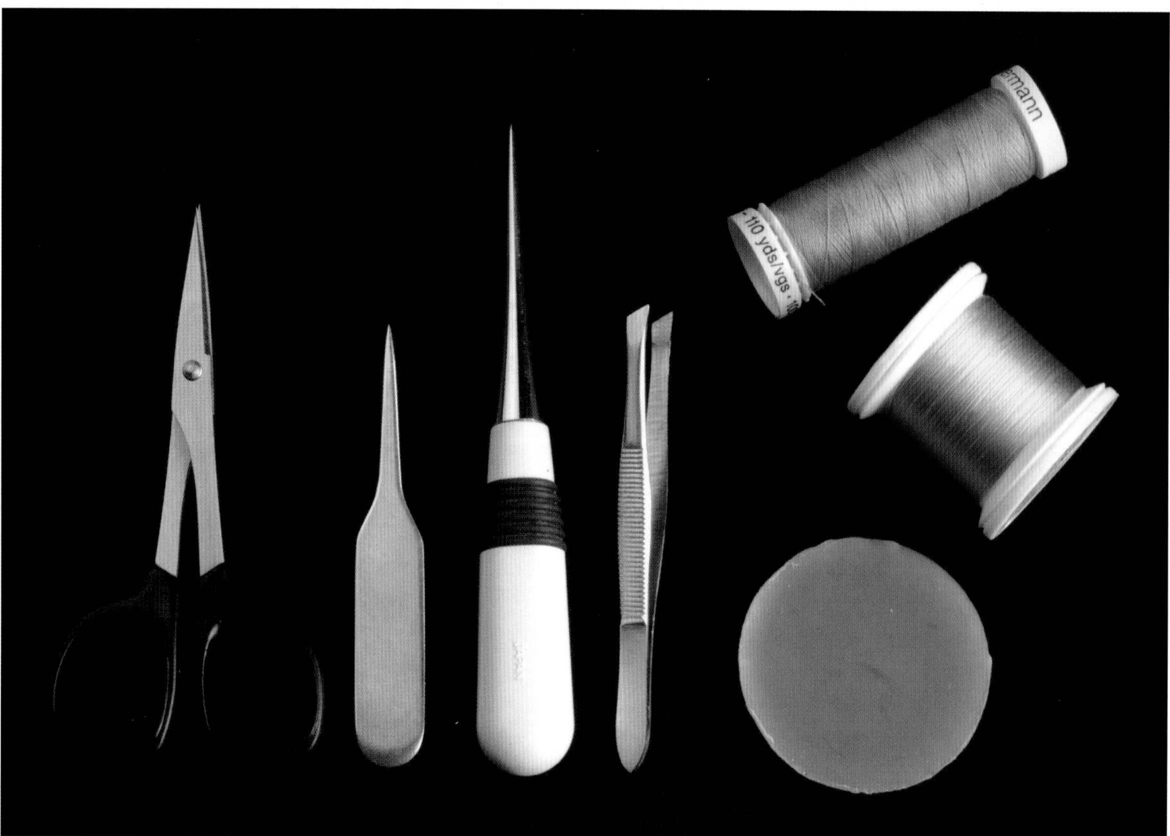

Scissors, mellor, stiletto, tweezers, beeswax and gold thread.

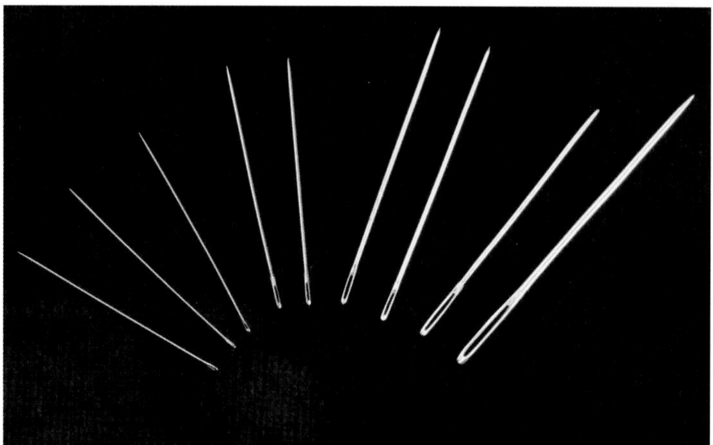

From left to right, the needles are: size 12 sharps, size 10 crewels, size 7 crewels, tapestry needle, chenille needle

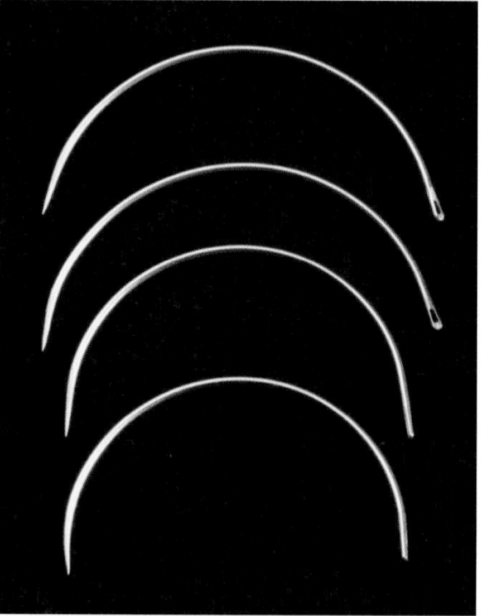

Curved needles

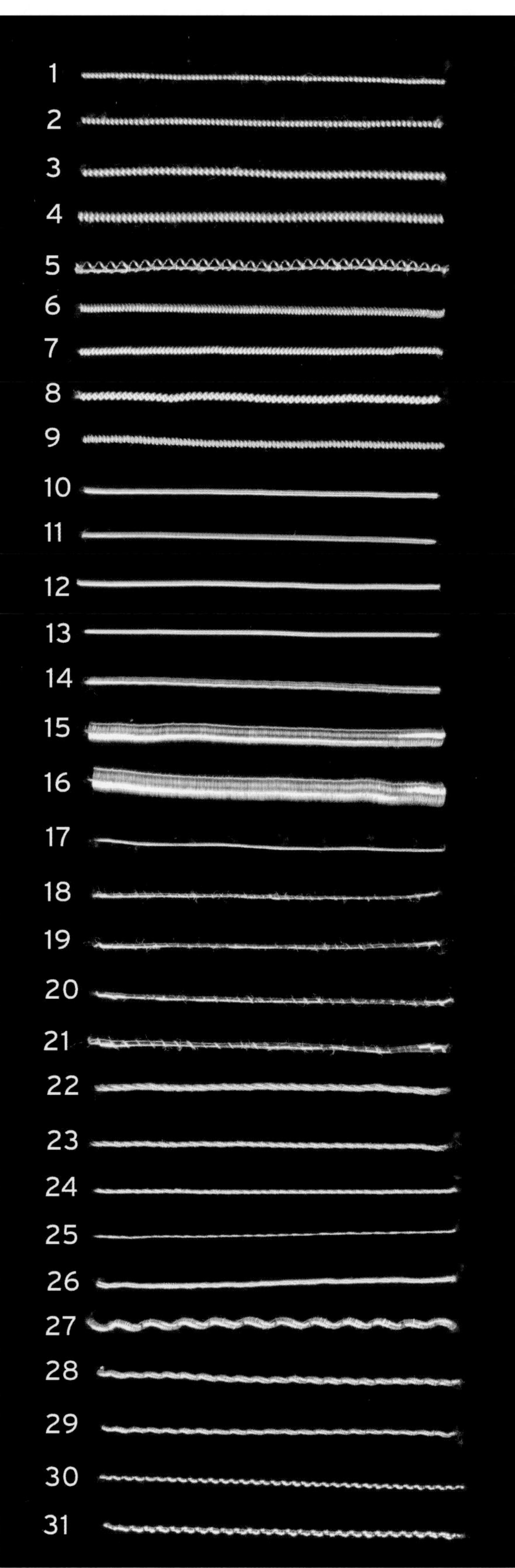

Threads

Examples of readily available gilt threads

1 Gilt super pearl purl
2 Gilt no. 1 pearl purl
3 Gilt no. 2 pearl purl
4 Gilt no. 3 pearl purl
5 Gilt milliary
6 Gilt no. 6 bright check
7 Gilt no. 8 bright check
8 Gilt no. 6 wire check
9 Gilt no. 8 wire check
10 Gilt no. 6 smooth purl
11 Gilt no. 8 smooth purl
12 Gilt no. 6 rough purl
13 Gilt no. 8 rough purl
14 Gilt no. 1 bright bullion
15 Gilt no. 6 bright bullion
16 Gilt no. 8 bright bullion
17 Gilt no. 5 smooth passing
18 Gilt no. 8 (k4) Japanese gold
19 Gilt no. 9 (k3) Japanese gold
20 Gilt no. 12 (k2) Japanese gold
21 Gilt no. 13 (k1) Japanese gold
22 Gilt 3-ply twist
23 Gilt no. 1½ twist
24 Gilt no. 1 twist
25 Gilt Elizabethan twist
26 Gold gimp
27 Gilt large rococo
28 Gilt medium rococo
29 Gilt fine rococo
30 Gilt no. 5 check
31 Gilt no. 7 check

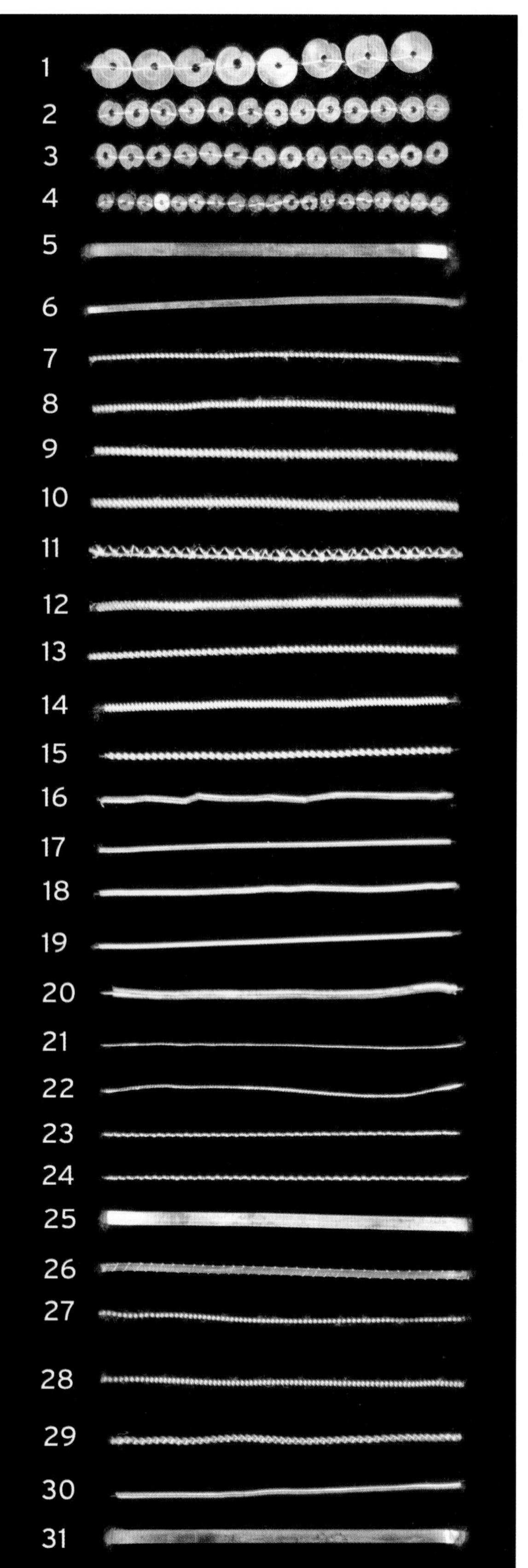

Gilt spangles, silver-plated and copper threads

1. Gilt 5mm spangles
2. Gilt 4mm spangles
3. Gilt 3mm spangles
4. Gilt 2mm spangles
5. Gilt broad plate
6. Gilt narrow plate
7. Silver-plated super pearl purl
8. Silver-plated no.1 pearl purl
9. Silver-plated no.2 pearl purl
10. Silver-plated no.3 pearl purl
11. Silver-plated milliary
12. Silver-plated no.6 bright check
13. Silver-plated no.8 bright check
14. Silver-plated no.6 wire check
15. Silver-plated no.8 wire check
16. Silver-plated no.6 smooth purl
17. Silver-plated no.8 smooth purl
18. Silver-plated no.6 rough purl
19. Silver-plated no.8 rough purl
20. Silver-plated no.1 bright bullion
21. Silver-plated tambour
22. Silver-plated no.5 smooth passing
23. Silver-plated no.5 check thread
24. Silver-plated no.7 check thread
25. Silver-plated broad plate
26. Silver-plated whipped plate
27. Copper super pearl purl
28. Copper no.1 pearl purl
29. Copper no.6 bright check
30. Copper no.6 smooth purl
31. Copper broad plate

Coloured metal threads

Twists, no. 20 couching threads, silk-covered purls, rough purls and wire check purls are available in a wide range of colours.

Some of the coloured metal threads available for use in goldwork embroidery: left, dark purple no.6 wire check purl; centre top, pink no.20 couching thread; centre middle, burgundy 3 ply twist; centre bottom, jade no.6 rough purl; right, red no.6 wire check

Storing metal threads

All metal threads need to be kept in acid-free tissue paper or the acid-free glassine available from art suppliers. Do not store them in plastic containers, as this causes them to become tarnished.

Metal threads are best kept in acid-free glassine bags

Materials commonly used in goldwork embroidery

- Calico or fine cotton is used as a supporting fabric for the embroidery fabric.
- The most popular fabrics for goldwork embroidery are: velvet, duchesse satin silk, dupion silk and linen. However, any stable fabric can be used. The more fragile fabrics such as silk organza and muslin can be applied or manipulated on a stable fabric for goldwork embroidery.
- Braids, ribbons, lace, kid leather, beads, crystals and 'found objects' are frequently used.
- Yellow felt is used for padding shapes that will be covered with gilt and copper threads, and white felt for silver-plated threads.
- Carpet felt is used for very high padding.
- DMC Soft Cotton or bumpf is used for string padding.

Dressing a square or slate frame

Goldwork requires both hands to be free to manipulate the metal threads. A square or slate frame, which can rest on trestles or two chairs of the appropriate height, is the ideal frame for goldwork. The larger projects in this book will require a quilter's frame if you do not have a slate frame. A quilter's frame is a large and deep circular frame with a diameter that far exceeds the diameters of ring/hoop frames. If you are using a quilter's or ring frame, you will need to weight it or clamp it to a table. For a ring frame, choose one with a deep rim and bind the inner ring with strips of calico or tape to hold the fabric more securely.

Materials for dressing a slate frame

- calico
- measuring tape
- pen
- pins and size 7 crewel needle
- a strong buttonhole thread
- wide webbing
- bracing needle (normally used by upholsterers)
- strong string or fine cord
- sewing thread for attaching the embroidery fabric

A slate frame has two rollers or bars, two arms and four pegs. The arms have a series of holes for the pegs. Webbing is stapled onto the rollers. Measure and make a permanent mark for the absolute centre on the webbing of both rollers.

In goldwork, the fabric to be embroidered is backed with pre-shrunk calico or cotton, which is put onto the frame first. This backing fabric must be *cut* on the weft and the warp. Do not rip it because this can distort the grain. Instead, draw threads on the weft and the warp and then cut. The backing fabric, which represents the width of the work, should not be wider than the webbing on the rollers. It is preferable that it be in a little from the edge on both sides of the webbing. The length of the backing fabric is not critical, because any excess can be rolled up on the rollers. Refer to Figure 1.

Fold a 1 cm (½ in) turning on the top and bottom edges of the calico or cotton to be attached to the rollers. Iron the turnings. Fold the turned edges of these sides in half to find the exact centre and mark with a pin. Match the pin on the fabric with the permanent mark on the webbing of the roller. Pin the turning of the backing fabric to the webbing at this point and continue pinning out to both edges. Starting in the centre, oversew the backing fabric and webbing together on one side with a substantial thread such as Gutermann Buttonhole and return to the centre to oversew the other side. This will prevent the backing fabric from 'walking' along the webbing. Repeat on the other roller. Make sure to thoroughly secure every beginning and end of your stitching with a repeated backstitch.

Once the backing fabric has been attached to both rollers in this way, roll up any excess length, and slip the arms of the frame through the ends of the rollers. Push pegs into the holes on the inner sides of the arms to hold the rollers evenly

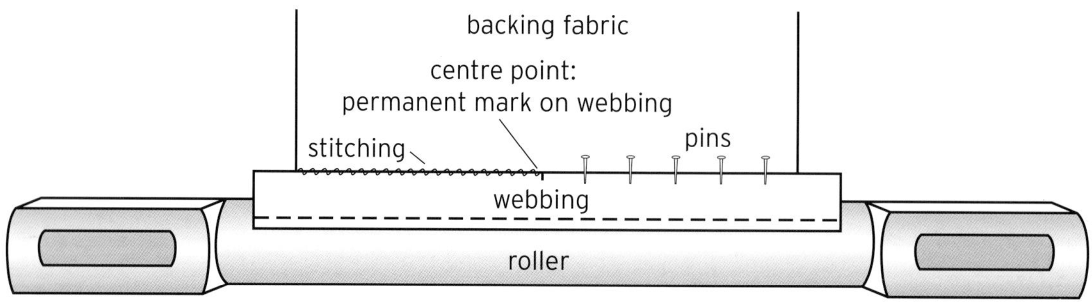

Figure 1 Attaching the backing fabric to the roller

apart. The backing fabric should be gently stretched between the two rollers but it should not be taut.

The sides of the backing fabric must be reinforced with webbing strips in preparation for lacing. Pin the webbing along the length of the backing fabric, allowing for two-thirds of its width to be sitting on the fabric. Refer to Figure 2. Using Gutermann Buttonhole, attach the webbing to the fabric with a wide basting stitch. Again, thoroughly secure the beginning and end of the basting by doing a backstitch repeatedly in the one place.

Next is the lacing stage. Thread a strong string or a very fine cord that will withstand extreme tension into a large bracing needle. Leaving a tail of at least 50 cm (20 in), take the bracing needle down through the webbing that extends beyond the side of the backing fabric, take the string under and over the arm of the frame and go back down through the webbing approximately 3 cm (1½ in) away from where you took the needle down previously. Repeat at 3 cm (1½ in) intervals along the entire length of the webbing. Leave another tail of at least 50 cm (20 in). Repeat the procedure along the other strip of webbing. Even up the lacing but at this stage still allow a little slack in the backing fabric. Wind the tails around the intersections of the rollers and arms and fasten off with a slip knot, which will allow you to retighten the strings easily later on. Refer to Figure 3.

The next step is to prepare the fabric to be embroidered. This, like the backing fabric, must also be *cut* on the weft and the warp. You may wish to transfer the design onto the fabric before it goes into the frame. (While the prick-and-pounce technique and the carbon method of transferring a design can both be used after the frame has been dressed and stretched to drum-tightness, you will have to place books of an appropriate size beneath the fabric to provide a firm surface to work on.)

As an aid to mounting the embroidery fabric on the straight, draw a thread in the backing fabric on one roller side and another on one of the laced sides to serve as guides. Line the embroidery fabric up with the drawn lines and pin these two sides first. Smooth out the embroidery fabric and pin the other two sides. Using a sewing thread, and starting at the corner of the two drawn lines, stitch along the roller

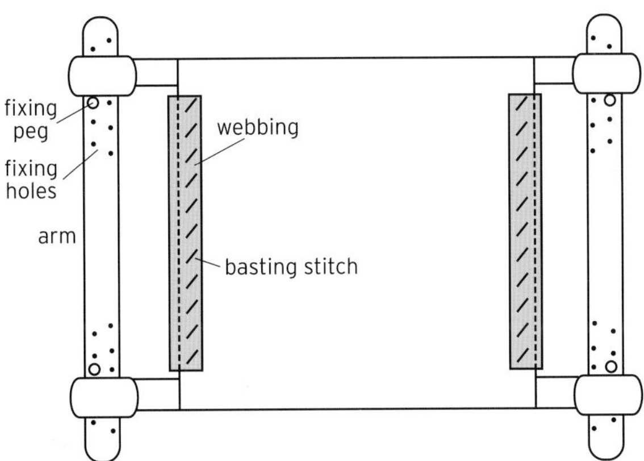

Figure 2 Attaching the webbing to the sides of the backing fabric

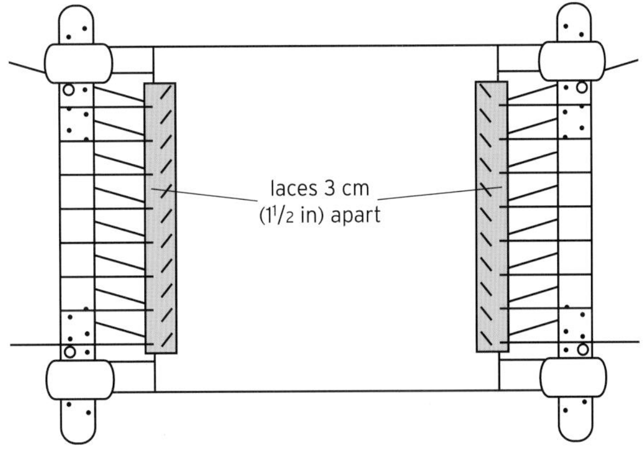

Figure 3 Lacing the backing fabric to the frame

side with alternating long and short stitch, coming up in the backing fabric and going down into the embroidery fabric. Space the stitches approximately 3 mm (⅛ in) apart. Starting from the same corner, stitch along the laced side. Stitch the remaining two sides, using a tape measure to check continually that the fabric remains smooth and on the straight. Refer to Figure 4.

The fabric in the frame is now ready to be tightened as taut as a drum. Move pegs down one hole on each side of one of the rollers (you may need to press on the end of the roller with your foot to do this). Release the slip knots, tighten the strings on both sides and retie the slip knots.

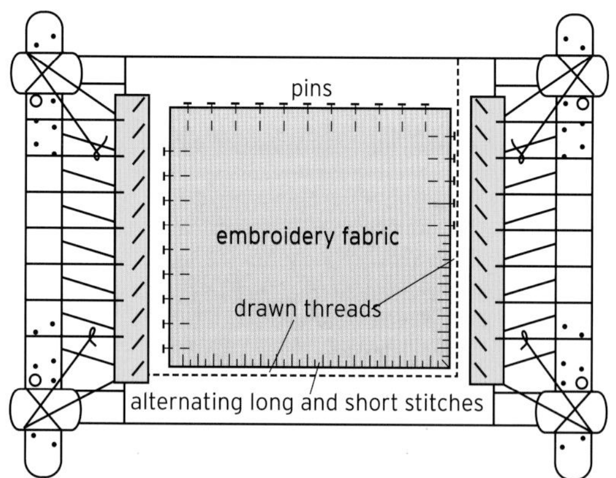

Figure 4 Mounting the embroidery fabric

Slate frame dressed, ready for embroidery to begin

Transferring a design

Prick-and-pounce technique

This traditional method of transferring a design is mostly used for transferring a design onto velvet. It is also ideal for transferring shapes onto the felt used for padding certain areas of a design.

Pounce is a mixture of powdered charcoal and powdered chalk or cuttlefish. For dark fabrics, the two should be mixed to a very light grey by adding very small amounts of charcoal to the chalk until it is the colour required. On lighter coloured fabrics, including felt, the pounce has to have a higher ratio of charcoal to chalk.

Trace the design onto tracing paper, preferably one of at least 110 gsm weight. Tracing paper less than 110 gsm is unsuitable because it buckles, especially in damp weather. Prick the design lines on the tracing paper with a size 9 crewel needle or a lace pricker, using a cork mat or card for support and spacing the pricks 1 mm (1⁄20 in) apart. Place the tracing paper, right side up, on the face of the velvet or felt, and weight the paper onto the fabric. Dip one end of a tightly rolled piece of felt into the pounce and rub over the entire design with circular movements. Lift off the tracing paper to reveal the outlines of the design formed by little dots. Gently blow any surplus pounce off the fabric.

The pounce will not remain on the surface of the fabric once embroidering commences, so the dots need to be fixed with paint. (There is no need to paint over the dots on felt shapes because they will be cut out and used immediately.) Yellow ochre watercolour paint is used when the design is to be embroidered with gold threads. The very fine yellow painted outlines will be entirely hidden under the metal threads. The paint will dry very quickly—once it has, pick up the fabric and give it a sharp flick to ensure that no excess pounce remains. The fabric is now ready to mount in the frame.

A design transferred onto velvet with several lines painted with yellow ochre watercolour paint

Dressmaker's carbon paper transfer technique

This method of transfer can be used on silk or linen backgrounds. Orange dressmaker's carbon works on most coloured embroidery fabrics. White dressmaker's carbon may be used if a design is worked entirely with silver-plated threads.

Trace the design onto 110 gsm tracing paper. Position the tracing on the embroidery fabric. Weight the tracing paper onto the fabric along the top only. Carefully slip the sheet of dressmaker's carbon paper, face down, between the tracing paper and the fabric. Use a fine tip biro to firmly and carefully trace over the design to transfer it onto the fabric.

4. Goldwork Embroidery Techniques

IMPORTANT!

- A *single* sewing thread is used for couching fibre-core threads.
- A *doubled* sewing thread is used for attaching all purls, spangles and beads.
- The sewing thread should be a golden yellow polyester or silk thread.
- To start and finish sewing threads such as Gutermann 968, work three little pin stitches, either on a design line or in the felt padding where they will be eventually hidden beneath metal threads. This applies to both single and doubled threads.
- The sewing threads must be waxed to keep them smooth and to protect them against the metal threads.

How to use pearl purl

Before using super pearl purl and no. 1 pearl purl threads, and threads that are finer still, stretch them a little to open them up for ease of couching. To stretch, hold the length of thread with both hands and gently pull in an outward direction with both hands. A 10 cm (4 in) length should be stretched to no more than 12 cm (4¾ in). It is not necessary to stretch the larger pearl purls (nos 2, 3 and 4).

Pearl purl sits entirely on the surface of the fabric, and is couched down using a single sewing thread. An easy way to start couching is to extend the length of pearl purl beyond the actual beginning of the design line, place a couching stitch over it where the design line begins and then twirl the pearl purl back to that point before you continue couching. The couching thread has to disappear completely between the 'beads'. (It is very reassuring to hear the 'clicking' noise as it sinks into the groove.) When couching, bring the needle up on the design line on the outside of the pearl purl and take it down on the inside. As the grooves of this metal thread are on an angle, the couching stitches must also be angled. Couch every third or fourth groove if you are working with a long and relatively straight length, or every second groove for a very short length or for a tight curve.

Aim to have a 'bead' showing at each end of

the couched length of pearl purl. It is not difficult to achieve that at the beginning because the pearl purl can be easily trimmed when in the hand. At the end, however, place your very sharp scissors carefully at a position on the pearl purl that will give you a 'bead' and not a hook.

When outlining a circle, start and finish at the bottom of the circle. Squares or rectangles should start and finish at one of the bottom corners. Pearl purl is a very flexible and robust thread and can be manipulated around the sharpest of corners with a pair of tweezers. For an acute angle, couch up to the very point of the angle, and anchor the point more securely by going back and couching a groove behind the point. Now it is possible to use the tweezers at the point to pivot the free pearl purl back on itself. Gently squeeze the point together with the tweezers for a sharper point and continue couching.

Pearl purl can be *overstretched* to create more textural interest or a more decorative outline. On overstretched lengths the couching stitches become visible, so more consideration needs to be given to their placement. Overstretched super or no. 1 pearl purl can be wound with a few threads of stranded cotton to also create a more decorative outline. This process may distort the thread, and to make it conform to the shape that you are outlining, couch the pearl purl in every groove with a strand of the same thread and colour that was wound around the pearl purl.

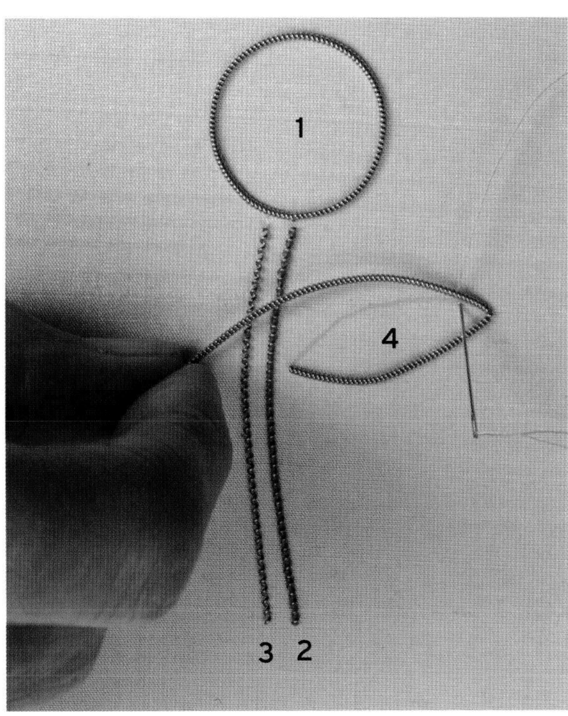

Pearl purl techniques, showing: 1, a circle couched with gilt no.1 pearl purl; 2, overstretched gilt no.1 pearl purl wound and couched with pink stranded cotton 3, overstretched gilt no. 1 pearl purl couched with Gutermann 968; 4, pearl purl manipulated around an acute angle.

Felt padding

In contemporary goldwork embroidery, yellow felt is used as padding underneath gilt/gold threads and white felt under silver threads. Padding is mostly used underneath cutwork and chip work because purls are more reflective over a curved surface, but it can also be used to raise laid work and appliqué work.

If the design is being worked on velvet, or any fabric with a heavy texture, the shapes in the design will need at least one layer of padding to prevent the metal threads being 'lost' in the fabric. If the purpose of the padding is to raise a section of the embroidery, more than one layer of felt will be required.

Felt padding is completed before commencing the embroidery. Start by tracing all the shapes to be padded onto 110 gsm tracing paper. Be very precise in tracing the shapes because they need to completely cover the design lines on the background fabric. If the shape is to be padded with more than one layer of felt, do the first tracing just on the outside of the design line for that shape. This will be the largest of the layers and the last to be attached. Make another tracing about 1–2 mm (1/16–1/8 in) (depending on the size of the shape) in from the design line for the second layer, and another a further 1–2 mm (1/16–1/8 in) inside that line if a third layer is required. The smallest layer is attached first. Occasionally a padded shape will require another padded shape on top of it; for example the centre of a flower.

The traced shapes can be transferred onto the felt using the prick-and-pounce technique or dressmaker's carbon (see chapter 3).

Cut the shapes out carefully and precisely. Use a single yellow sewing thread for yellow felt, white sewing thread for white felt, and attach the shapes to the background with small stab stitches. The needle must come up in the background fabric and be taken down in the felt. Do not work the reverse way because the felt will move out of place. Also, taking the needle down in the felt allows you to pull the felt over very gently, if need be, to hide the paint lines on the embroidery fabric. (This only applies to the last layer.)

The hidden layers of felt require only a stab stitch in each quarter of the shape, and one or two stitches in between them. When you position the last layer for that shape, work a stab stitch in each quarter and then stab stitch around the entire shape. The stitches need to be about 2 mm (1/8 in) apart.

Padding with four or five layers of felt can be worked in this way. If a thickness of more than five layers is required for a particular design, it is better to use carpet felt. The first layer of carpet felt padding is the largest. To 'carve' the shape, the edges of each layer of carpet felt need to be bevelled. Each layer is attached with large basting stitches. Cover the padded shape with a single layer of yellow or white felt.

Felt padding: the upper layers have been partially sewn down, then turned back to demonstrate the staggered sizes of the layers

Cutwork

In all forms of cutwork the sewing thread needs to be doubled. After a hollow purl has been picked up on the needle it must be dropped to the bottom of the sewing thread so that it is resting on the embroidery fabric before the needle is taken back through the fabric. Support the thread with a mellor, chenille or tapestry needle as it is drawn through.

Chipwork

Both bright check purl and wire check purl are used for chipwork, which uses purl chips cut into pieces as long as they are wide. Felt shapes designated for chipwork should be outlined first with a metal thread such as pearl purl or twist. The chips must be densely packed if they are laid on felt padding, otherwise they can be scattered across the surface. Either way, they need to be laid down in different directions. When stitching a chip, bring the sewing thread up through the fabric, thread the chip, drop it to the bottom of the thread, and take the needle down at a

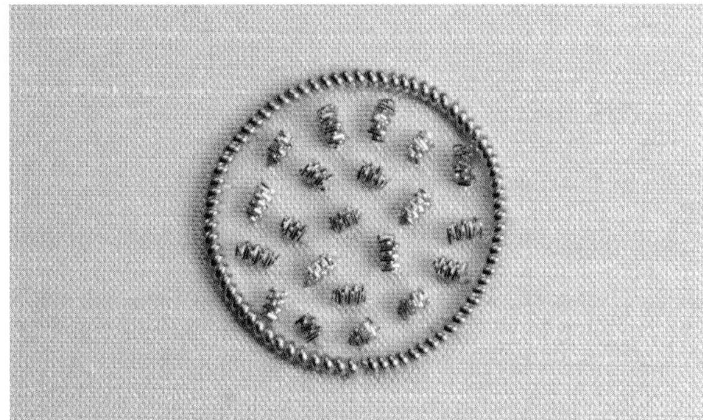

Chipwork: densely packed chips on an outlined and padded background, and random placement within a couched circle

distance equal to the length of the purl so that the chip will lie flat on the surface. In dense chipwork, bring the needle up beside the chip just laid in preparation for the next chip, which needs to sit in a different direction.

Cutwork over felt padding

All four types of purl thread—bright check purl, wire check purl, smooth purl and rough purl—can be used for this technique. Longer lengths of purl than those used in chipwork are used for cutwork over felt; chips of purl may also be needed to fill in the sharper corners of some shapes.

This type of cutwork can look very effective when two different kinds of purl are alternated, as shown here in the sample flower. With only one or two layers of felt, the ends of the cut purls will be visible and it may be desirable to outline the shape before commencing the cutwork. Felt padding with three or more layers may be so high that the cut ends of the purls are not visible, and can thus be treated in the same way as cutwork over string padding (see next section).

Traditionally, the purls in cutwork over felt padding are taken directly across it. It is best to start by placing a purl in the centre of the shape and work out to one side, then the other. The centre purl sets the direction of the cutwork for that shape. To stitch each purl, come up on the inside of the metal thread outlining the felt shape. Thread up the purl and lay it across the padding to see if it is the correct length. If the cut purl is sitting proud of the padding, it will fracture; if it is too short, the felt padding will be seen at the edge. A purl that is too long can be moved back up and a little beyond the point of the needle and snipped back to the required length. (Keep any chips because they can be used elsewhere.) Once the length is correct, take the needle down through the felt on the opposite side, just inside the outline thread. In preparation

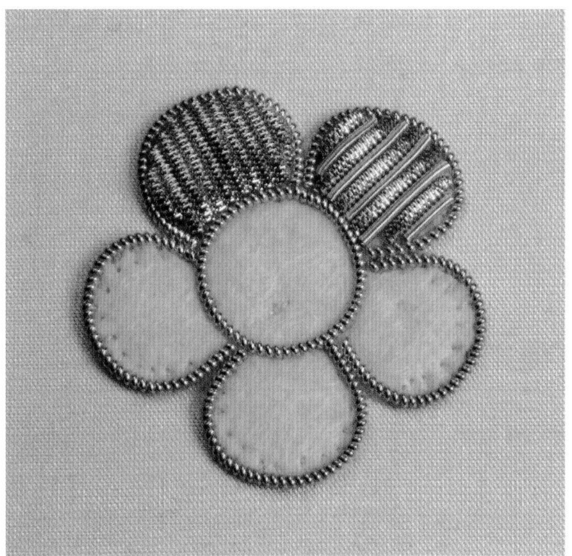

A flower partly worked in cutwork over felt padding

for stitching the next purl, bring the needle up close beside the previous one. In other words, succeeding purls are laid down 'head to toe'.

Horizontal cutwork over string padding

For string padding, take several equal lengths of DMC soft cotton or bumpf padding (ten lengths will generally be enough for the projects in this book) and lay them within the drawn design lines for the cutwork. Allow enough space between the padding and the design lines for the purls to sit perfectly on the background fabric. Make sure the strings are not twisted around each other. Couch along the length of the string padding with a doubled sewing thread. Wrap the bundle of strings with the couching stitches by angling the needle as you bring it up through the fabric beneath the bundle, and angling the needle under the bundle as the thread is taken back through the fabric. Trim off the excess strings at both ends, and couch again to hold the cut ends together. Place a horizontal stitch into the bundle at either end. See the top sample in the photograph marked with an arrow.

The first step in the embroidery is to create a template for the cut purls. Bring up a threaded needle in the centre and close to the string padding on the lower side. Thread up a purl and lay it over the string padding from bottom left to top right at a 45° angle. This is the traditional direction for horizontal cutwork. Hold the thread down on the background with another needle to see if the purl is the correct length. If the purl is too long it will sit proud of the string padding and will fracture; if too short, it will not sit directly onto the fabric and the padding will be exposed. Once the correct length has been determined, slide the purl off the needle and use it as a template for cutting the other purls.

Thread a purl on your needle and drop it to the bottom of the sewing thread. Lay the purl across the padding at the 45° angle from bottom left to top right, in the centre of the padding. Take the needle down close to the padding. This centre purl sets the angle of the cutwork.

When working to the right of the centre purl, the 45° angle will be maintained by bringing the needle up very close to the previous purl on the bottom side of the string padding and taking the needle down on the top side, leaving a space that is the width of a purl. Each purl to the right is worked in this manner. See the middle sample in the photograph.

When working to the left of the centre purl, the reverse will apply. The wider space between the purls is now on the bottom side and the needle is taken down close to previous purls on the top side.

Finish with a half length of purl at either end, as can be seen in the bottom sample in the photograph, to prevent the last full-length purl from sliding off the padding.

This form of cutwork is not outlined.

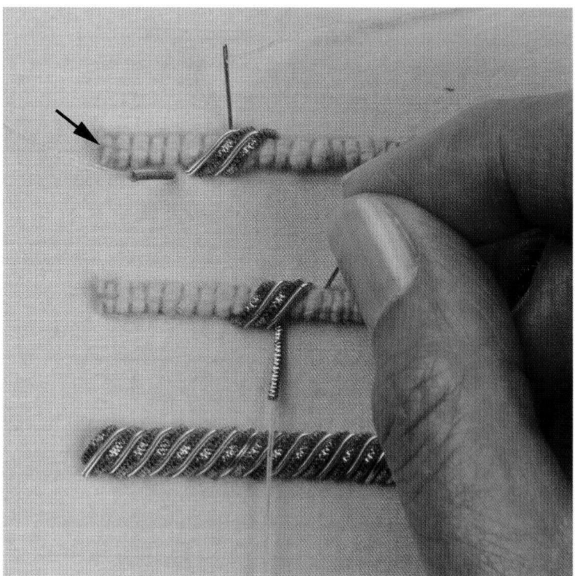

Stages in working horizontal cutwork over string padding

Vertical cutwork over string padding

String padding for vertical cutwork is worked in the same way as string padding for horizontal cutwork (see above).

Again, the first step in the embroidery is to create a template for the cut purls. Bring up the threaded needle in the centre and close to the string padding on the right side. Thread up a purl and lay it over the string padding from top right to bottom left at a 45° angle. This is the traditional direction for vertical cutwork. Hold the thread down on the background with another needle to see if the purl is the correct length. Once the correct length of purl has been determined, slide it off the needle and use it as a template for cutting the other purls.

Thread a purl on your needle and drop it to the bottom of the sewing thread. Lay the purl across the padding at the 45° angle, from top right to bottom left, in the centre of the padding. Take the needle down close to the padding. This centre purl sets the angle of the cutwork.

When working above the centre purl, bring the needle up a purl-width away from the centre purl on the right side of the string padding and take the needle down on the left side, tucking the needle in snugly beside the centre purl. Come up every time on the right side of the padding, leaving a wider space between the purls on this side than on the left side to ensure that the angle remains the same as the centre purl for the remaining length of the padding.

When working below the centre purl, bring the needle up on the left side of the string padding a purl-width away from the previous purl. Thread up a purl and take the needle down very closely to the previous purl on the right side of the string padding. Come up every time on the left side of the padding, leaving a wider space between the purls on this side than on the right side to ensure that the angle remains the same as the centre purl down the remaining length of the padding.

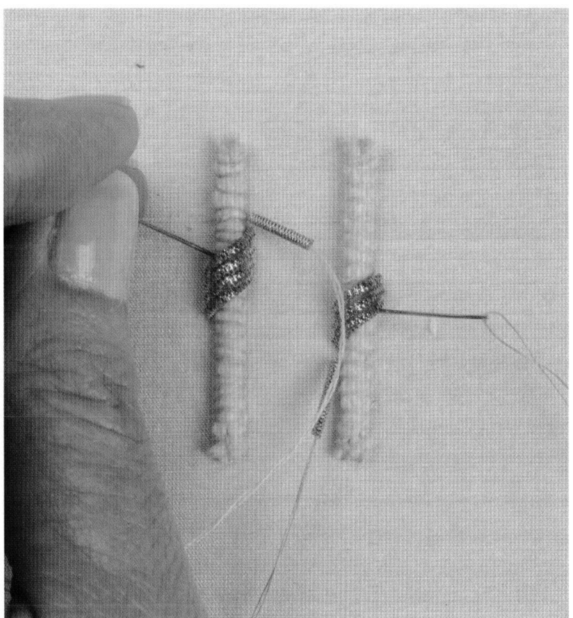

Vertical cutwork over string padding

Finish with a half length of purl at either end as for horizontal string padding to prevent the last full-length purl from sliding off the padding.

S-ing

S-ing is a form of cutwork which looks like stem stitch. All four different types of purls can be used. The purls are cut all the same length, traditionally 5–6 mm (¼ in) For a horizontal row of S-ing, work from left to right; for a vertical or diagonal row, work from top to bottom.

Bring up the needle on the design line one purl length from the beginning of the design line. Thread up a purl and take the needle down at the beginning of the design line.

For the second purl, bring the needle up on the design line half a cut purl length away from the first purl. Thread up the second purl and take the needle down on the design line above and halfway along the first purl if it is a horizontal row. If the row of S-ing is being worked vertically, the needle will go down on the right side of the purl. Angle the needle just under the first purl. Support the sewing thread with the mellor or a chenille needle as you take the thread through, then allow the purl to curve over the mellor or needle as it just tucks under the first purl.

For the third purl, bring the needle up on the design line half a cut purl length away from the second purl. Thread up the third purl and take the needle down on the design line above and halfway along the second purl. The beginning of the third purl will meet up with the end of the first purl. It will now be possible to see the purls taking on the characteristic S shape. Repeat in the same manner along the entire design line.

A half length of purl may need to be used at the beginning and end of a row of S-ing, certainly in the case of a straight row. For the start of a horizontal row, bring the needle up at the beginning of the design line on the bottom side of the first purl. If it is a vertical row of S-ing, the needle will come up on the left side of the first purl. Thread up the half purl and drop it to the bottom of the sewing thread. Angle the needle halfway along and underneath the first purl. Support the sewing thread with the mellor or a chenille needle as you take the thread through and then allow the purl to curve over the mellor or needle as it tucks under the first purl. The same applies at the end of the row. For a horizontal row of S-ing, bring the needle up at the end of the design line on the top side of the last purl; if it is a vertical row, the needle comes up on the right side of the last purl.

S-ing is very effective for creating a single decorative line; working several rows of S-ing close together creates a beautiful texture.

S-ing can also form the outline of a circle. Begin at the bottom and proceed in an anti-clockwise direction around the circle. Work in the same manner as for S-ing a horizontal line until there is only one purl to add to complete the circle. Aim to have what will be the second last purl meeting the first purl that started the outline (end-to-end). To complete the circle, bring the needle up halfway underneath and on the bottom side of the first purl. Thread up the final purl and drop it to the bottom of the sewing thread. Angle the needle down halfway along the second last purl, approaching from the top side of the purl. Use the mellor to gently push aside the second last purl to allow the last purl to go into its S-shape.

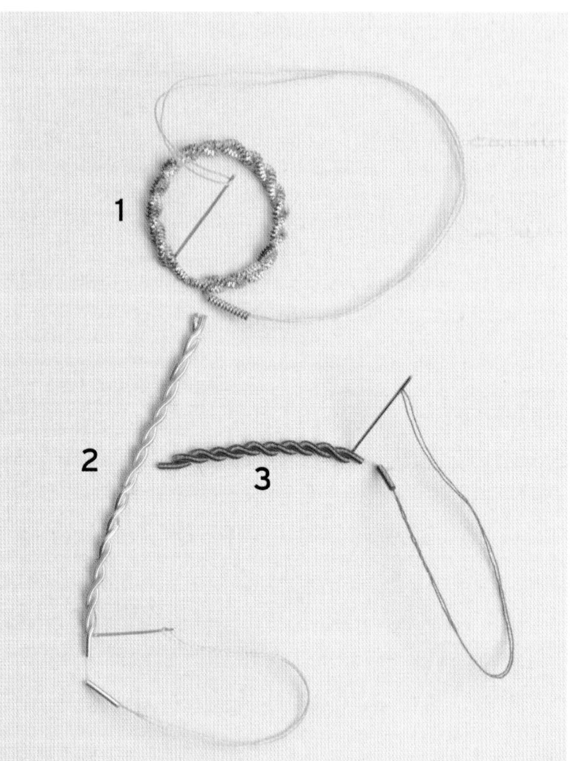

S-ing: 1, circle of S-ing with the needle in place for the last purl; 2, vertical S-ing with the needle in place for the last purl; 3, horizontal S-ing with the needle in place for the last purl.

S-ing with spangles or sequins

In preparation for this work, cut the purls into lengths slightly greater than the diameter of the spangles. Use a doubled sewing thread. For a horizontal row of S-ing with spangles, work from left to right; for a vertical or diagonal row, as seen in the photograph, work from top to bottom.

Bring the needle up through the fabric on the design line at a distance the length of a cut purl away from the beginning of the line. Thread up a spangle and then a purl. Drop them to the bottom of the sewing thread and take the needle down to the beginning of what will be a row of spangles with S-ing.

For the next step, bring the needle up at the bottom of the first spangle. Thread up the spangle first, then the purl, and drop them to the bottom of the sewing thread. Take the needle down at the top of the first spangle. Support the thread with a mellor or a chenille needle as it is pulled through, allowing the purl to curve over the mellor or needle as it tucks into the first purl.

Now bring the needle up at the bottom of the second spangle. Thread up the third spangle and purl. Drop them to the bottom of the sewing thread. Take the needle down through the hole of the first spangle. Come up at the bottom of the third spangle and thread up the fourth spangle and purl. Drop them to the bottom of the thread and take the needle down through the hole of the second spangle. Repeat in the same manner for the rest of the row. Notice that the purls tuck into each other to form an S shape.

Spangles and loops of purl

In preparation for this work, cut the purl thread into the lengths required for the particular design.

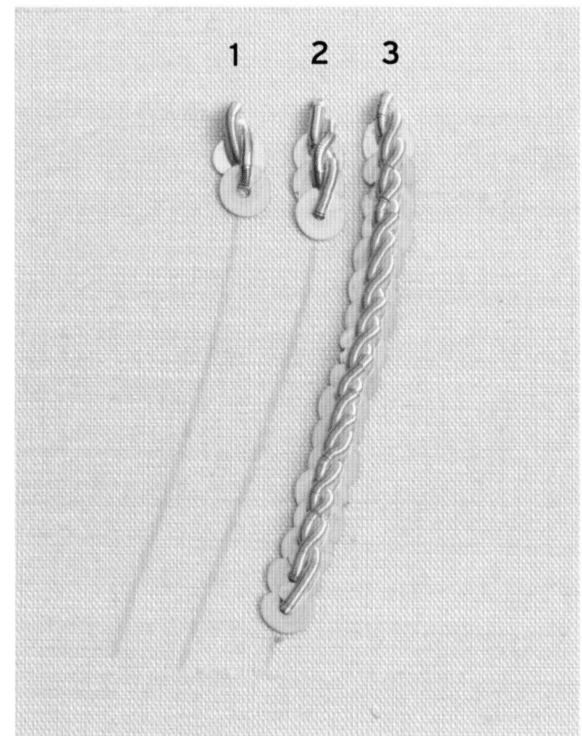

S-ing with spangles: 1, left, the first two spangles and purls attached; 2, centre: the third spangle and purl attached; 3, right, more spangles and purls attached

For the single spangles, bring the needle up through the fabric. First, thread up a spangle and then a length of purl. Drop them to the bottom of the sewing thread and take the needle back down through the hole of the spangle. Use a mellor or a chenille needle to support the doubled sewing thread as it is pulled through, and then allow the purl to curve over the mellor or needle. Once the thread has been pulled right through, there will be a loop of purl standing proud on top of the spangle. The loop of purl is also anchoring the spangle onto the background fabric.

For a cluster of spangles and loops of purl, attach a centre spangle and purl in the same manner as explained above. The centre spangle is surrounded by a circle of spangles and loops which are worked in a clockwise direction. The

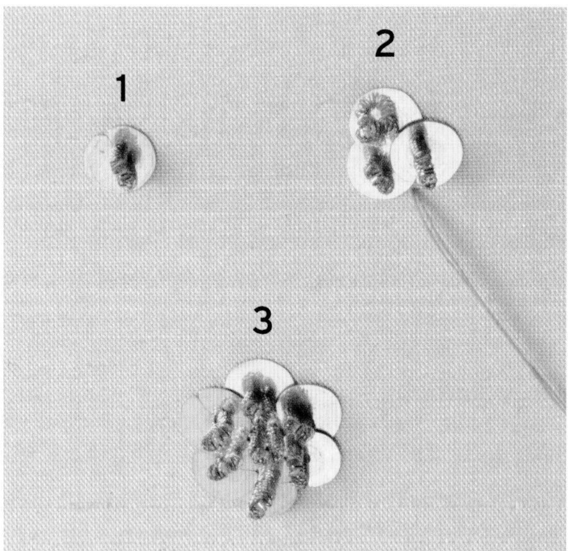

Spangles and loops of purl: 1, top left, the attachment of centre spangle and loop of purl; 2, top right, the attachment of the first and second spangle and loop of purl for the outside circle of spangles and loops—note the position of needle and thread coming through for the third spangle and loop of purl; 3, bottom centre, the completed cluster of spangles and loops.

circle of spangles should overlap each other as well as the centre spangle, although the last spangle is not overlapped. The centre spangle is almost completely hidden under the circle of spangles. It usually requires six spangles to complete a circle.

Laid work

Fibre-core metal threads are used for laid work. When pairs of fibre-core metal threads such as Japanese gold or passing are laid down and couched to form a line, the technique is referred to as *couching*, but when pairs of those same threads are laid side by side to fill a shape, it is known as *laid work*.

Flat laid work

Laid work can be worked directly onto the background fabric or over felt padding. Usually two fibre-core metal threads, such as Japanese gold or smooth passing, are laid side by side and couched over as if one thread. It is advisable to wind the two metal threads onto a spool.

The couching thread is usually a golden yellow sewing thread for gold threads and white or grey sewing thread for silver threads, but a contrasting colour can also be used. The couching stitches are at right angles to the metal threads and are evenly spaced about 5 mm (¼ in) apart. Traditionally, couching stitches create a brick pattern. This is achieved by placing the couching stitches of the second row of laid work in between the couching stitches of the first row. Repeat the pattern of couching stitches of the first two rows for the rest of the laid work.

Tails of approximately 5 cm (2 in) are left at the beginning and the end of laid work, to be plunged through to the back of the work. The technique of plunging is explained at the end of the section on flat laid work.

Two main techniques are used in flat laid work.

Technique 1

This technique gives the best definition at the edges of the laid work and is certainly the best technique to use if the shape is tapered or irregular.

The first row should define the edge of one side of the shape. If the laid work is over felt padding, the first row should sit on the felt. To couch the first row, bring the needle with the couching thread up on the outside of the two metal threads and take the needle down on the inside of the metal threads. Repeat every 5 mm (¼ in) keeping in mind that the couching stitches

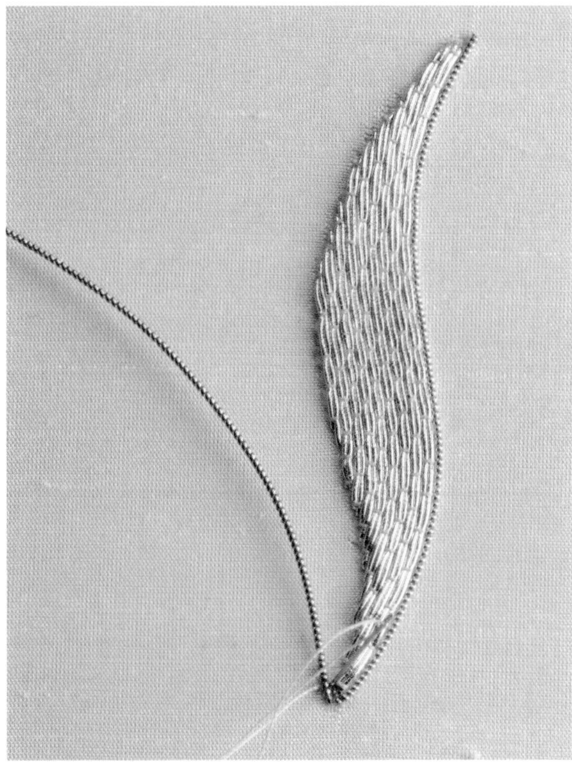

Leaf shape in flat laid work: technique 1

are to remain perpendicular to the metal threads. Leave tails of the metal threads at the beginning and the end of the first row.

The second row will also have tails. For the second row bring the needle up on the inside of the two metal threads, then take it down between this row and the first row, angling the needle slightly so that the second row is pulled up against the first. Work in this manner along the entire length of the second row and for all remaining rows.

This technique leaves you with an inordinate number of metal thread tails to plunge through to the back of the work. Instructions on how to plunge the threads are to follow.

Technique 2

Start the laid work on the edge of the shape, leaving tails of the two metal threads at the beginning of the first row.

To couch the first row, bring the needle with the couching thread up on the outside of the two metal threads and take it down on the inside of the metal threads. Repeat every 5 mm (¼ in) to the end of the row.

The two metal threads are now turned back on themselves. Be careful not to allow them to cross over each other. Before couching the metal threads at the turn, hold a mellor at the turn and pull the threads in the opposite direction around it. The two metal threads are couched separately on the turn. Bring the needle up on the outside of the outer metal thread and take it down on the inside of this thread; for the inner metal thread, come up on the inside and go down on the outside of the inner thread. If necessary pinch the two metal threads at the turn with tweezers.

To work the second row, bring the needle up on the inside of the two metal threads and then take it down between this row and the first row, angling the needle slightly so that the second row is pulled up against the first row. Turn the metal

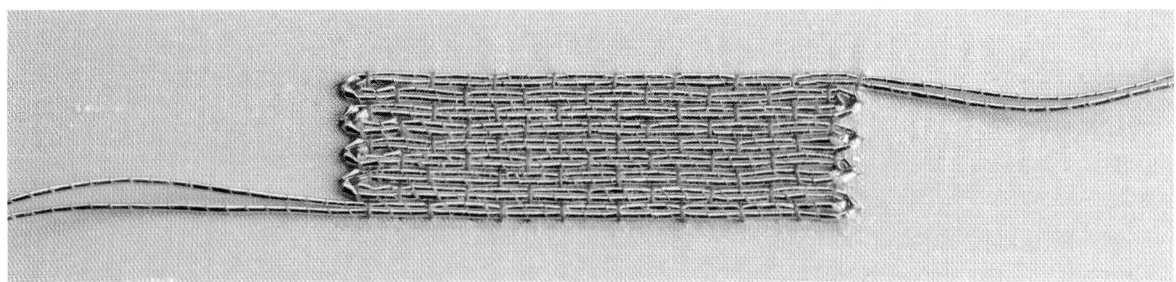

Rectangular shape in flat laid work: technique 2

threads at the end of every row. Leave tails for plunging at the very end of the laid work.

This technique works well for squares and rectangles, but not so well for a tapered shape, where it produces a stepped edge.

Couching a leaf shape from the outside in

Start the laid work on the edge of the shape, leaving tails of the two metal threads at the beginning of the first row.

To couch the first row, bring the needle with the couching thread up on the outside of the two metal threads and take it down on the inside of the metal threads. Repeat every 5 mm (¼ in) to the end of the row.

The two metal threads are now turned to be taken down the other side of the leaf shape. Before couching the metal threads at the turn, hold a mellor at the turn and pull the threads around it. The two metal threads are couched separately on the turn, as in technique 2 above.

When the first row around the perimeter of the leaf shape has been completed, turn the threads again in the same way as at the other end of the leaf, and start the second row around the leaf. Couch the second row by bringing the needle with the couching thread up through the fabric the width of the two metal threads away from the first row, and then take the needle down between the second and first rows. Angle the needle slightly so that the second row is pulled up against the first. Starting with the second row, create a 'brick' pattern with the couching stitches.

Continue couching rows around the leaf shape and turn the metal threads at each end of the leaf. At the centre of the leaf shape, leave the outside metal thread at one end of the leaf and continue couching the inside metal thread up to the other end. Cut both threads in the centre at either end, leaving 5 cm (2 in) tails to plunge.

Couching a circle from the outside in

Two metal threads are laid side by side and are couched over as if one thread. The couching stitches for the first row are spaced 5 mm (¼ in) apart, but the gap between couching stitches will close in as the laid work spirals towards the centre of the circle. The couching stitches are to remain perpendicular to the metal threads.

Start with only one of the metal threads on the outside of the circle, leaving a 5 cm (2 in) tail for plunging to the back of the work when the spiral is completed. Couch over this thread and only introduce the second thread when the first thread has been couched two or three times. The second thread is on the outside of the first. (The first thread now becomes the inside thread of the pair.) The two metal threads are now couched as

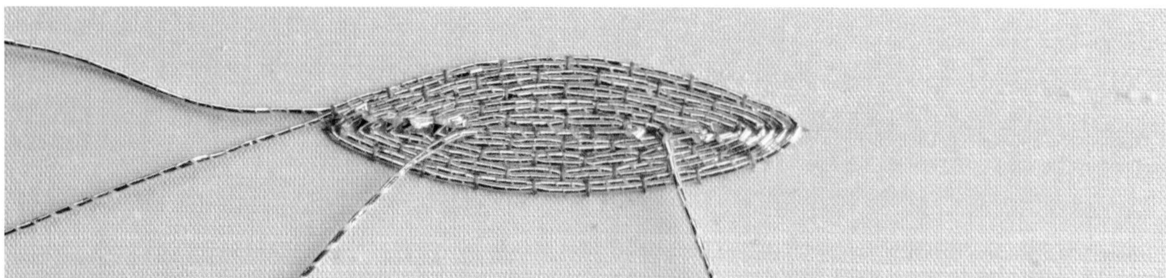

Couching a leaf shape from the outside in. The position of the tails to be plunged indicates the beginning and the end of the couching work.

Couching a circle; here only the ends remain to be plunged

one. For the first row the metal threads are couched from the outside to the inside.

After the first row has been worked, proceed to couch the second row by bringing the needle up on the inside of the two metal threads already laid, leaving enough space for the two metal threads of the second row to be able to sit nicely. Angling the needle just under the first row, gently pull the second row up against the first. To create a brick pattern with the couching stitches, beginning with the second row, couch in between two couching stitches of the previous row.

When the spiral has reached the centre, plunge the tail of the inner gold thread just before plunging the tail of the outside gold thread. Finish by plunging the two tails at the beginning.

Couching a diaper pattern

A diaper is an allover pattern. Common diaper patterns for laid work are diamonds and chevrons. The lines for the diaper pattern are drawn onto the embroidery fabric before commencing the laid work. Thread up a yellow sewing thread for couching the areas between the lines for the diaper patterns, and thread up a coloured thread for the couching of the patterns themselves. Once you begin couching the metal threads, only put in a coloured couching stitch where you have come up against a line for the diaper pattern. The coloured couching stitches must remain perpendicular to the metal threads even if the lines for the diaper patterns are on the diagonal.

Plunging the tails of fibre-core metal threads

Each thread must be dealt with separately when plunging the tails of metal threads to the back of the work. Create a hole exactly where the tail is to be plunged with an awl, stiletto or size 18 chenille needle. Make a lasso by threading two ends of buttonhole or very strong sewing thread into a size 18 chenille needle. Place *only* the tip of the tail of metal thread into the lasso and

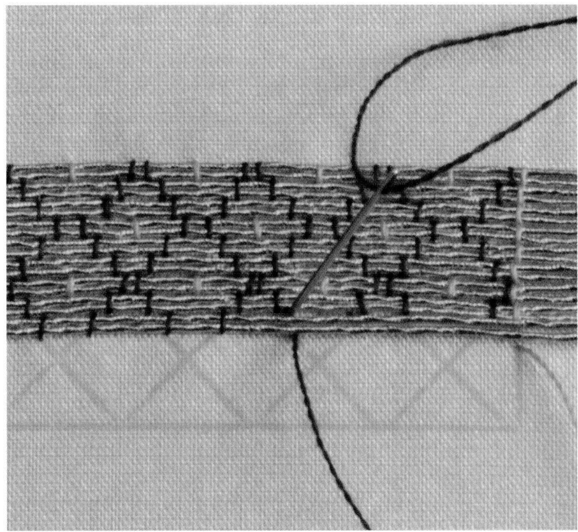

Couching a diaper pattern of diamonds, showing the stepped effect created by keeping the pattern stitches vertical

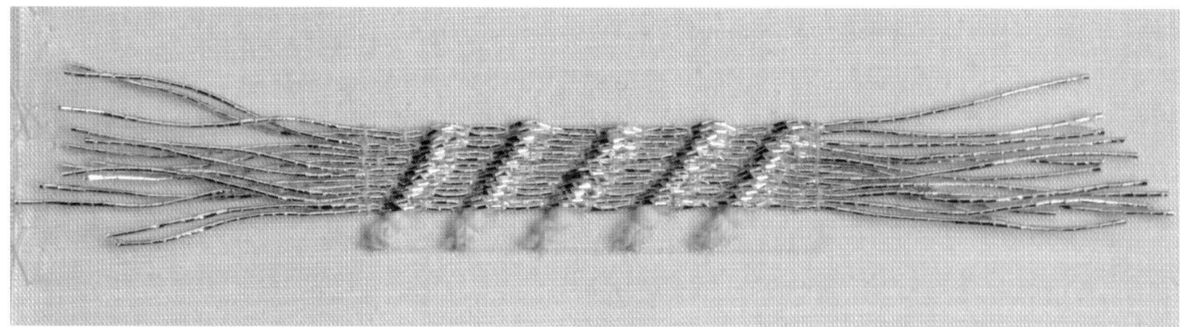

Laid work over simple diagonal string padding

carefully pull it through to the back. Turn the work over and couch the tail to the back of the work. A curved needle will make this task much easier.

Raised laid work

Fibre-core metal threads can be raised over string padding, acid-free card or pelmet vilene.

String padding

For string padding, use several equal lengths of either bumpf or DMC soft cotton, or a single cotton cord. Lay the string padding on the design line. Couch along the length of the string padding with a doubled sewing thread. Trim off the excess at both ends and couch again to hold the cut ends together. Place a horizontal stitch into the soft cotton or cord at either end.

Simple string padding

Traditionally, rows of string padding are laid at evenly spaced intervals perpendicular to the direction of the laid work or diagonally across the laid work, as seen in the photograph. Using technique 1 or 2 for flat laid work, take pairs of metal threads over the string padding. Couch the metal threads on either side of the string padding. The couching stitches remain perpendicular to the metal threads even when the string padding is on the diagonal. If the spaces are wide between the rows of string padding, couch and brick as for flat laid work.

Basket weave

Rows of string padding are placed on the perpendicular at evenly spaced intervals across the area to be covered with this pattern. Each

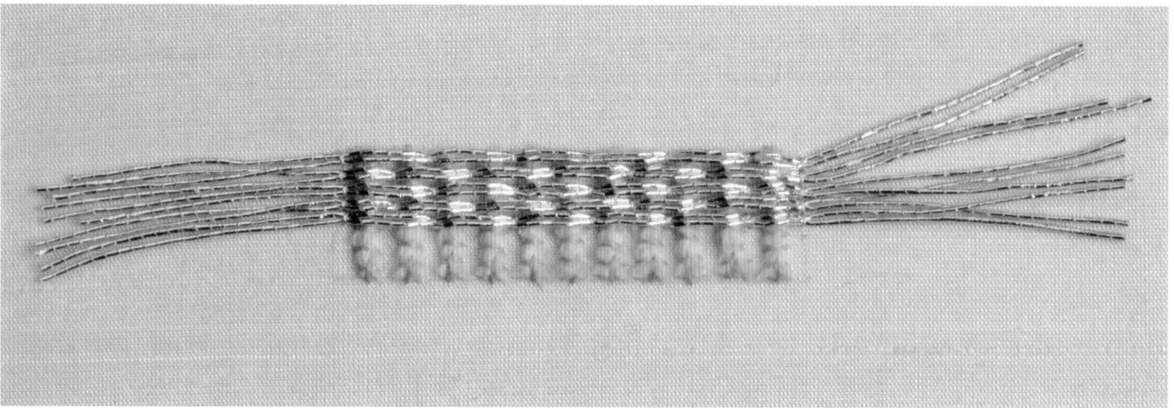

Basket-weave pattern of laid work

space is the width of the string. Using technique 1 or 2 for flat laid work, take pairs of metal threads over the string padding. To create the basket-weave pattern, take the metal threads over two strings and couch firmly to create a valley. Repeat this pattern of couching along the row. For the next row, couch between the couching stitches of the previous row. The third row is couched to line up with the couching stitches of the first row. Repeat the pattern across the entire area.

Sewing twist invisibly

The preferred technique for sewing twist is to work invisible couching with a single sewing thread. To begin couching in this way, hold the twist in one hand, and with the other hand bring the needle with the sewing thread up through the fabric at the beginning of the design line for the twist. Then thread the needle through one of the strands of the twist (remember to leave a tail), then lay the twist on the design line and take the needle down through the fabric 1 mm away from where the needle came up. Continue by placing a couching stitch approximately every 4 mm

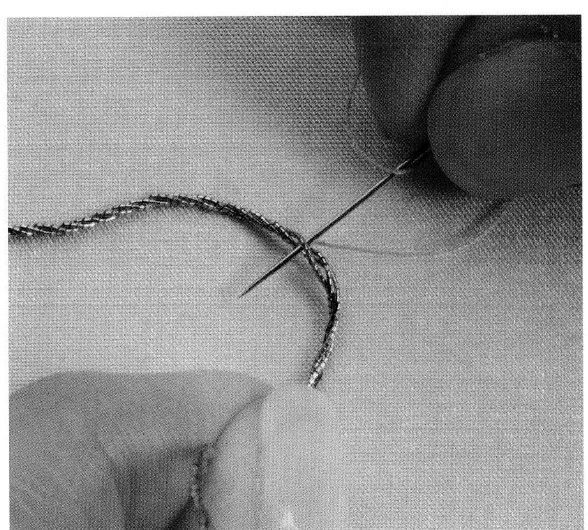

Sewing twist invisibly

(2⁄10 in). To make the couching stitch invisible, gently roll the twist to separate the strands, bring the needle up through one of the strands and then roll the twist back to close the strands and take the needle down through the fabric 1 mm away from where the needle came up. Leave a tail at the end to plunge.

Closed plate work

This form of plate work is usually worked over felt padding. Use only a single sewing thread for couching plate. In plate work always start at the narrow end of the shape and work out to the widest part of the shape.

To begin the plate work, form a 2–3 mm (1⁄8 in) hook at the end of the plate with tweezers. Lay the plate, with the hook turned upwards, against the felt padding, facing it in the opposite direction to the way it will be worked. It will make it easier to catch the hook. Couch the hooked end of the plate down at the edge of the felt and further secure it with a little pin stitch in the felt, which will be covered eventually. Bring the plate up and over the padding and couch across it at the edge of the other side of the felt padding as shown in the left example in the photograph. Pull the couching thread firmly from underneath. While performing this action, fold the plate back over the couching stitch and angle the plate so that it will partially cover the plate beside it. (It is advisable in plate work to secure every couching stitch with a pin stitch in the felt or at the edge of the felt where it will not be seen; otherwise the plate may lift off the felt.) Couch over the plate on the other side of the felt padding as shown in the middle example in the photograph, this time bringing the needle up against the plate previously couched and taking the needle down on the other side of the plate. (Note that if the shape you are working has no

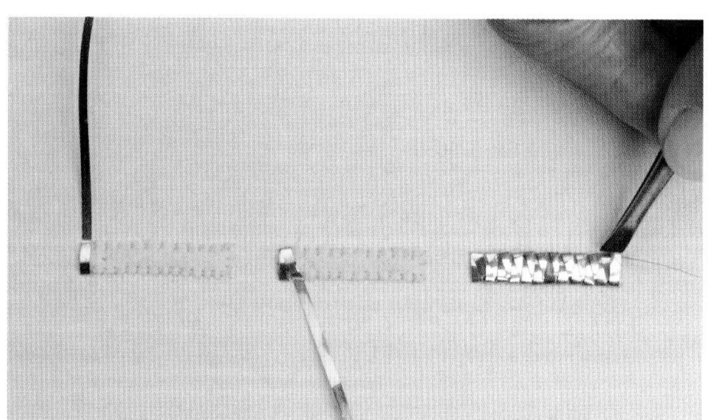

Closed plate work: 1, left, the first step of closed plate work; 2, centre, the second step of closed plate work; 3, right, the plate has been cut in preparation for forming a hook to complete the work

variation in width, it is necessary to bring the needle up a minute distance in from the edge of the felt padding and to take it down at the edge of the felt. This prevents the plate work from increasing in width.) While pulling the couching thread firmly from underneath, fold the plate over the couching stitch so that it sits perpendicular to the previous plate, partially covering it in the process. Repeat this zigzag movement across the felt.

To finish, cut the plate, allowing 3 mm (⅛ in) to turn under to form a hook at the end as shown in the right example in the photograph. Couching this hook can be the most difficult part of plate work. Bring the needle and thread up on the edge of the felt, preferably on the outside, and take the needle down beside the plate just laid, leaving a large loop on the surface. (A mellor or a large chenille needle is helpful at this stage to support the loop as you take the needle through to anchor the hook.) Catch the hook with the loop (leave the needle and thread dangling under the work while you use both hands to do this part of the task). With the mellor in one hand, hold the loop out to the side where the thread came up and with the other hand take the needle underneath and carefully bring the thread through, thus pulling the hooked end of the plate down onto the felt padding. It may take a little practice to master this action.

Cutting and attaching kid leather

Trace the shapes for kid leather onto tracing paper. Place the tracing paper onto the leather and pinprick the shapes through the tracing paper onto the right side of the leather. Cut around the pin-pricked outline with a sharp pair of small scissors. If it is difficult to see the pin-pricked outline on the right side, it may be clearer on the wrong side. Placing a piece of tracing paper over the right side, however, will surprisingly make the pin pricks very easy to see, in which case hold the tracing paper over the kid leather while cutting out.

To hold the kid leather in place before stitching it down, work threads across the leather, going up and down into the background fabric (do not pierce the kid leather at this stage). Then stitch the kid leather down with minute stab stitches, no more than 1–2 mm apart, around the entire shape, coming up in the background fabric and going down through the kid leather. Remove the holding threads once the shape has been completely stab stitched onto the background fabric.

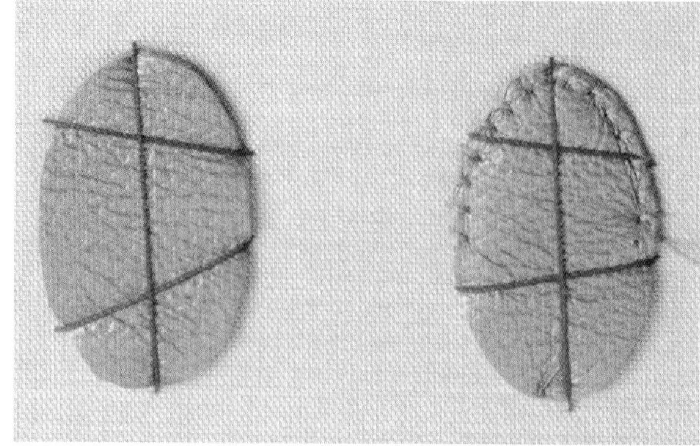

Attaching a kid leather shape, showing the holding stitches and the partially worked stab stitches

SECTION II:

THE PROJECTS

Contemporary Jewel

A pure geometrical shape has become a jewel. It only required two goldwork techniques to make this transformation—laid work and burden stitch.

The 'jewel' is framed with lines worked in Grecian gimp, a magnificent gold thread.

The 'jewel' could be worked without the scroll lines and be made into a contemporary brooch.

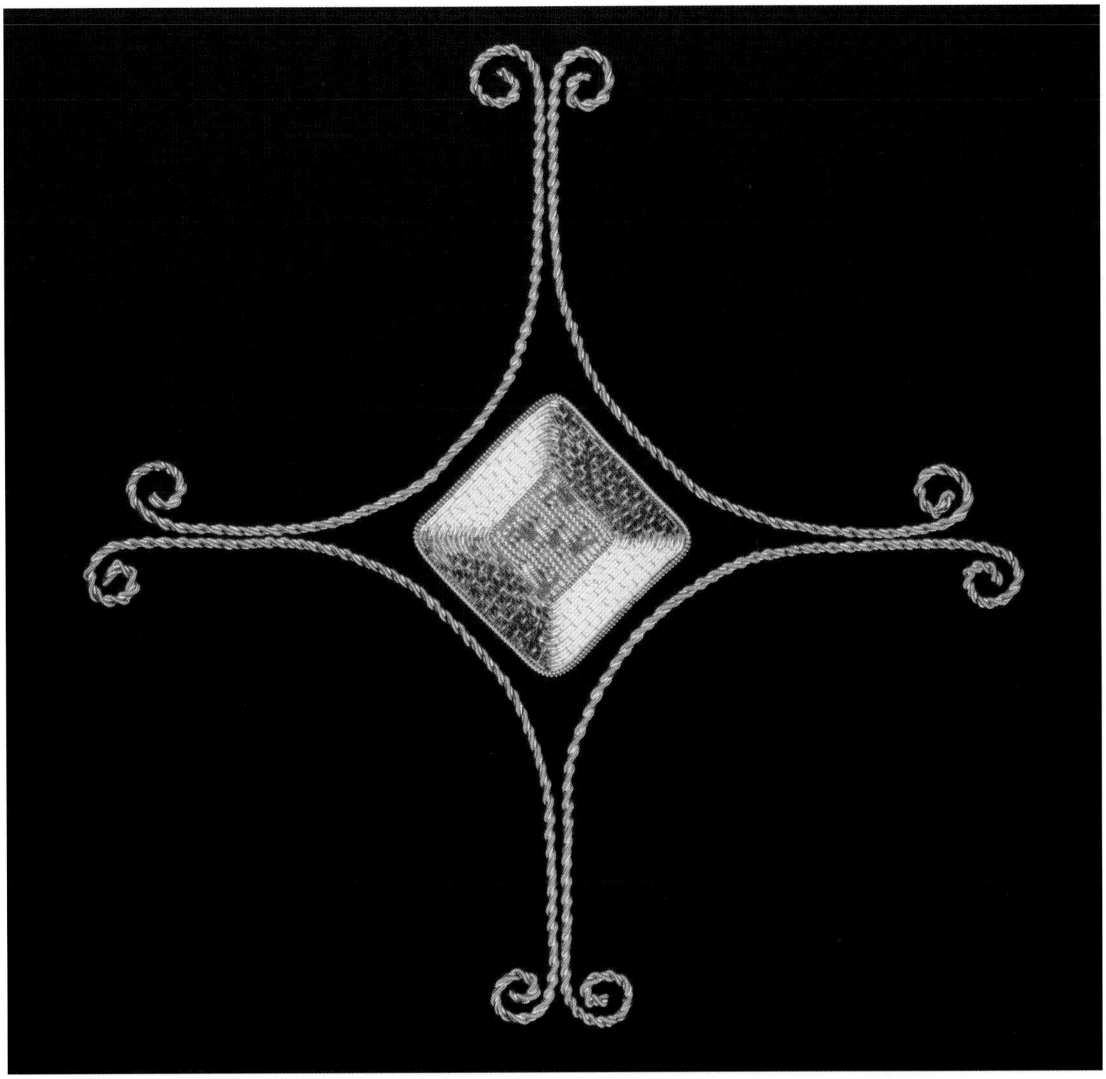

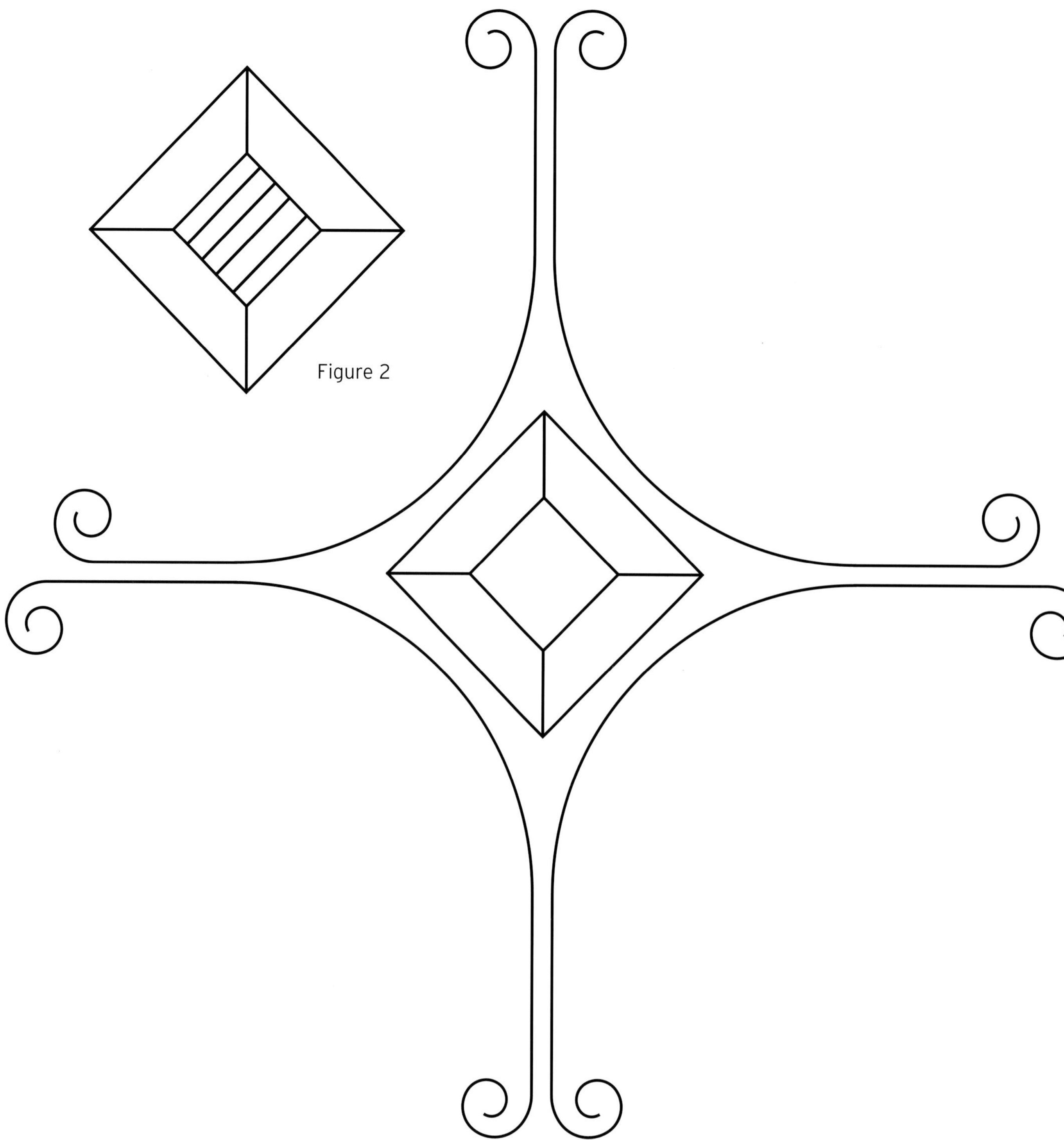

Figure 2

Figure 1

EQUIPMENT AND MATERIALS

76 cm (30 in) slate frame or 36 cm (14 in) ring frame
calico to fit frame
square of dark purple duchesse silk satin an appropriate size for the frame
8 cm (3 ¼ in) square yellow felt
1 skein of yellow DMC soft cotton or yellow bumpf
2 x A4 sheets 110 gsm tracing paper
white dressmaker's carbon
orange dressmaker's carbon
Gutermann thread to match the dark purple silk
Gutermann 968
YLI silk thread 078
size 10 crewel needles
mellor or size 18 chenille needle
awl or stiletto

METAL THREADS

20 cm (8 in) gilt no. 1 pearl purl
25 cm (10 in) gilt no. 2 pearl purl
1.2 m (47 in) Grecian gimp
2.2 m (94 in) no. 9 Japanese gold
20 cm (8 in) gilt no. 6 bright check
20 cm (8 in) gilt no. 6 wire check

METHOD

Dark purple duchesse satin silk background

This design is best transferred onto the silk after it has been stretched taut on the frame because of the long straight lines in the design. Refer to the instructions for dressing a slate frame in the preparation chapter. Trace the lines in Figure 1 onto tracing paper and then transfer the design onto the silk using white dressmaker's carbon (white will be easier to see on this dark background, but ensure that these lines are covered by the metal threads). Use a book for support under the fabric in the frame.

Felt padding

Trace the diamond shape in Figure 2 onto tracing paper and then transfer these design lines onto the square of yellow felt, using orange dressmaker's carbon. Press heavily when tracing onto felt otherwise the orange carbon will not show on the yellow felt. Cut the shape out of the felt. Use a single sewing thread to attach the felt shape onto the silk. Refer to the instructions for felt padding in chapter 3.

String padding

The four lines across the centre diamond are to be covered with string padding. Use four lengths of yellow DMC soft cotton or yellow bumpf. Refer to the instructions for simple string padding (under raised laid work) in chapter 3. Cut the string padding on the inside of the design line for the centre diamond. An outline of pearl purl will be couched on this design line.

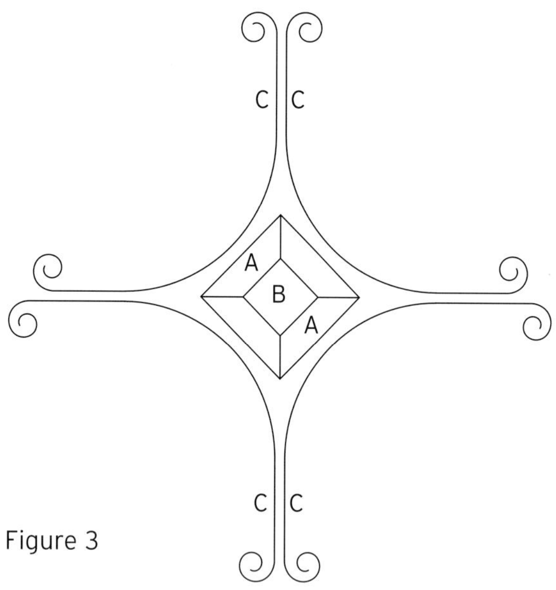

Figure 3

Embroidery

The elements of the design to be embroidered are listed alphabetically in Figure 3 and are matched to the alphabetical order of work which follows.

A Use no. 9 Japanese gold for the laid work and couch with YLI silk thread 078. Refer to the instructions for flat laid work in chapter 3. Start the laid work on one corner. Lay the two threads of Japanese gold on the edge of the felt and leave 3–5 cm (1¼–2 in) tails. Place the first couching stitch 2 mm (1/10 in) in from where the tails will be plunged. Refer to Figure 4. Leave intervals of 3 mm (⅛ in) between couching stitches. The two threads of Japanese gold are to be couched continuously around the diamond shape in the same manner as the leaf-shape in chapter 3. Refer to the instructions for working the leaf-shape because this is the technique that you are using for the diamond. Pay particular attention on how to turn the metal threads around the corners. They are couched separately. The couching stitches follow the diagonal lines at each corner. Refer to Figure 4. The end of the laid work is to be at the same corner as the beginning of the laid work. The beginning and the end of the laid work are marked with an **X** on Figure 4. Leave tails at the end to plunge. Refer to the instructions for plunging fibre-core metal threads in chapter 3. Tails must be plunged before outlining the laid work. Outline the inside of the laid work with gilt no. 1 pearl purl and outline the outside of the laid work with gilt no. 2 pearl purl. There is no need to stretch the no. 2 pearl purl because the couching stitches slip very readily into the grooves of the larger pearl purls. The * on Figure 4 marks where to begin and end the outlining. By beginning and ending at this point you will achieve four round corners. It will not be necessary to use tweezers to take the pearl purl gently around the corners.

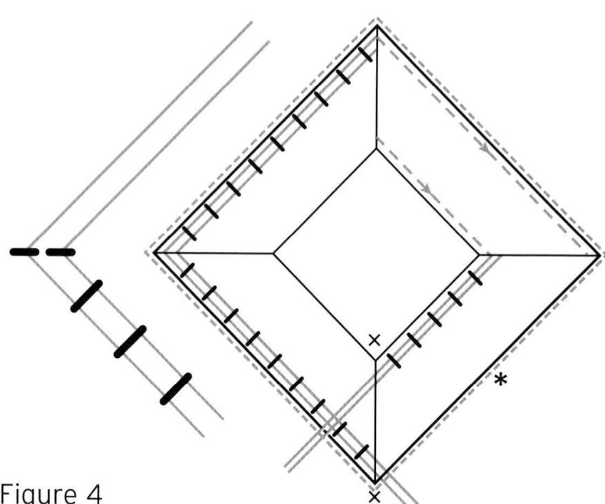

Figure 4

B The centre diamond is filled with burden stitch over the string padding. Use gilt no. 6 bright check and gilt no. 6 wire check for this work. Refer to the instructions for cutwork over felt padding in the Technique chapter for attaching the hollow purl threads. Figure 5 shows the direction of the burden stitch and illustrates the steps for working burden stitch, using the

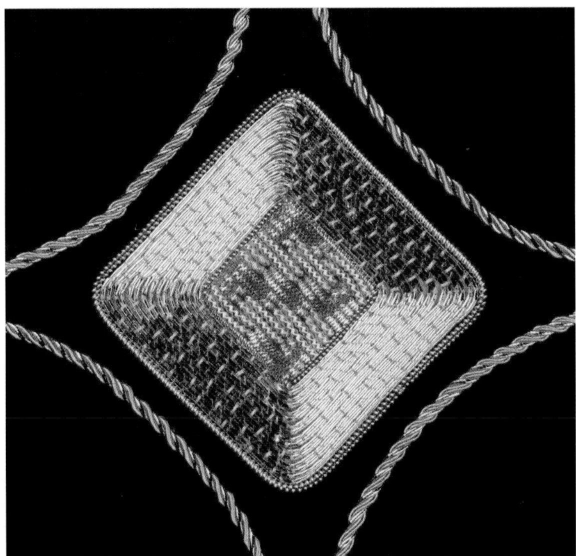

two different check purls. The pattern is worked from left to right. Two lengths of gilt bright check are laid over strings 1 and 2, followed by two lengths of gilt wire check over strings 3 and 4. In the next row, two lengths of gilt bright check are laid over string 1, followed by two lengths of gilt wire check over strings 2 and 3 and two lengths of gilt bright check over string 4. Continue working in this manner across the shape as shown in the last illustration in Figure 5.

C The four lines terminating in scrolls are worked with Grecian gimp. This is best attached invisibly but if this proves to be too difficult, it will be perfectly acceptable to couch diagonally over the gimp with YLI silk thread 078. To begin the line of Grecian gimp, carefully create a hole large enough to accommodate the gimp, with an awl or stiletto. Catch the end of the gimp in a lasso and plunge it to the back of the work. Pull 2.5 cm (1 in) of the gimp through and couch it at the back of the work. Now proceed to couch the gimp along the design line. Refer to the instructions for sewing twist invisibly in chapter 3. At the end of the line, create another large hole with an awl/stiletto and take a 2.5 cm (1 in) tail of gimp to the back of the work and couch. Keep this thread twisted as it is plunged.

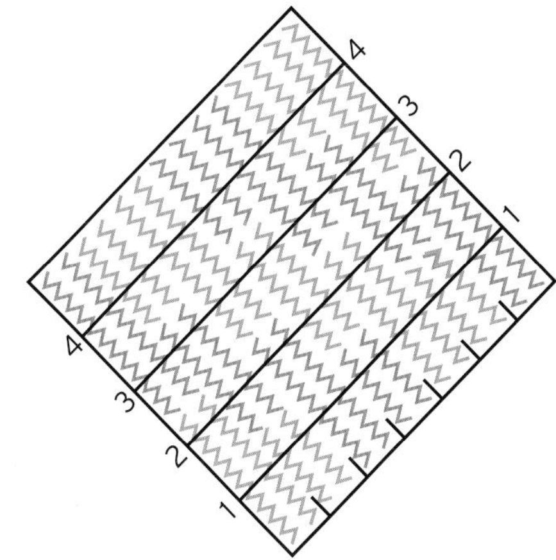

Figure 5

Circle of Hearts

A charming and youthful design inspired by the work of the haute couture designer Christian Lacroix. With a little modification this design would be ideal as a brooch. The use of sumptuous materials such as purple velvet, gold and metallic pink kid leather, wire check bullion, gold gimp, tinsel, purls and crystals transform this small design into a precious piece.

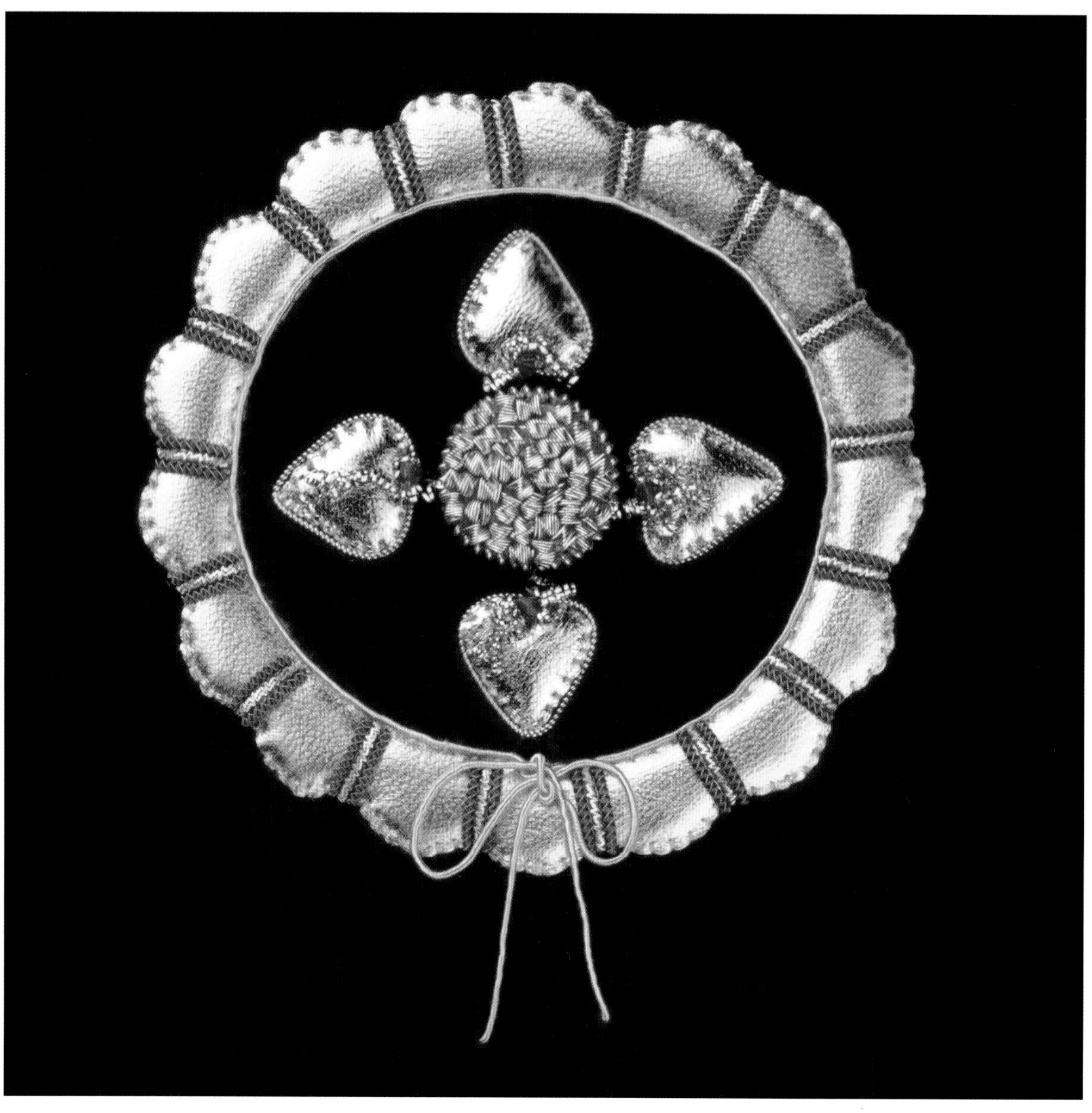

EQUIPMENT AND MATERIALS

76 cm (30 in) slate frame or 30 cm (12 in) ring frame
calico to fit frame
square of purple velvet an appropriate size for the frame
3 cm (1⅛ in) square yellow felt
1 x A4 sheet 110 gsm tracing paper
1 gram pounce (and roll of felt to apply pounce)
1 tube yellow ochre watercolour paint
1 size 000 paintbrush
10 cm (4 in) square gold kid leather
5 cm (2 in) square metallic pink kid leather
4 small red Swarovski bicone crystals
Gutermann 968
pink Gutermann to match the pink kid leather
dark purple Gutermann to match the plum twist purl
1 reel YLI gold silk thread 078
size 10 crewel needle
mellor or size 18 chenille needle

Figure 1

METAL THREADS

4 cm (1⅝ in) gilt no. 4 pearl purl
18 cm (7 in) gilt super pearl purl
60 cm (24 in) gold gimp
15 cm (6 in) gold wire check bullion
40 cm (16 in) plum twist purl
20 cm (8 in) gilt façonnée
12 cm (5 in) no. 20 black and gold couching thread

METHOD

Purple velvet background

Mount the velvet square and the calico into your frame. Refer to the instructions for dressing a slate frame in chapter 3.

Trace the design lines in Figure 1 onto tracing paper. Use the prick-and-pounce method to transfer the design on to the velvet. Refer to the instructions for the prick-and-pounce method in chapter 3. The transferring of the design can be done after mounting the velvet onto the slate frame. Place books beneath the frame to support the fabric while pouncing and painting the design lines.

Further secure the velvet to the calico by pin-stitching along the design lines, allowing approximately 3 mm (⅛ in) between each pin-stitch. The pin-stitches will eventually be hidden.

Felt padding

Trace the small circle in Figure 1 onto a small piece of tracing paper. Cut it out and use it as a template to cut a circle out of the felt square. Attach the circle of felt onto the velvet background with minute stab stitches. Bring needle and thread up in the velvet and take the needle down in the felt.

Gold kid leather scalloped circular frame

Trace the scalloped circle in Figure 1 onto tracing paper. Place the tracing paper over the kid leather and prick the outlines onto the leather. Now follow the instructions for cutting and attaching kid leather in chapter 3. To ensure that the kid leather shape does not move on the velvet background, place a holding stitch over every scallop and then work a stab stitch at every juncture of two scallops as shown in Figure 2. Use Gutermann 968 for the stab stitching.

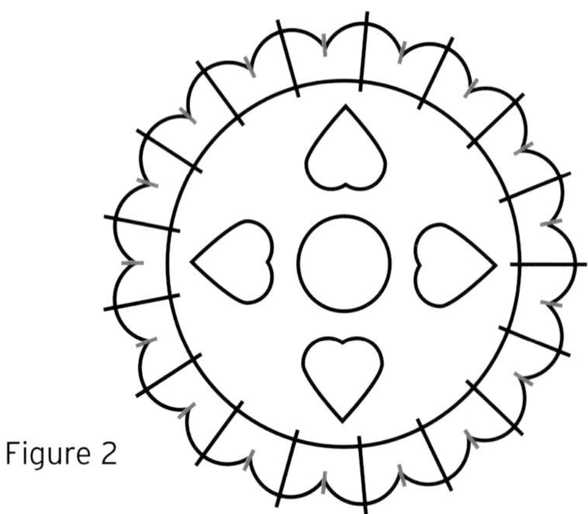

Figure 2

Pink kid leather hearts

Trace the four hearts in Figure 1 onto tracing paper. Place the tracing paper over the kid leather and prick the outlines onto the leather. Again, follow the instructions for cutting and attaching kid leather in chapter 3. Use a single thread of matching pink Gutermann for attaching the kid leather.

Centre circle

Stretch the 4 cm (1⅝ in) length of gilt no. 4 pearl purl to 7 cm (3 in). Outline the circle of felt with the now overstretched pearl purl. Couch the pearl purl in every second groove with Gutermann 968. Cut the gold wire check bullion into 3 mm (⅛ in) chips to fill the small circle. Use a doubled thread of Gutermann 968 to attach the bullion chips.

Decoration on the hearts

At this point, outline the four pink kid leather hearts with gilt super pearl purl.

Cut the 12 cm (5 in) length of no. 20 black and gold couching thread into 3 cm (1¼ in) lengths. Remove the gold metal thread from its black fibre-core. It is like tinsel once it is removed from the core. Roll it lightly between thumb and finger to make it into a 'ball' of tinsel and then attach it at the top of the heart with a couple of small stab stitches using Gutermann 968. Attach a red Swarovski bicone crystal in the midst of the tinsel.

Inside of circular frame

Outline the inside of the circular frame with gold gimp. Leave 15 cm (6 in) tails of the gimp at the beginning and the end. Couch the gimp with YLI gold silk thread 078. Leave a space interval of 4 mm (2/10 in) between couching stitches. The gimp is couched on the edge of the kid leather. Bring the needle up at the edge of the kid leather and take the needle down in the kid leather. Tie the two 15 cm (6 in) tails into a bow. Couch the knot and the bow in several places to hold it in place. Determine where you want the tails of the bow to sit and to finish, make a hole with a stiletto or mellor, plunge the remainder of the tails through and couch them at the back of the work.

Decoration on circular frame

Cut seventeen 1 cm (9/20 in) lengths of gilt façonnée and thirty-four lengths of plum twist purl that are a fraction over 1 cm (9/20 in). Attach the façonnée over the junctions of the scallops with a doubled thread of Gutermann 968. Plum twist purl is then attached on both sides of the façonnée with a doubled thread of matching Gutermann.

Spray of Flowers

So many twentieth-century embroidered gowns that I studied in British collections featured sprays of flowers. I made numerous sketches of the designs on these magnificent gowns which I referenced when designing this spray of flowers.

Coloured metal threads have been joyously combined with the gilt threads. Never in the history of goldwork embroidery has there been such an array of coloured metal threads to work with, as is available today.

This design introduces the beginner in goldwork embroidery to such techniques as couching, cutwork, chip work and S-ing.

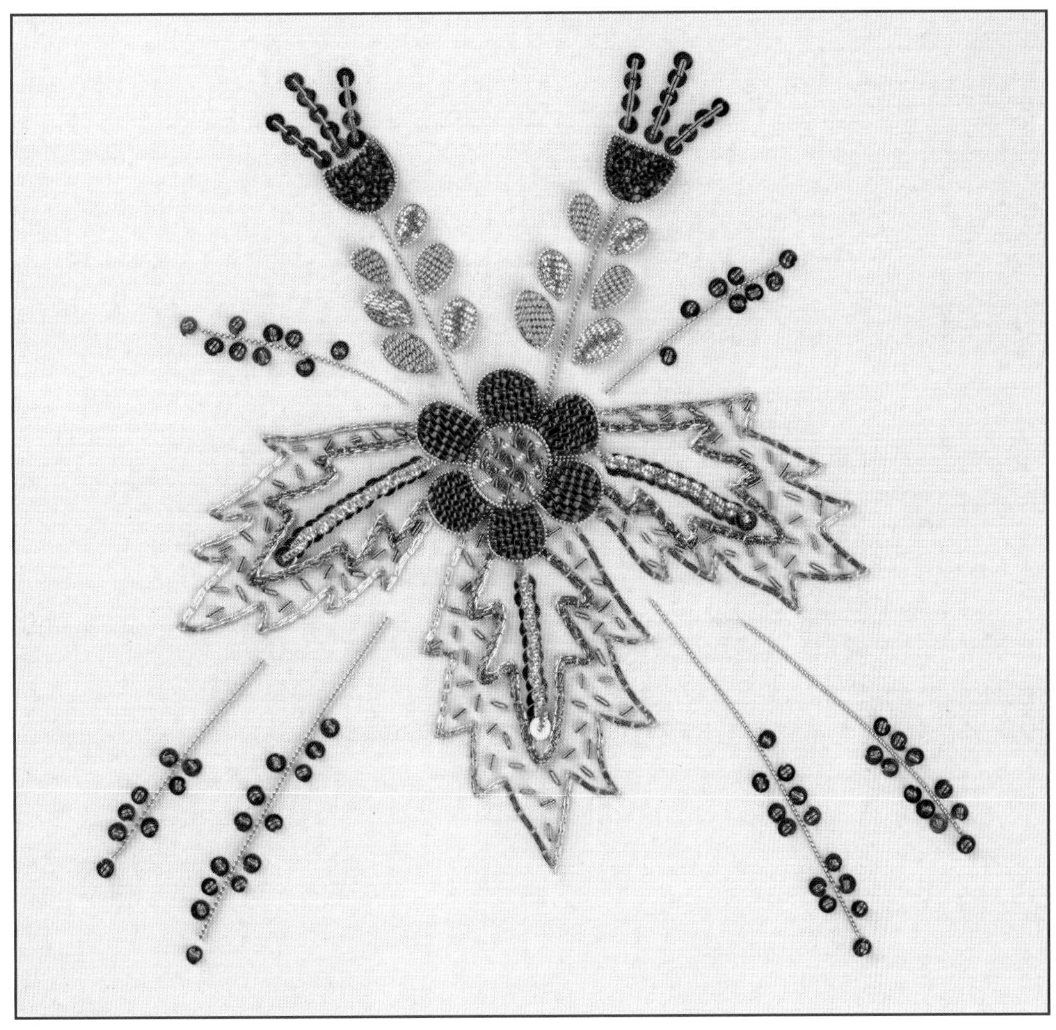

EQUIPMENT AND MATERIALS

76 cm (30 in) slate frame or 36 cm (14 in) ring frame
calico to fit frame
square of white dupion silk an appropriate size for the frame
2 x A4 sheets 110 gsm tracing paper
orange dressmaker's carbon
10 cm (4 in) square yellow felt
Gutermann 968
dark pink Gutermann
Gutermann polyester metallic thread 9970
2 grams of 4 mm (2⁄10 in) gilt spangles
2 grams of 3 mm (1⁄8 in) gilt spangles
1 packet of 2 mm (1⁄10 in) pink sequins
size 12 sharps needle (for the no. 8 purls and pink sequins)
size 10 crewel needle
mellor or size 18 chenille needle

METAL THREADS

35 cm (13¾ in) gilt extra super pearl purl
80 cm (31½ in) gilt super pearl purl
8 cm (3 ¼ in) gilt no. 1 pearl purl
3 m (118 in) gilt no. 6 wavy passing
1 m (40 in) gilt fine rococo

Figure 1

1 metre (40 in) metallic green 3-ply twist
50 cm (20 in) gilt no. 8 bright check
20 cm (8 in) gilt no. 8 wire check
60 cm (24 in) wine no. 6 wire check
50 cm (20 in) carnation pink no. 6 rough purl

METHOD

White dupion silk background

Trace the design lines in Figure 1 onto tracing paper and then transfer the design onto the silk, using orange dressmaker's carbon. Mount the silk square and the calico into a hoop/ring frame or sew the silk square onto calico which has already been laced up on a square or slate frame. Refer to the instructions for dressing a slate frame in chapter 3.

Felt padding

Trace the shapes in Figure 2 onto tracing paper and then transfer these design lines onto the square of yellow, using orange dressmaker's carbon. Cut the shapes out of the felt. Use a single sewing thread to attach the felt shapes onto the silk. Refer to the instructions for felt padding in chapter 3.

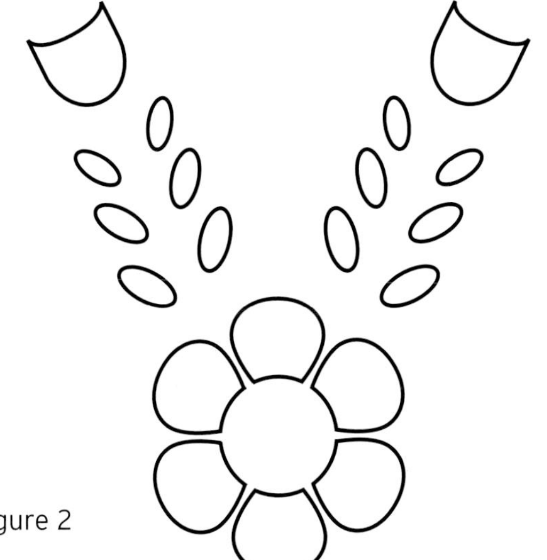

Figure 2

Embroidery

The elements of the design to be embroidered are listed alphabetically in Figure 3 (on next page) and are matched to the alphabetical order of work which follows.

A *The outlines and seeding of the three large leaves.* The main outline is worked with two threads of gilt no. 6 wavy passing couched every 3 mm (⅛ in) with Gutermann 968. Take the couching stitches over both metal threads but at the corners couch each metal thread separately as shown in Figure 4 for the inside lines. Refer to the instructions for technique 2 for laid work in chapter 3.

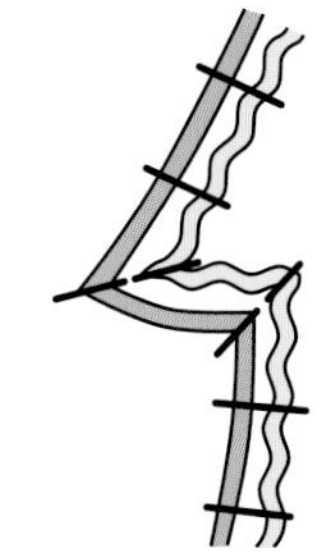

Figure 4

The internal lines of the leaves are worked in the same manner using metallic green 3-ply twist and gilt fine rococo. These two metal threads are couched with Gutermann polyester metallic thread 9970.

The seeding between the two outlines is worked with 2 mm (1/10 in) lengths of carnation pink no. 6 rough purl. Attach these small lengths of purl with dark pink Gutermann. Lay the purls in different directions.

Note that the row of S-ing with spangles running through the centre of each leaf is not worked until the centre flower has been embroidered.

B *The centre flower.* Outline the centre of the circle with gilt no. 1 pearl purl and outline the petals with gilt super pearl purl.

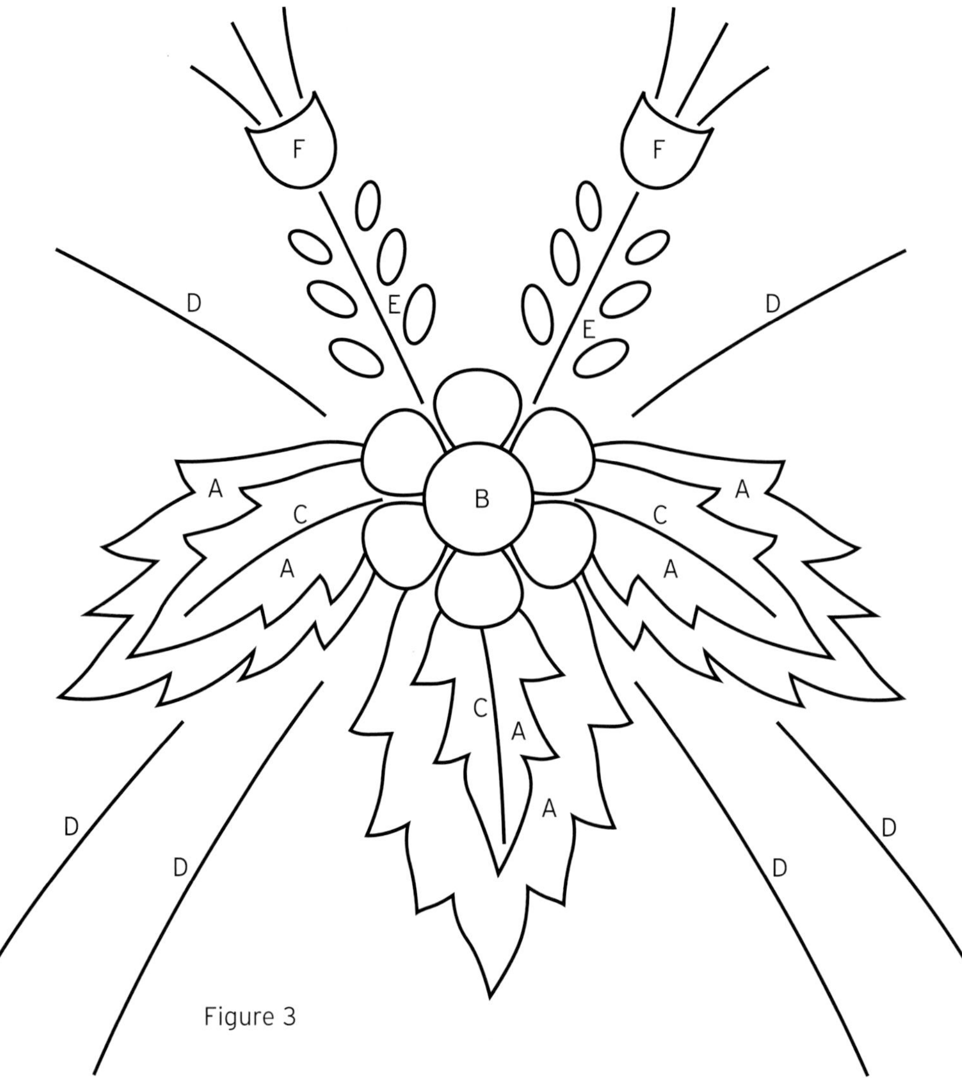

Figure 3

The flower's centre features a trellis pattern. Long lengths of gilt no. 8 bright check are used for the trellis and 5 mm (¼ in) lengths of carnation pink no. 6 rough purl are looped over the intersections of the trellis. Refer to Figure 5(a), (b) and (c) to work the trellis pattern.

The petals are worked in cutwork using wine no. 6 wire check. Use a doubled thread of dark pink Gutermann. Refer to the instructions for cutwork over felt padding in chapter 3 and to Figure 6 for the direction of the cutwork.

C *The centre veins of the three large leaves* are worked with spangles and S-ing. Use 4 mm (²⁄₁₀ in) spangles. The S-ing is worked with gilt no. 8 bright check. Cut the bright check into lengths

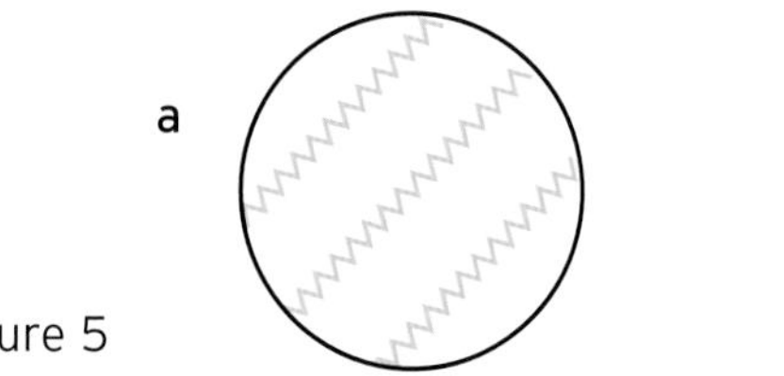

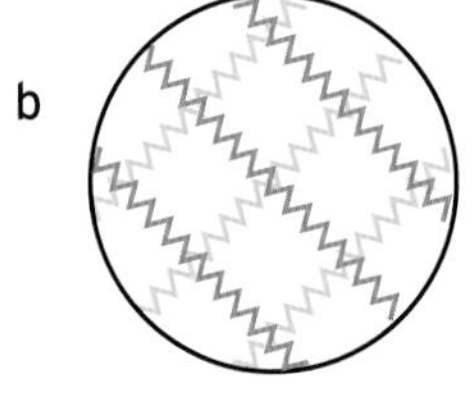

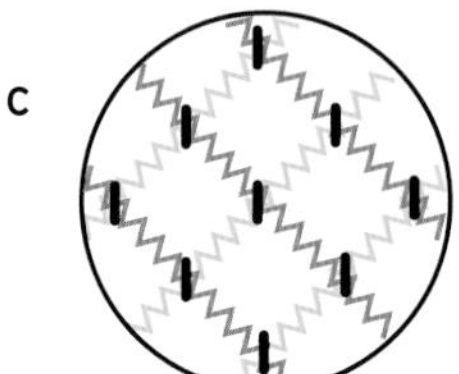

Figure 5

Figure 6

Figure 7

that are slightly longer than the diameter of the spangles. Refer to the instructions for S-ing with spangles in chapter 3.

D *The ornamental grass stems* are worked with overstretched gilt super pearl purl. Take a 30 cm (12 in) length of gilt super pearl purl and stretch it out to 45 cm (18 in). Lay the pearl purl on the design line and couch every third groove with Gutermann 968.

The grass seeds are worked with 3 mm (a fraction over ⅛ in) spangles, 2 mm (1/10 in) pink sequins and 1 mm (1/20 in) lengths of carnation pink no. 6 rough purl. Arrange them creatively along both sides of the stem. Also attach one at the tip of the stem. Using a doubled thread of dark pink Gutermann pick up a spangle, a sequin and a purl, in that order. Drop the three components to the bottom of the thread and take the needle down through the holes of the sequin and spangle. From beneath, gently pull the thread to make the purl become a loop.

E *Stems with small leaves*. The stems are also worked with overstretched gilt super pearl purl. Couch every third groove of the pearl purl. Outline the small leaves with gilt extra super pearl purl. Begin and end the outline at the point closest to the stem. The small leaves are filled in with cutwork. The leaves are either worked with gilt no. 8 bright check or gilt no. 8 wire check. Figure 7 identifies which check purl is used for each leaf and also shows the direction of the cutwork.

F *Two cup-shaped flowers with spangles*. Outline the flowers with gilt super pearl purl and fill the flowers with chips of wine no. 6 wire check.

Each flower has three lines of spangles and purls. The centre line has five spangles and the lines on either side have four spangles. Use 3 mm (a fraction over ⅛ in) spangles and carnation pink no. 6 rough purl for this work. The first purl in the line is 3 mm (a fraction over ⅛ in) and the succeeding purls are cut a little shorter than the first purl. Use a double thread of dark pink Gutermann. Bring the needle up on the design line 2 mm (1/10 in) away from the top of the flower, pick up a spangle and the 3 mm purl and drop both to the bottom of the thread. Using your needle, place another spangle beside the spangle on the thread and take the needle down through the hole of the second spangle. (If all three components were picked up the second spangle would slide over the purl.) Bring the needle up again on the design line at a distance of half the length of a 3mm spangle away from the second spangle. (The spangles are not meant to overlap.) Pick up a spangle and one of the shorter lengths of purl. Drop both to the bottom of the thread. Take the needle down through the hole of the second spangle. Repeat this last step for the fourth and fifth spangles and purls.

Silver Flower

This design was inspired by the embroidered flowers on Queen Maud of Norway's magnificent coronation dress, which was on display in the Style and Splendour *exhibition in 2005–2006 at the Victoria & Albert Museum in London.*

EQUIPMENT AND MATERIALS

76 cm (30 in) slate frame or 36 cm (14 in) ring frame
calico to fit the frame
square of light blue duchesse satin silk an appropriate size for the frame
1 x A4 sheet 110 gsm tracing paper
orange dressmaker's carbon
white dressmaker's carbon
10 cm (4 in) square white felt
Gutermann 800
1 x 4 mm (¼ in) flat crystal set in a metal claw with two channels
2 grams of 3 mm (⅛ in) silver spangles
size 10 crewel needle
mellor or size 18 chenille needle

METAL THREADS

55 cm (22 in) silver-plated super pearl purl
55 cm (22 in) silver-plated no. 7 check thread
60 cm (24 in) silver-plated no. 6 bright check
60 cm (24 in) silver-plated no. 6 rough purl
40 cm (16 in) silver-plated no. 6 smooth purl

METHOD

Light blue duchesse satin silk background

Trace the lines in Figure 1 onto tracing paper and then transfer the design onto the silk, using white dressmaker's carbon. Mount the silk square and the calico into a hoop/ring frame or sew the silk square onto calico which has already been laced up on a square or slate frame. Refer to the instructions for dressing a slate frame in chapter 3.

Figure 1

Layers of felt padding for the left-side shape in the flower's centre.

Figure 2(a)

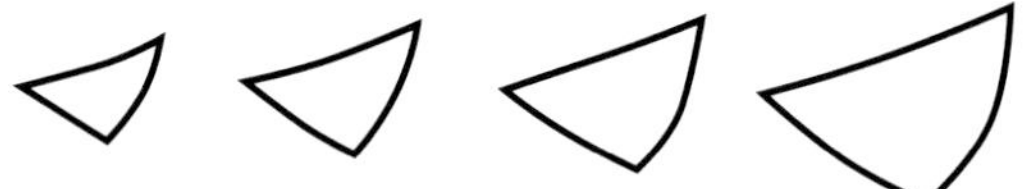

Layers of felt padding for the right-side shape in the flower's centre.

Figure 2(b)

Felt padding

Trace the shapes in Figure 2(a) and (b) onto tracing paper and then transfer these design lines onto the square of white felt, using orange dressmaker's carbon. Cut the shapes out of the felt. Use a single sewing thread to attach the felt shapes onto the silk. Both padded parts in the centre of the flower have four layers of felt. The smallest layer is attached first.

Cutwork over padded shape on left side of flower's centre

Follow the instructions for cutwork over felt padding in chapter 3. However, as the felt padding is so high, there will be no need to outline the shape. Two lengths of silver-plated no. 6 bright check are used to one length of silver-plated no. 6 rough purl for the cutwork. The lengths of purl are laid directly over the padding.

Loops of purls over padded shape on right side of flower's centre

Cut silver-plated no. 6 smooth purl and silver-plated no. 6 rough purl into 4 mm (2⁄10 in) and 5 mm (¼ in) lengths. Mix the purls and loop them over one another, and in different directions. The longer lengths of purl are looped over the shorter lengths of purl.

Attaching the crystal

A small **X** in the flower's centre in Figure 1 indicates the position of the crystal. The type of crystal used for this design is one that has been set into a metal claw with two channels which form a cross at the back of the crystal. Use a waxed doubled thread for attaching the crystal. Bring the needle up beside one of the channels, pass the needle through the channel and take the needle directly down through the fabric. Bring the needle up again beside the other channel, pass the needle through and take it directly down through the fabric.

The same needle and thread can be brought up again close to the crystal to attach the circle of silver-plated no. 6 bright check around the crystal. The length of this bright check purl is 17 mm (¾ in). Thread the cut length of bright check. Drop it to the bottom of the sewing thread, and with a mellor or chenille needle, hold the bright check purl in a loop around the crystal, while taking the needle back down through the same hole. Come up again on the opposite side, and very gently put in a couching stitch over the bright check purl. It should not be a visible couching stitch.

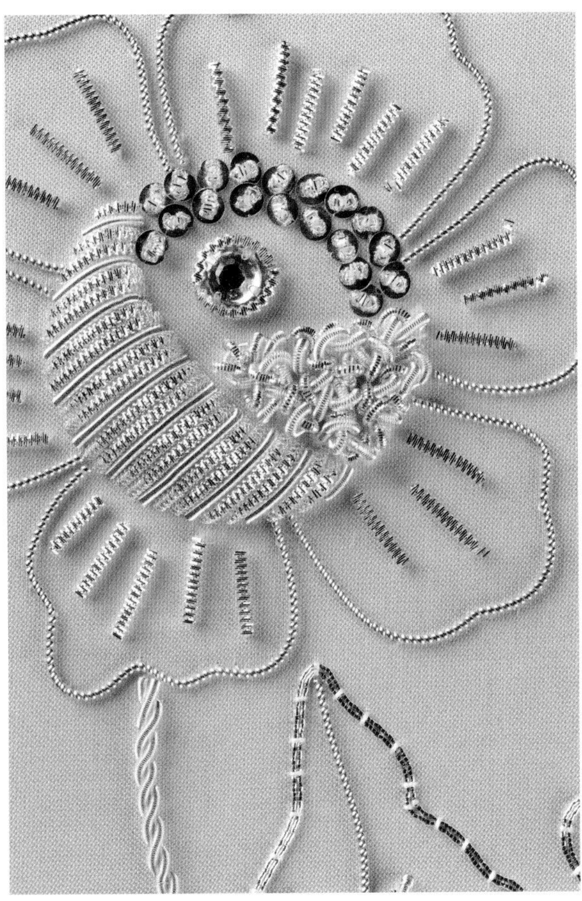

Double row of spangles

A double row of spangles anchored with loops of purls is worked along the curved design line at the top of the flower's centre. Refer to the instructions for attaching spangles and loops of purl in chapter 3. Use 3 mm (1/8 in) silver spangles and 3 mm (1/8 in) lengths of silver-plated no. 6 bright check for the loops.

Petals outlined with silver-plated super pearl purl

The six petals are outlined with silver-plated super pearl purl. Use a pair of tweezers to manipulate the pearl purl around the many curves of the petals. Cut 9 mm (3/8 in) lengths of silver-plated no. 6 bright check for the design lines within the petals.

Flower stem

The stem of the flower is worked with a row of S-ing using 4 mm (2/10 in) lengths of silver-plated no. 6 rough purl. Follow the instructions for vertical S-ing in chapter 3.

Leaves

The two leaves are outlined with two threads of silver-plated no. 7 check thread couched as one with Gutermann 800. To couch the corners of the leaves, refer to the instructions for couching a laid-worked leaf shape in chapter 3. Plunge the tails of the check threads through to the back of the work.

Work the centre vein of the upright leaf with silver-plated super pearl purl. The stem that carries the two leaves continues into the other leaf to become its centre vein. Work this line with silver-plated super pearl purl.

Work a chain stitch on both sides of the leave's centre vein. There are small design lines on either side of the veins to indicate the position of the chain stitches. Cut 8 mm (3/8 in) lengths of silver-plated no. 6 bright check for the chains and 4 mm (2/10 in) lengths of silver-plated no. 6 smooth purl to hold the chains in place. Create each chain stitch by bringing the needle up at the end of the design line closest to the vein to thread up the cut length of bright check. Drop the purl to the bottom of the sewing thread, and with a mellor or a chenille needle hold the bright check purl in a loop, while taking the needle down through the same hole. Once the loop has been formed, hold it down with a mellor or chenille needle, bring needle and thread through on the inside of the loop, thread up the smooth purl and take the needle down on the outside, 1 mm (1/20 in) away from the loop.

White Poppy

This single white poppy is the ideal design for the beginner in goldwork to embroider. The 'petals' of the flower are an appliquéd muslin suffolk puff. Coloured metal threads are now frequently used in goldwork embroidery. The silver threads in this work are enhanced by the use of dark pink metal threads. The flower head is worked in laid work with the very centre filled with loops of pink purls. This is an excellent design for learning how to manipulate pearl purl.

EQUIPMENT AND MATERIALS

76 cm (30 in) slate frame or 30 cm (12 in) ring frame
square of calico to fit the frame
square of dark pink duchesse silk satin an appropriate size for the frame
20 cm (8 in) square cream muslin
10 cm (4 in) square white felt
white dressmaker's carbon
orange dressmaker's carbon
2 x A4 sheets 110 gsm tracing paper
Gutermann 800
pink Gutermann to match pink no. 6 rough purl
50 cm (20 in) silver Au Papillon thread
1 packet YLI silk floss no. 6
size 10 crewel needle
mellor or size 18 chenille needle

METAL THREADS

1 m (40 in) silver and pink 3-ply twist
30 cm (12 in) silver-plated no. 7 check thread
2 m (2¼ yd) silver-plated no. 5 smooth passing
30 cm (12 in) silver-plated super pearl purl
30 cm (12 in) silver-plated no. 1 pearl purl
6 cm (2½ in) silver-plated no. 2 pearl purl
30 cm (12 in) silver-plated no. 6 bright check
30 cm (12 in) pink no. 6 rough purl
30 cm (12 in) bright violet no. 6 wire check

METHOD

Dark pink duchesse silk background

Trace the lines in Figure 1 onto tracing paper and then transfer the design onto the silk, using white dressmaker's carbon. Mount the silk square and the calico into a hoop frame or sew the silk square onto calico which has already been laced up on a square or slate frame. Refer to the instructions for dressing a slate frame in chapter 3.

Cream muslin flower head

Place a saucer approximately 16 cm (6½ in) in diameter on top of the cream muslin, and trace around the saucer with a coloured pen. Cut the circle out and turn a 5 mm (¼ in) hem on the muslin circle and tack the hem around the entire circle using small stitches. Pull the tacking thread up and secure. A 'suffolk puff' has been created! Centre the muslin suffolk puff, with gathered

side up, over the drawn circle on the dark pink silk background. Pin and tack the suffolk puff on the circle on the dark pink background. All tacking threads will remain because they will be hidden underneath the felt padding. Trim away the gathered layer of the muslin within the circle of tacking so that there will be very little bulk under the flower head's felt padding.

White felt padding

Trace the shapes in Figure 2 onto tracing paper and then transfer these shapes onto the square of white felt, using orange dressmaker's carbon. Press more heavily when tracing onto felt, otherwise the orange carbon will not show up on the felt. Cut the shapes out of the felt. Use a single sewing thread to attach the felt shapes onto the silk background. The flower head has three layers of felt. The three circles are numbered in Figure 2. Work from 1 to 3. The right side leaf has one layer of felt.

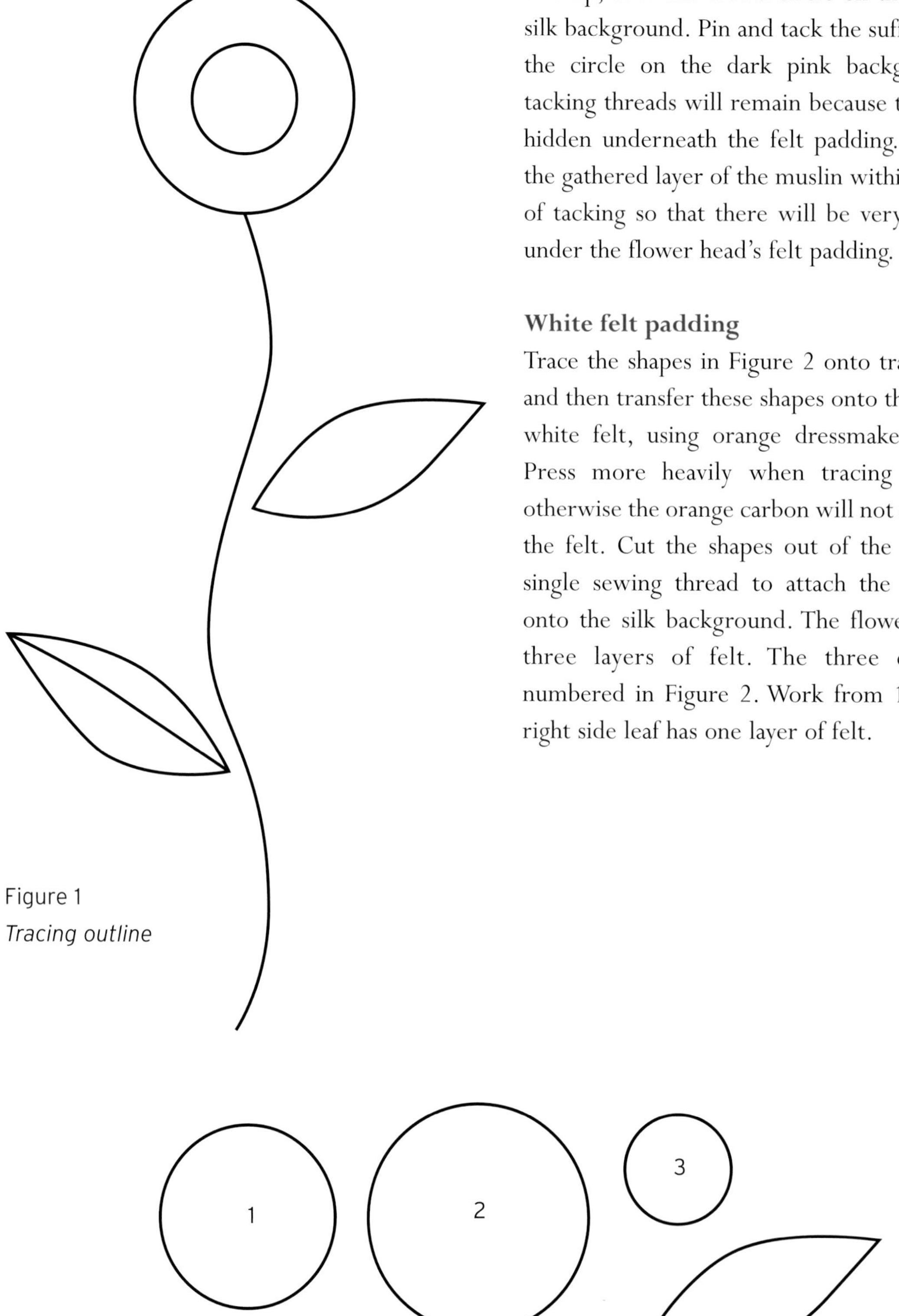

Figure 1
Tracing outline

Figure 2
Shapes for felt padding

Flower head

Work the flower head in the following order:

- The outer area of the padded circle is worked as laid work using no. 5 silver smooth passing. Refer to the instructions for couching a circle from the outside in chapter 3. Work the laid work up to the centre felt circle of the flower head. Plunge the four tails of silver passing and couch at the back of the work.
- Outline the smaller circle on the felt padding with overstretched silver no. 2 pearl purl. Take a 6 cm (2½ in) piece of this pearl purl and stretch it to 10 cm (4 in). Couch every second groove with a single thread of Gutermann 800.
- The smaller centre circle of the flower head is filled with concentric rows of loops of pink no. 6 rough purl. Cut the pink purl into 3 mm (⅛ in) lengths and work from the outside of the inner circle to the inside. Use a double sewing thread of matching pink Gutermann. To form a loop, bring the needle up through the fabric, pick up a purl, drop it to the bottom of the thread, and take the needle down through the fabric 1 mm (1/20 in) away from where the needle came up. Support the thread with a mellor or chenille needle as it is taken through. Allow the purl to curve over the mellor or chenille needle. After the first row has been completed around the circle, 'brick' the remaining rows of loops.
- Outline the larger circle of the flower head with S-ing using bright violet no. 6 wire check. Cut the wire check into 5 mm (¼ in) lengths. Use a double thread of matching pink Gutermann. Bring the needle up for all the purls about 1 mm (1/20 in) away from the edge of the laid work. The directions for S-ing a circle are in chapter 3.
- The twelve stamens radiating from the laid work circle are worked with 1 cm (4/10 in) lengths of silver no. 6 bright check and 2 mm (1/10 in) chips of bright violet no. 6 wire check. To achieve equal spacing between the stamens, place pins in the muslin at the compass points, and then place two pins in each quadrant. Attach the silver bright check lengths first, and then attach the chips of wire check across the ends of the stamens.

Leaf on right side

This leaf is worked as laid work using silver and pink 3-ply twist. Use silver Au Papillon thread to couch the twist so that the couching stitches will be invisible, which means that there is no need to 'brick' the couching stitches. The directions for couching a leaf shape are in chapter 3. Once the four tails of the metal threads have been plunged and couched at the back of the work, outline the leaf with silver no. 1 pearl purl, starting at the end close to the stem.

Leaf on left side

This unpadded leaf is worked in the following order:

- outline the entire leaf with silver no. 1 pearl purl
- work the centre vein with silver no. 1 pearl purl
- fill the areas on either side of the centre vein with cut lengths of overstretched silver no. 6 bright check threaded up with a doubled thread of YLI silk floss no. 6. The bright check should be opened up sufficiently to be able to see the dark pink thread. The cut lengths run along the length of the leaf shape. Either lay the bright check purls so that they sit flat on the surface, or allow them to stand slightly proud of the surface. It will look more textured if you do the latter.

Stem

The centre line of the stem is worked in silver no. 7 check thread. The line of the stem starts beneath the muslin 'petals'. Leave 5 cm (2 in) tails at the start and finish of the line, to plunge through to the back of the work. The outline each side of the check thread is worked in silver super pearl purl. Start and finish the outline of pearl purl beneath the muslin 'petals'.

Horus Eye

This design was inspired by a Horus-eye amulet from the Saite-Ptolemaic period that I saw displayed in the Metropolitan Museum in New York.
An intense blue was chosen as the background for the gold threads because these two colours are associated with Egyptian art objects.

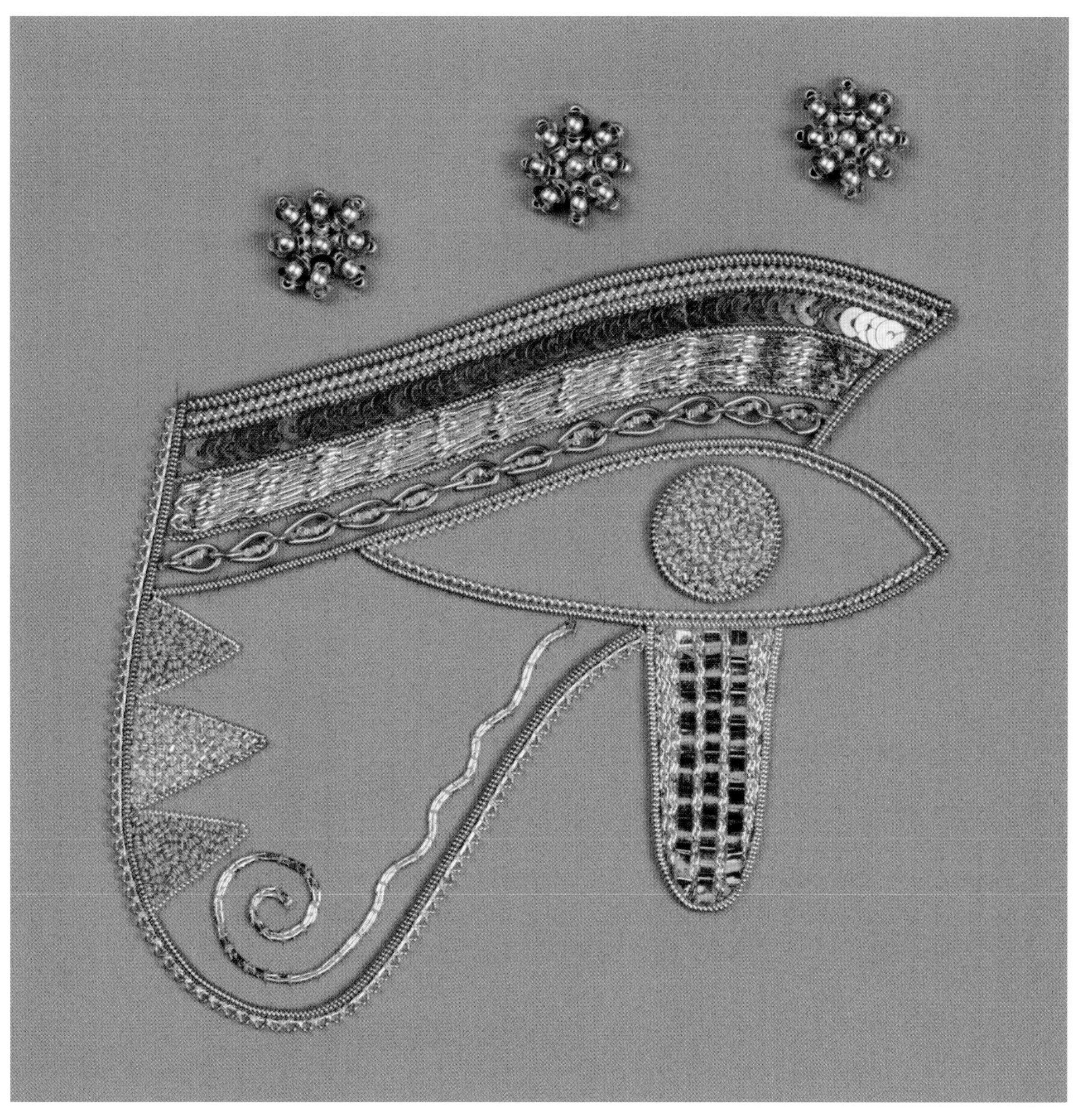

EQUIPMENT AND MATERIALS

76 cm (30 in) slate frame or 36 cm (14 in) ring frame
calico to fit the frame
square of turquoise blue duchesse satin silk an appropriate size for the frame
2 x A4 sheets of 110 gsm tracing paper
orange dressmaker's carbon
5 cm (2 in) square white felt
10 cm (4 in) square yellow felt
1 skein yellow DMC soft cotton
Gutermann 968
Gutermann 800
3 grams of 4 mm ($^{2}/_{10}$ in) gilt spangles
3 grams of 3 mm ($^{1}/_{8}$ in) gilt spangles
3 grams standard size matte champagne seed beads
size 12 sharps and size 10 crewel needles
mellor or size 18 chenille needle

METAL THREADS

5 cm (2 in) gilt super pearl purl
25 cm (10 in) gilt no. 1 pearl purl
20 cm (8 in) gilt no. 2 pearl purl
20 cm (8 in) gilt no. 3 pearl purl
10 cm (4 in) silver-plated super pearl purl
25 cm (10 in) silver-plated no. 1 pearl purl
15 cm (6 in) silver-plated no. 3 pearl purl
20 cm (8 in) silver-plated milliary
2.5 m (100 in) no. 8 Japanese gold
1.2 m (48 in) gilt no. 7 check thread
15 cm (6 in) gilt broad plate, ribbled (see note under instruction O, The teardrop shape)
40 cm (16 in) gilt no. 8 smooth purl
20 cm (8 in) gilt no. 8 wire check
20 cm (8 in) silver-plated no. 8 wire check
15 cm (6 in) gilt no. 6 wire check

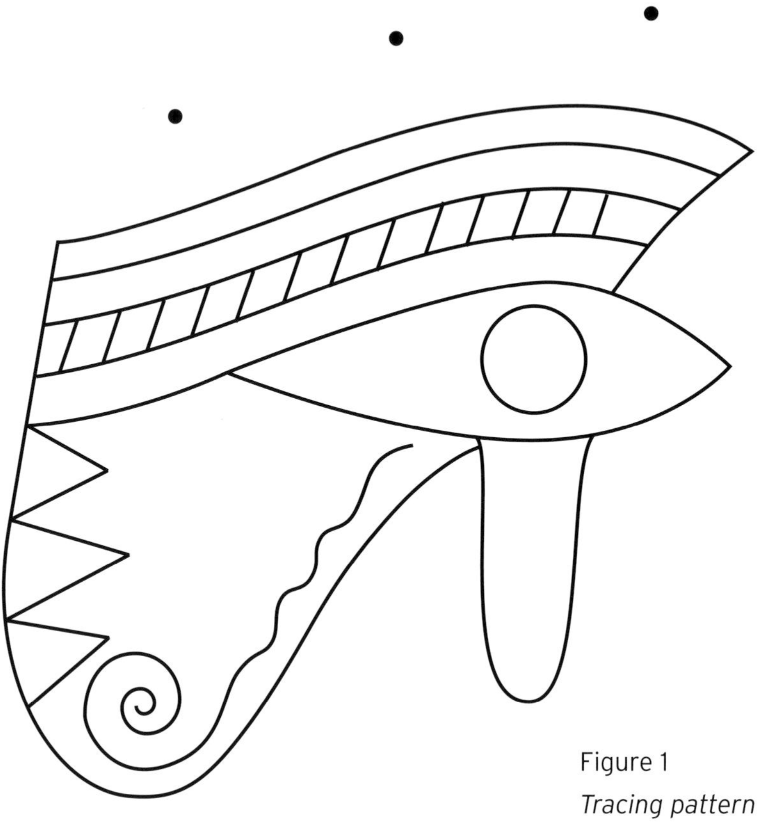

Figure 1
Tracing pattern

Figure 2

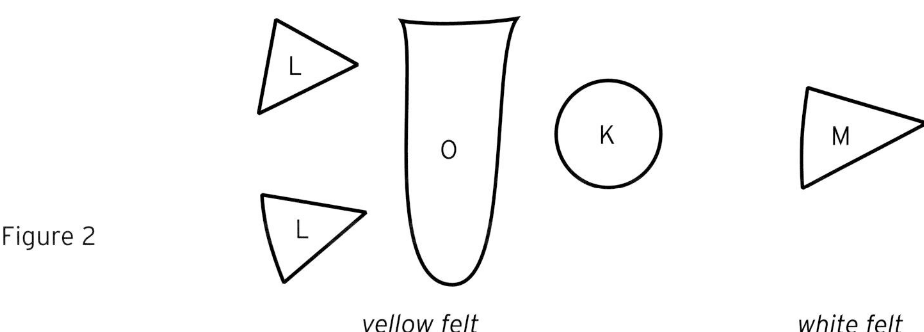

METHOD

Turquoise blue duchesse silk background

Trace the design lines in Figure 1 onto tracing paper and then transfer the design onto the silk, using orange dressmaker's carbon. Mount the silk square and the calico into a hoop/ring frame or sew the silk square onto calico which has already been laced up on a square or slate frame. Refer to the instructions for dressing a slate frame in chapter 3.

Felt padding

Trace the shapes in Figure 2 onto tracing paper and then transfer these design lines onto the squares of yellow and white felt, using orange dressmaker's carbon. Cut the shapes out of the felt. Use a single sewing thread to attach the felt shapes onto the silk. The shapes in Figure 2 are identified with capital letters which also appear in Figure 3. Refer to Figure 3 when attaching the felt shapes.

Figure 3

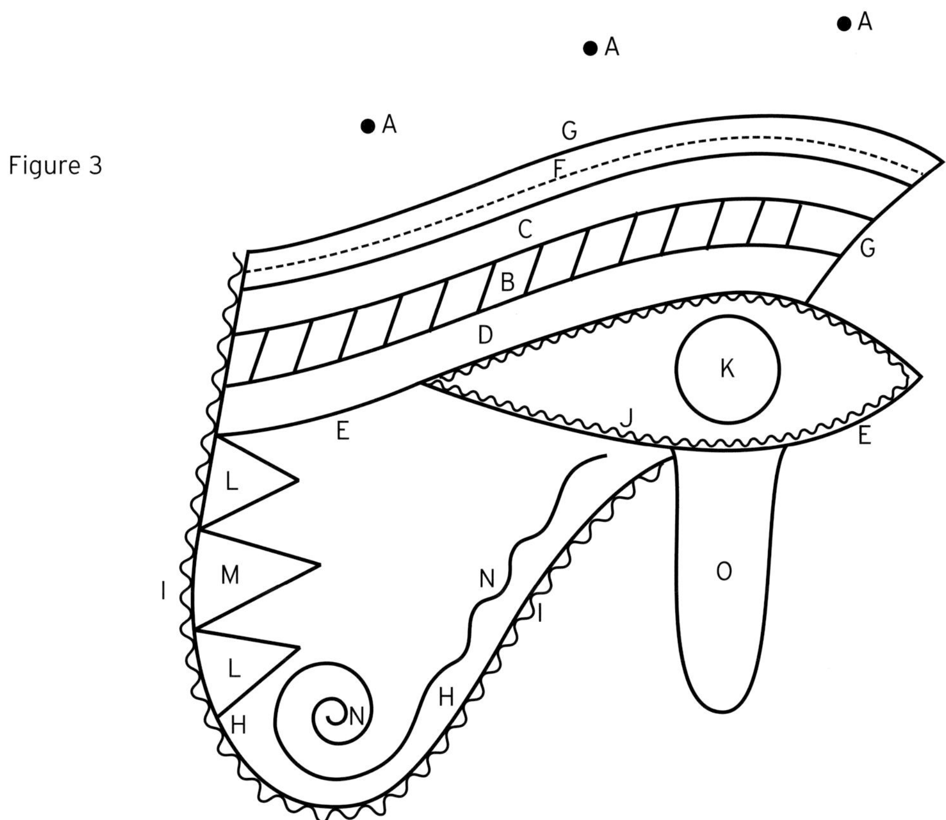

String padding

Each diagonal line in area B of the design is padded with three lengths of yellow DMC soft cotton or yellow bumpf couched with a doubled thread of Gutermann 968. Follow the instructions for string padding in chapter 3.

Embroidery

The elements of the design to be embroidered are listed alphabetically in Figure 3 and are matched to the alphabetical order of work which follows.

A *The rosettes*. Refer to Figure 4. Use 3 mm (⅛ in) gilt spangles and champagne seed beads for the rosettes. Use a double thread of Gutermann 968. Bring needle and thread through at the dot which marks the centre of the rosette, pick up a gilt spangle and then a champagne seed bead. Take needle and thread down through the hole of the spangle. Eight spokes are to be worked from the centre spangle and bead. Work the ones that are at right angles to the centre first, and then those that are at a 45° angle to the centre. All spokes are worked out from the centre. For each spoke, bring the needle and thread up close to the edge of the centre spangle and thread up a bead, a spangle, a bead, a spangle and bead. Take the needle down at a distance that will make the two spangles and centre bead stand proud.

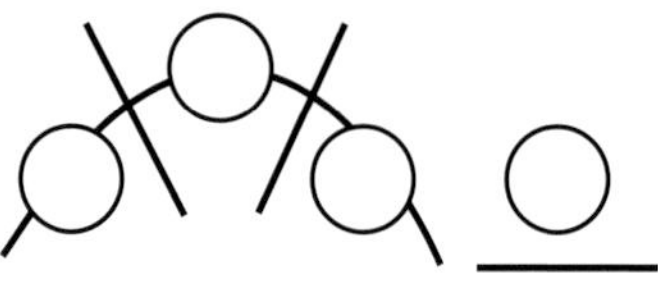

Figure 4

B *Laid work over string padding on the 'entablature' above the eye*. Use no. 8 Japanese gold for the laid work and couch with Gutermann 968. Follow the instructions for simple string padding in chapter 3. Turn the threads at the end of each row as described in the instructions for technique 2 for flat laid work in chapter 3. Outline both sides of the laid work with gilt no. 1 pearl purl. Note that the laid work and the outlines of pearl purl must not encroach on the G and H outlines.

C *Spangles*. A row of spangles is worked in this space. Attach 4 mm (²⁄₁₀ in) gilt spangles with a single thread of Gutermann 968. Working from left to right, bring the needle up in the fabric, thread up a spangle, and drop the spangle to the bottom of the thread. Take the thread across the spangle at a 45° angle, as shown in Figure 5. Take the needle down, and bring the needle up again, as close as possible to the previous spangle. Thread up another spangle and attach it in the same way as the first. Repeat this last step across the row. The outline above the spangles, is

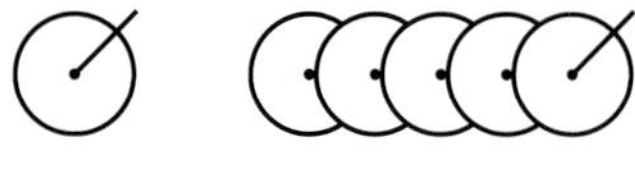

Figure 5

worked with Gilt No. 2 pearl purl. Note that the spangles and the outline of pearl purl must not encroach on the G and H outlines.

D *A row of chain stitches* is worked in this space. In preparation for this work cut 12 mm (½ in) lengths of gilt no. 8 smooth purl for the loops, 5 mm (²⁄₁₀ in) lengths of gilt no. 8 smooth purl for the links and 3 mm (⅛ in) lengths of silver-plated no. 8 wire check to fill the inside of the chains. Thread up a size 12 crewel needle with a doubled thread of Gutermann 968. Refer to the six steps in Figure 6.

Step 1 Start the row of chain stitches 2 mm (1/10 in) in from the left side of the space. Bring the needle through, thread up a 12 mm (1/2 in) length of gilt no. 8 smooth purl, drop it to the bottom of the thread and take the needle down close to where it came up. Allow the purl to wrap around a mellor or chenille needle.

Step 2 Bring the needle up again 1.5 mm (a fraction under 1/10 in) away from where the loop of the chain will sit after it has been linked to the next chain. (Temporarily hold the loop down with a mellor or chenille needle to determine where to bring up the needle for the next chain.) Make another loop.

Step 3 Before proceeding onto the next chain, return to the beginning of the row. Bring the needle up 1 mm (1/20 in) out from the beginning of the first chain, thread up a 5 mm (2/10 in) length of gilt no. 8 smooth purl, drop it to the bottom of the thread and take the needle down just on the inside of the first chain.

Step 4 Hold the loop of the first chain down with the mellor or chenille needle while bringing the needle up again on the inside of this loop. Thread up another 5 mm (2/10 in) length of gilt no. 8 smooth purl, drop it to the bottom of the thread and take the needle down just on the inside of the second chain.

Step 5 Bring the needle up again 1.5 mm (a fraction under 1/10 in) away from where the second loop of the chain will sit after it has been linked to the next chain. (Temporarily hold the loop down with a mellor or chenille needle to determine where to bring up the needle for the next chain.) Make another loop.

Step 6 Repeat these steps for the chains and links for the remainder of the row. Once the chains and links have been completed, fill each chain with a 3 mm (1/8 in) gilt no. 8 bright check.

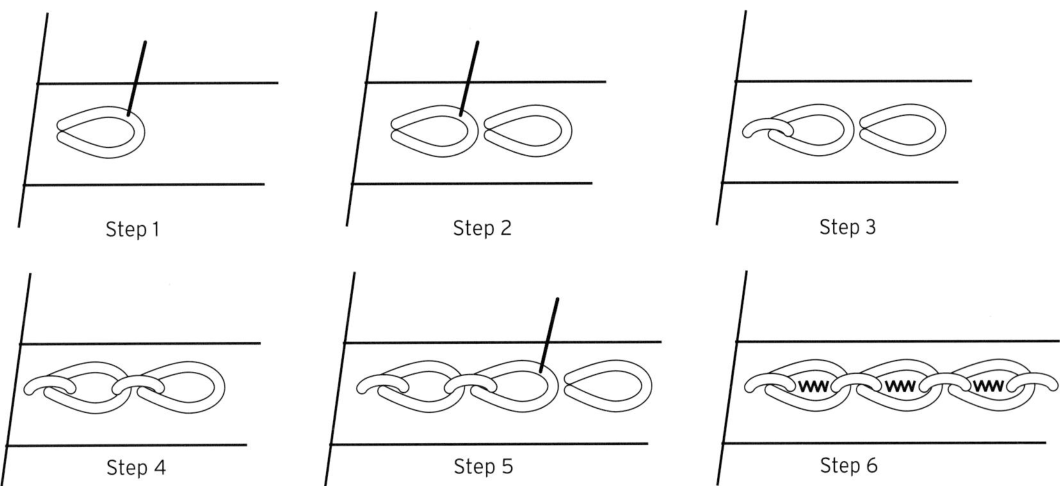

Figure 6

E The *outline of the eye* is worked with gilt no. 1 pearl purl. This line also outlines the bottom side of the row of chain stitches. Use the tweezers to manipulate the pearl purl around the inside corner of the eye.

F *Return* to the outline of gilt no. 2 pearl purl (above the row of spangles), and work a row of overstretched silver-plated no. 3 pearl purl.

G The *completed 'entablature'* is now outlined in gilt no. 3 pearl purl. Use the tweezers to manipulate the pearl purl around the corner.

H This *outline of gilt no. 1 pearl purl* starts from the left side of the G outline and ends under the eye beside the tear-drop shape.

I The *outline of silver-plated milliary* is worked on the outside of the H outline of gilt no. 1 pearl purl. Couch every second groove of the milliary with Gutermann 800.

J The *inside outline of the eye* is worked with overstretched silver-plated no. 1 pearl purl. Use the tweezers to manipulate the pearl purl around the inside corner of the eye.

K The *iris* of the eye is outlined with gilt no. 2 pearl purl and is filled in with chips of gilt no. 6 wire check.

L The *two small triangles* are outlined with silver-plated super pearl purl and filled in with chips of gilt no. 8 wire check.

M The *centre triangle* is outlined with gilt super pearl purl and filled in with chips of silver-plated no. 8 wire check.

N The *serpentine line* is a couched line of no. 8 Japanese gold. Use Gutermann 968 to couch the metal threads. Allow a 3 mm (⅛ in) interval between each couching stitch. Fold the length of Japanese Gold in half. Start the couching with the folded end beneath the eye. The end of the row will have tails to plunge to the back of the work.

O The *tear-drop shape* is outlined with silver-plated no. 1 pearl purl.

Couch a length of ribbled (crinkled) gilt broad plate with a single thread of Gutermann 968 down the centre of the shape. (If this design is purchased as a kit, the plate will be supplied in a ribbled state—that is, it will have been taken through a small ribbler machine, hence the unusual expression 'ribbled'!) Before couching, turn one end of the plate under to form a hook. Couch the hooked end immediately beneath the eye and proceed to couch every groove of the ribbled plate. Cut the plate at the end of the row. Do not attempt to form a hook at this end.

Couch a row of gilt no. 7 check thread on both sides of the plate. Fold the small lengths of check thread in half for this work. Start the couching with the folded end of the check thread beneath the eye. Use Gutermann 968 to couch the metal threads. The end of the rows will have tails to plunge to the back of the work.

Couch another row of plate on either side of these couched check threads. Fill the remainder of the tear-drop shape with rows of couched check thread on both sides of the three rows of plate.

Medallion

A wealth of inspiration for goldwork designs is to be found in the applied ornament of architecture, especially from the Victorian, Art Nouveau and Art Deco periods. Victorian octagonal floor tiles were the inspiration for this design but the accretion of metal threads on this work transformed the utilitarian tile into a piece of sumptuous jewellery. Imagine this design as a motif which can be repeated. To add further visual appeal and to give you the opportunity to make this work uniquely your own, create one or two other variations of this design to bring into the repeat.

EQUIPMENT AND MATERIALS

76 cm (30 in) slate frame or 36 cm (14 in) ring frame
calico to fit the frame
square of red velvet an appropriate size for the frame
2 x A4 sheets of 110gsm tracing paper
1 gram pounce (and roll of felt to apply pounce)
1 tube yellow ochre watercolour paint
1 x 000 paintbrush
orange dressmaker's carbon
10 cm (4 in) square yellow felt
Gutermann 968
2 grams of 4 mm (2⁄10 in) gilt spangles
7grams of 5–6 mm (5⁄20 in) gilt spangles
size 12 sharps (for the gilt no. 8 bright check) and size 10 crewel needles
mellor or size 18 chenille needle

METAL THREADS

90 cm (36 in) gilt no. 1 pearl purl
1.2 m (48 in) gilt no. 2 pearl purl
1.5 m (60 in) gilt no. 5 check thread
45 cm (18 in) gilt no. 1 bright bullion
50 cm (20 in) gilt no. 6 façonnée
110 cm (44 in) gilt no. 6 bright check
20 cm (8 in) gilt no. 8 bright check
30 cm (12 in) gilt broad plate, ribbled (see note under instruction B, Felt padded border)

METHOD

Red velvet background

Mount the velvet square and the calico into a ring/hoop frame or sew the velvet square onto calico which has already been laced up on a

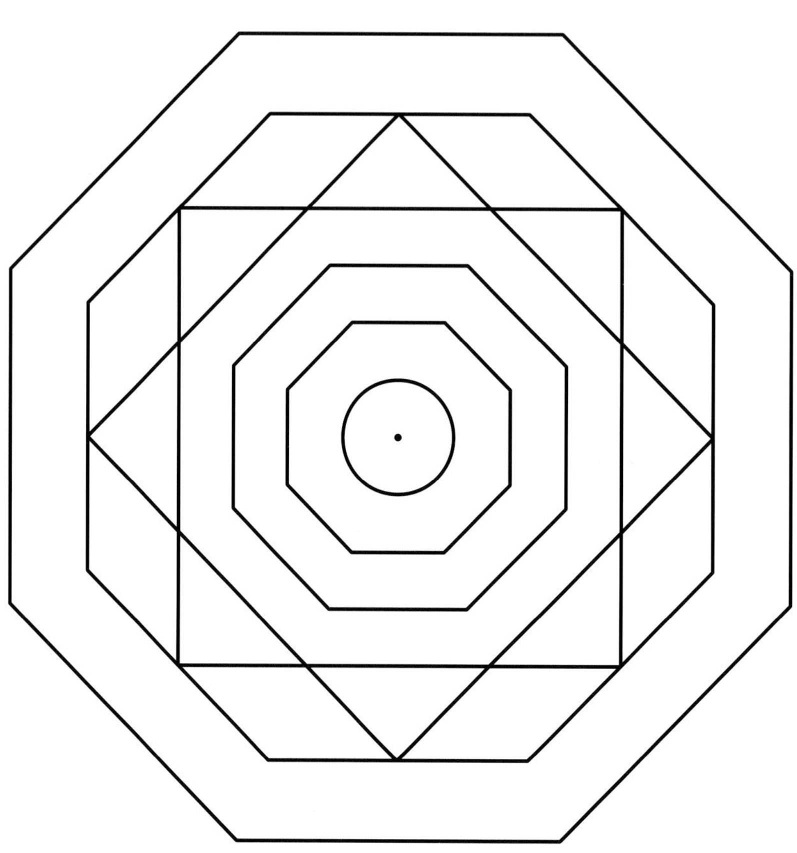

Figure 1
Tracing shape

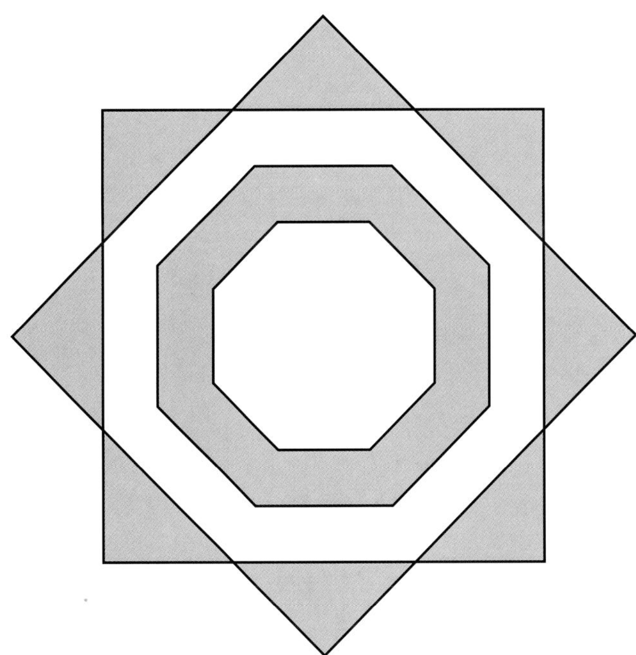

Figure 2 *Shapes for felt padding; trace and cut each of the triangular shapes separately*

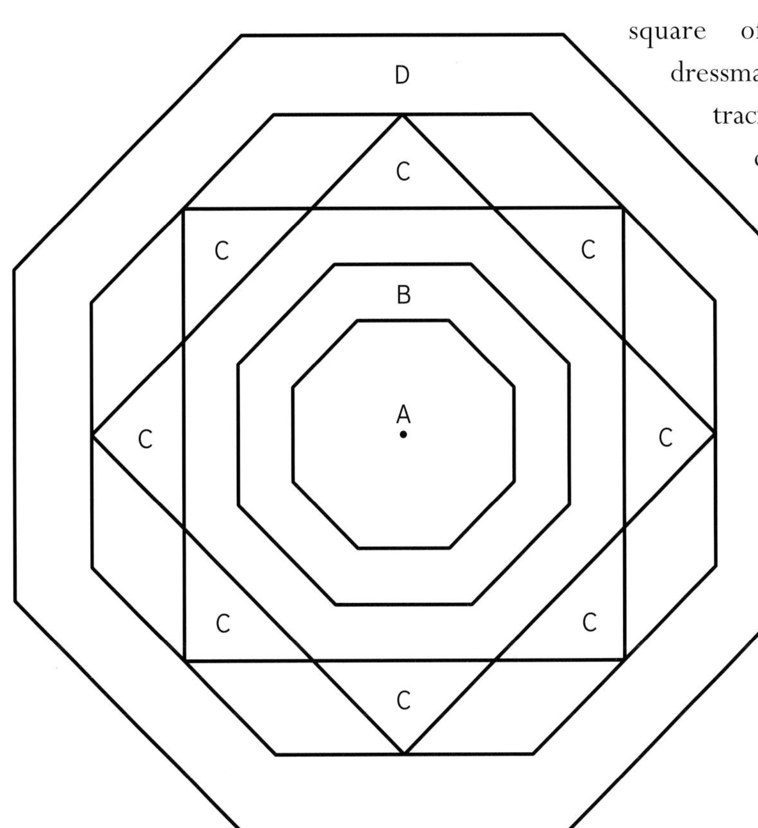

Figure 3

square or slate frame. Refer to the instructions for dressing a slate frame in chapter 3.

Trace the lines in Figure 1 onto tracing paper. Use the prick-and-pounce method to transfer the design on to the velvet. Refer to the instructions for the prick-and-pounce method in chapter 3. The transferring of the design can be done after mounting the velvet onto the slate frame. Place books beneath the frame to support the fabric while pouncing and painting the design lines.

Further secure the velvet to the calico by pin stitching along the design lines, allowing approximately 3 cm (⅛ in) in between each pin-stitch. The pin stitches will eventually be hidden.

Felt padding

Trace the shapes in Figure 2 onto tracing paper and then transfer these design lines onto the square of yellow felt, using orange dressmaker's carbon. Press heavily when tracing onto felt otherwise the orange carbon will not show on the yellow felt. Cut the shapes out of the felt. Use a single sewing thread to attach the felt shapes onto the velvet. Refer to the instructions for felt padding in chapter 3.

Embroidery

The elements of the design to be embroidered are listed alphabetically in Figure 3 and are matched to the alphabetical order of work which follows.

A The *centre of the medallion*. This is a cluster of spangles and purls. It is worked differently to the cluster of spangles described in chapter 3. Follow the steps in Figure 4 to work this cluster. Use 5–6 mm (5/20 in) gilt spangles, 6 mm (5/20 in) lengths of gilt no. 6 façonnée and a doubled thread of Gutermann 968 for the cluster.

Step 1 Bring needle and thread through at the dot in the centre of the medallion. Thread up a spangle and a 6 mm (5/20 in) length of gilt façonnée. Drop both to the bottom of the thread. Take the needle down through the hole of the spangle. Support the thread with a mellor or chenille needle and allow the façonnée to loop over it as the thread is taken through.

Step 2 The circle line in the centre of the medallion indicates where the needle will come up for the circle of spangles which will surround the centre spangle. (Note that the needle will be taken down at the edge of the centre spangle.) Start at the top of the centre spangle and work in a clockwise direction. Bring the needle up on the circle line. Thread up a spangle and a length of façonnée. Take the needle down so that the façonnée is sitting diagonally on and across the spangle and resting at the edge of the centre spangle. The façonnée extends beyond its spangle a distance of half the diameter of the spangle.

Step 3 Bring the needle up on the circle line beside the first spangle. Thread up a spangle and a length of façonnée. Drop both to the bottom of the thread. Allow the spangle to sit beneath the façonnée. (Note that the spangles in the circle overlap each other but they do not overlap the centre spangle.) Take the needle down approximately 2 mm (1/10 in) in front of the previous length of façonnée.

Step 4 Repeat Step 3 until the last spangle which will become the tenth spangle. Thread up the spangle. Use the mellor or chenille needle to tuck the last spangle beneath the first spangle. Thread up the last length of façonnée. It will extend beneath the first length of façonnée.

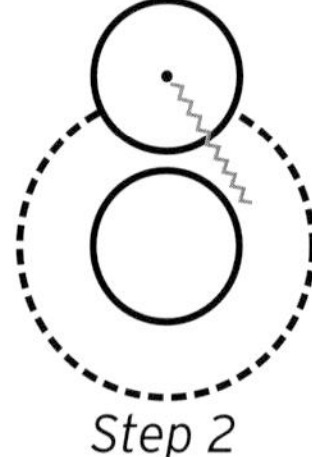

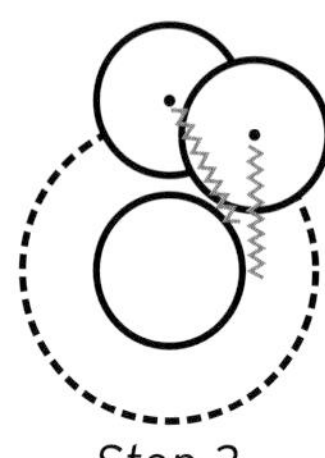

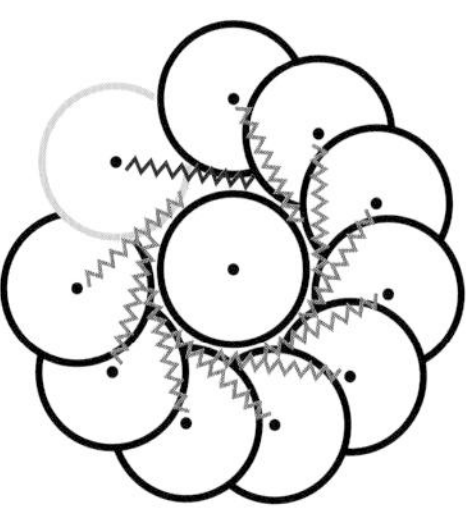

Figure 4

B The *felt padded border* around the cluster of spangles. The gilt broad plate needs to be ribbled (crinkled) for this work. (If this design is purchased as a kit, the plate will be supplied in a ribbled state—that is, it will have been taken through a small ribbler machine, hence the unusual expression 'ribbled'!) Turn the end of the plate under with a pair of tweezers. The plate runs through the centre of the border. To attach the plate couch over every groove of the ribbled plate with Gutermann 968. Before couching the last groove, turn this end of the plate under with tweezers.

Cut the length of gilt no. 8 bright check into 2 mm (1/10 in) pieces. Attach these small lengths of bright check over every groove of the ribbled plate using a doubled thread of Gutermann 968.

Gilt no. 5 check thread is couched on both sides of the plate. Cut the length of check thread in half. Fold each half in two and commence couching with the folded ends of the check thread. Use a single thread of Gutermann 968 to couch the check thread. Leave a space interval of 3 mm (1/8 in) between couching stitches. Refer to Figure 5. Finish with 3 cm (1¼ in) tails and plunge these through to the back of the work. Refer to the instructions for plunging the tails of fibre-core threads in chapter 3.

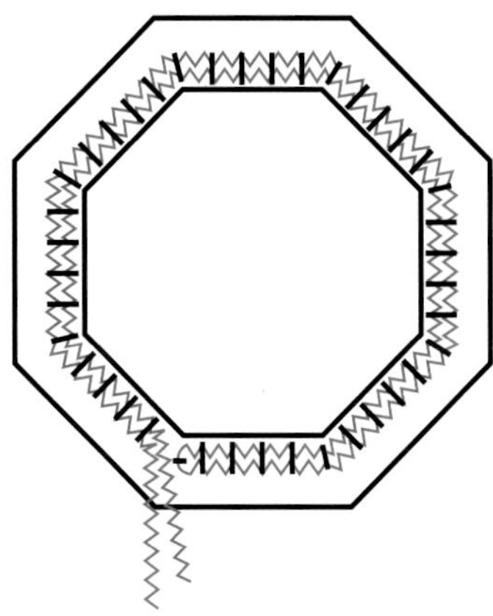

Figure 5

Outline the border on both sides of the couched check thread, first with gilt no. 1 pearl purl, followed by a row of overstretched gilt no. 1 pearl purl. Prepare for the latter by stretching a 20 cm (8 in) length of gilt no. 1 pearl purl to 30 cm (12 in).

C The *pattern of triangles*. Outline the triangles with gilt no. 1 pearl purl. The triangles are not outlined individually. Figure 6 shows the two design lines for outlining these shapes.

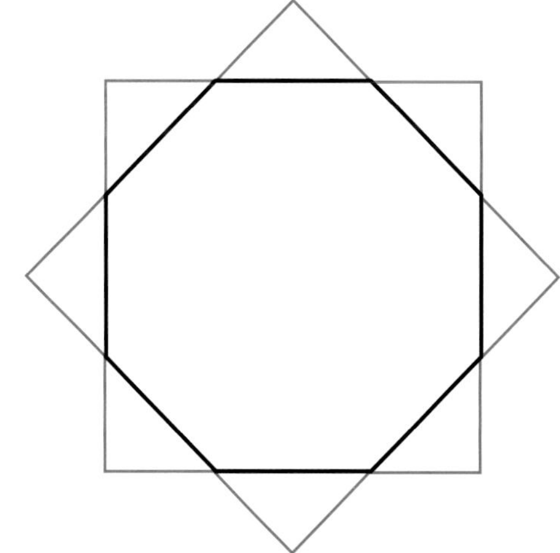

Figure 6

The centre of each triangle features a cluster of spangles with loops of gilt no. 6 bright check. Use 4 mm (2/10 in) gilt spangles and cut 6 mm (3/10 in) lengths of bright check for the loops. Refer to the instructions for spangles and loops of purl in chapter 3. Fill the remainder of each triangle with chips of gilt no. 6 bright check.

D The *outside border* of the medallion. Firstly, cover the two design lines for the border with overstretched gilt no. 2 pearl purl. For the inside design line, stretch a 20 cm (8 in) length of gilt no. 2 pearl purl to 35 cm (14 in), and for the outside design line stretch a 25 cm (10 in) length of gilt no. 2 pearl purl to 45 cm (18 in). Couch every third groove of the overstretched pearl purl with Gutermann 968. Secondly, couch gilt no. 2 pearl purl on the inside and close to both outlines of overstretched gilt no. 2 pearl purl.

A row of S-ing with spangles is worked within the pearl purl outlines. Refer to the instructions for S-ing with spangles in chapter 3. However, as this will be a continuous row of S-ing, you will also need to follow the steps for starting and finishing the row of S-ing in Figure 7. Use 5–6 mm (5/20 in) gilt spangles and a doubled thread of Gutermann 968 for this work. Cut the gilt no. 1 bright bullion and the gilt no. 6 façonnée into 6 mm (5/20 in) lengths. The bright bullion and the façonnée will be used alternately for the S-ing.

Step 1 Start at a corner on your left side of the medallion and work in an anti-clockwise direction. Attach two spangles without a bullion or façonnée purl. They must overlap.

Step 2 Bring the needle through, close to the second spangle. Thread up the third spangle and a bright bullion or façonnée purl. Take the needle down through the hole of the first spangle.

Figure 7

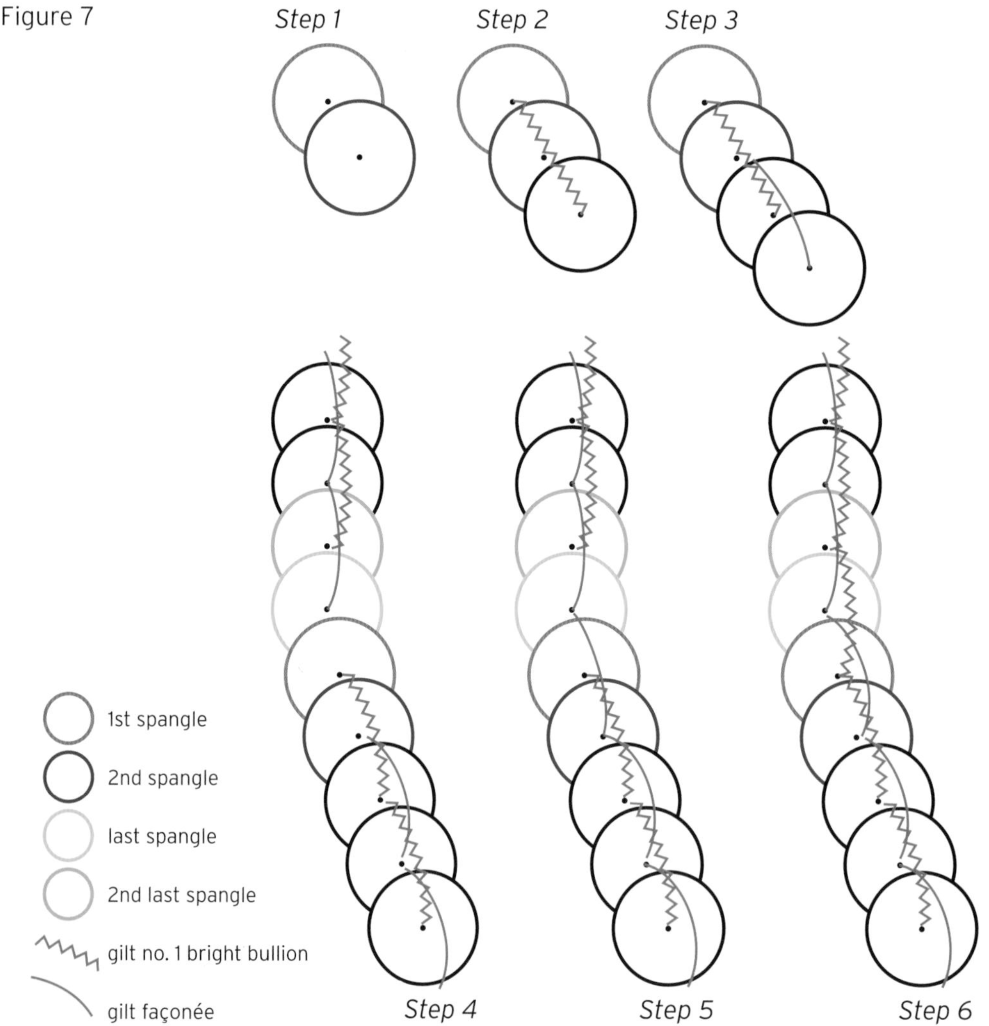

Step 3 Bring the needle through, close to the third spangle. Thread up the fourth spangle and a length of bullion or façonnée purl. Take the needle down through the hole of the second spangle. (By Step 3, you need to be referring to the instructions for S-ing with spangles in chapter 3.) Continue in this manner around the border until you arrive at the last spangle.

Step 4 Thread up the last spangle. Use a mellor or chenille needle to assist in tucking the last spangle beneath the first one. Once that has been achieved, thread up a bright bullion or façonnée purl and take the needle down though the hole of the third last spangle.

Step 5 Bring the needle up through the hole of the second spangle on the left side of the bright bullion or façonnée purl. Thread up a bright bullion or façonnée purl. Drop it to the bottom of the thread. Take the needle down through the hole of the last spangle.

Step 6 Bring the needle up through the hole of the first spangle on the left side of the bright bullion or façonnée purl. Thread up a bright bullion or façonnée purl. Drop it to the bottom of the thread. Take the needle down through the hole of the second last spangle on right side of the bright bullion or façonnée purl already in position. This completes the row of S-ing and it is no longer discernable as to where the line began and finished.

Ornamental Fan

Throughout history fans have been the one fashion accessory to always carry ornament. This fan design has been encrusted with pure ornament—clusters of spangles, sequins, pearls, beads and metal bullions and purls. Plate work circles superimposed with bullions are added to the sumptuous mix.

The fan has a pretty edging of milliary and overstretched pearl purl wound with a pink metal couching thread. The base of the fan is cutwork over a large size pearl purl, the bullions slightly spaced apart to reveal glimpses of metal beneath.

The muslin ground is a reference to lacy fans.

This is a playful piece so you are encouraged to take as many liberties as you can when working the design. Enjoy!

EQUIPMENT AND MATERIALS

76 cm (30 in) slate frame or 30 cm (12 in) ring frame
square of calico to fit the frame
square of light pink duchesse silk satin an appropriate size for the frame
20 x 15 cm (8 x 6 in) cream muslin
10 cm (4 in) square yellow felt
1 sheet tissue paper
HB pencil
small piece of 110 gsm tracing paper
Gutermann 968
Gutermann 800
1 gram of 5 mm (2⁄10 in) pink cup sequins
1 gram of 3 mm (1⁄8 in) pink bugle beads
1 gram standard size champagne gold matte seed beads
8 large gold ball beads
3 medium size pearls
1 gram of 3 mm (1⁄8 in) gilt spangles
1 gram of 5 mm (2⁄10 in) gilt spangles
size 10 crewel needle
size 7 crewel needle for the no. 20 pink couching thread
mellor or tapestry needle

METAL THREADS

45 cm (17½ in) gilt no. 3 pearl purl
15 cm (6 in) gilt no. 4 pearl purl
3.5 m (approximately 4 yd) no. 20 pink couching thread
1.4 m (56 in) gilt milliary
90 cm (36 in) gilt no. 1 bright bullion
50 cm (20 in) gilt façonnée purl
25 cm (10 in) pink no. 6 rough purl
25 cm (10 in) fuchsia no. 6 rough purl
1.2 m (48 in) gilt narrow plate

(a) tracing outline

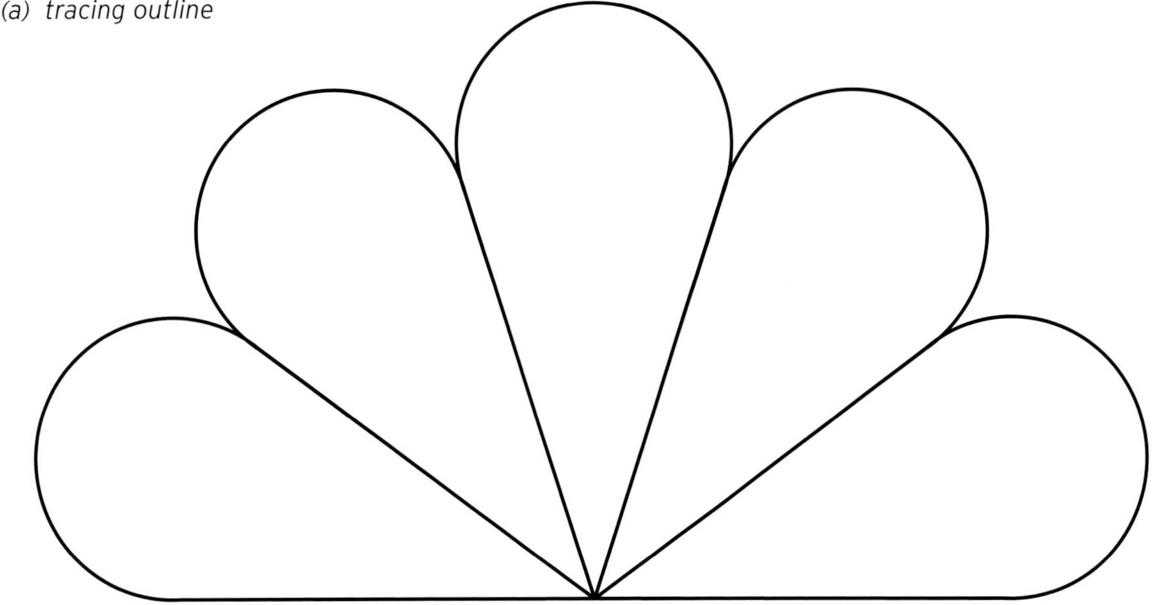

Figure 1

(b) felt padding shape

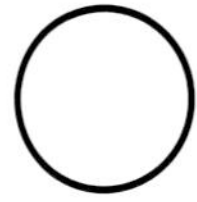

METHOD

Light pink duchesse silk background

Mount the silk square and the calico into a hoop/ring frame or sew the silk square onto calico which has already been laced up on a square or slate frame. Refer to the instructions for dressing a slate frame in chapter 3.

Transferring design and attaching muslin to silk background

Trace Figure 1(a) onto tissue paper with pencil. Centre the rectangle of muslin on the silk background. Place the tissue paper with the traced design onto the muslin. Push pins down through the three layers. Pin-stitch every 3 cm (1¼ in) along the design lines to attach the tissue paper and muslin onto the silk background. Remove the pins as you pin stitch. The next step is to work small tacking stitches with Gutermann 800 around and along all design lines. Make the tacking stitches 2 mm (1/10 in) on top and 1 mm (1/20 in) beneath. When tacking has been completed, remove the tissue paper. With the utmost care, trim away the excess muslin 1 mm (1/20 in) away from the tacking around the base line and scalloped edges.

Felt padding

Trace the circle in Figure 1(b) onto tracing paper. Cut it out and use it as a template to cut five circles out of the felt square. These circles are for the felt padding beneath the plate work. Attach one circle in each segment of the fan. Vary the position of the circles but attach them in the top half of the segment because this is the part that will be heavily embellished with ornaments.

Base line of fan

Couch gilt no. 4 pearl purl along the base line. Cutwork using alternate lengths of gilt façonnée and gilt no. 1 bright bullion is worked over the pearl purl. Follow the directions for horizontal cutwork over string padding in chapter 3. However, as the cutwork is being worked over pearl purl, allow small spaces between the façonnée purls and bright bullions so that glimpses of metal can be seen through the cutwork.

Outlining the segments of the fan

In preparation for outlining the five segments, stretch the 45 cm (17½ in) length of gilt no. 3 pearl purl to 70 cm (28 in). Cut the overstretched pearl purl so that you have a 40 cm (16 in) and a 30 cm (12 in) length. The 30 cm (12 in) length will be used for two segments and the 40 cm (16 in) length will be used for two segments, plus the short curved line at the top of the middle segment. Wind no. 20 pink couching thread around both lengths of the overstretched pearl purl. Gain purchase for the pink couching thread in the closed end of the pearl purl (the part that was held by your thumb and finger when you stretched the pearl purl).

First outline the fan according to the design lines in Figure 2 with the overstretched and wrapped gilt no. 3 pearl purl. The beginning and the end of each design line is marked with an **X**. Couch the pearl purl on the muslin. Couch every second groove of the pearl purl with no. 20 pink couching thread. The gilt no. 3 pearl purl outline should connect to the gilt no. 4 pearl purl on the base line.

Couch gilt milliary on the outside of the overstretched pearl purl around the scalloped edge. Use Gutermann 968 to couch every second groove of the milliary.

Figure 2

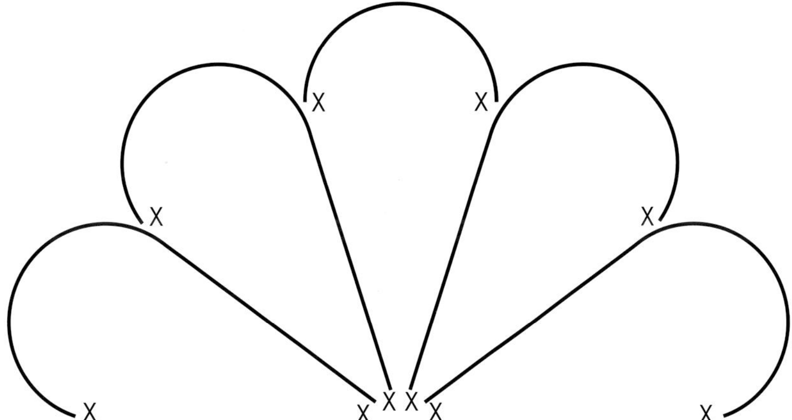

Finally, couch milliary on the inside of the overstretched pearl purl outlines of the segments. When the milliary work has been completed, all the overstretched pearl purl outlines should have milliary on both sides.

Plate work, bullion and purl work over the felt padding

Refer to Figure 3 for the direction that the plate work should follow in each segment. Follow the instructions for closed plate work in chapter 3. As you are couching plate over a circle of felt padding, the sides of the plate work will be slightly stepped.

In preparation for the bullion and purl work, cut 12 mm (½ in) lengths of gilt no. 1 bright bullion and 9 mm (a fraction over ⅜ in) lengths of gilt façonnée. Attach the bright bullion lengths in the same way as a large bugle bead over the plate work in a square formation as shown in Figure 4. The façonnée lengths are looped around the bright bullions as shown in Figure 4. Work loops of façonnée around each intersection first. Bring the needle up on the outside and into the intersection, thread up the façonnée purl, drop it to the bottom of the doubled sewing thread, take the needle and thread over and under the intersection and return the needle close to where it came up. Support the thread with a mellor or tapestry needle as it is pulled through the fabric. Use the same tool to assist the façonnée purl to tuck under the bright bullion.

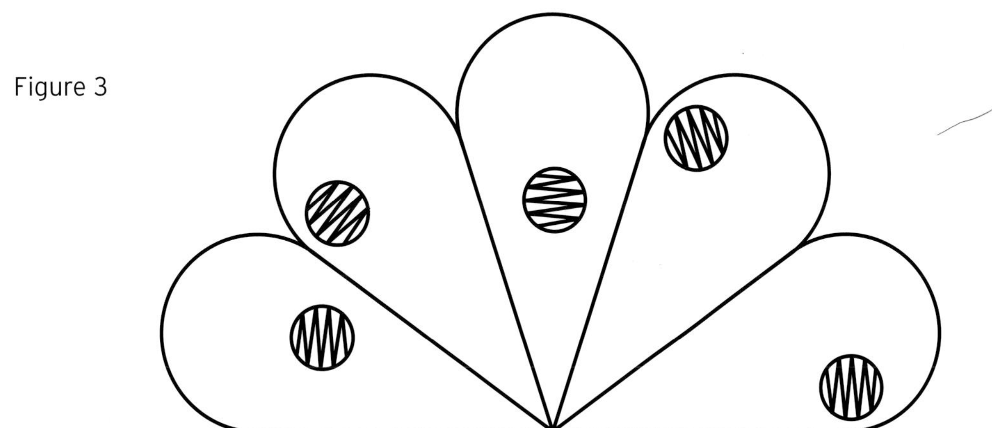
Figure 3

Figure 4

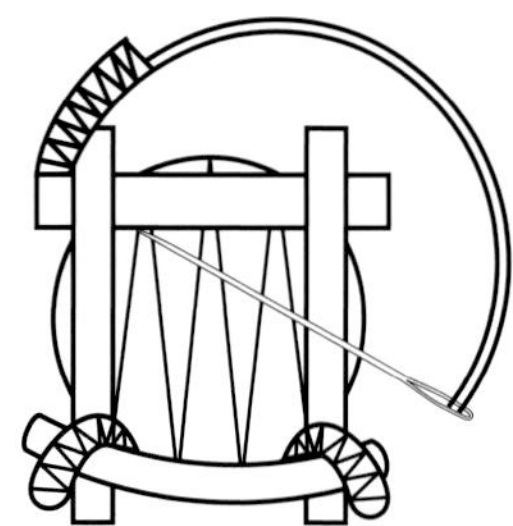

Note that the bullions can take more handling than the smaller purls. Loop two façonnée purls over and under each length of bright bullion around the plate-worked circle. The loops of façonnée will pull the bright bullions out to form a circular shape over the plate work.

Remaining ornaments

There are eight different ornaments, other than the plate-worked circles, that appear in the upper half of each segment of the fan. Several appear in all segments and others are used in alternate segments. Figure 5 identifies the components that are used for the ornaments. Use a doubled thread of Gutermann 968 in a size 10 crewel needle for the threading and the attachment of the components of the ornaments.

The eight ornaments are identified alphabetically, A to H. Figure 6 demonstrates their dispersal on the fan.

Ornament A

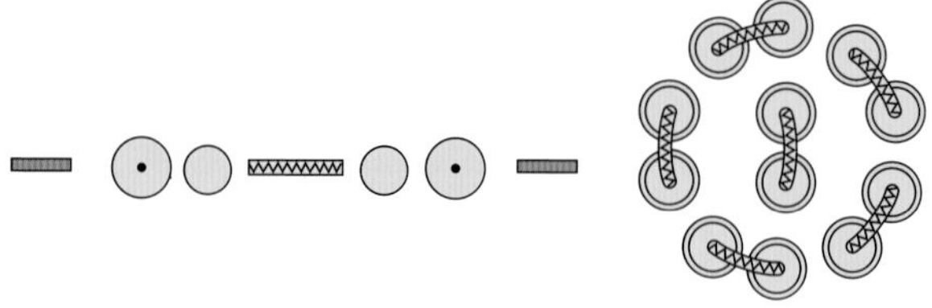

Cut the gilt façonnée into 4 mm (2/10 in) lengths.

Bring the needle through, thread up the components above, in the order that they have been shown, drop them to the bottom of the thread and take the needle down close to where the needle came through. Support the thread with a mellor or tapestry needle as it is taken through the fabric.

To create a cluster, have one set of components in the centre and arrange five sets around this centre one.

Ornament B

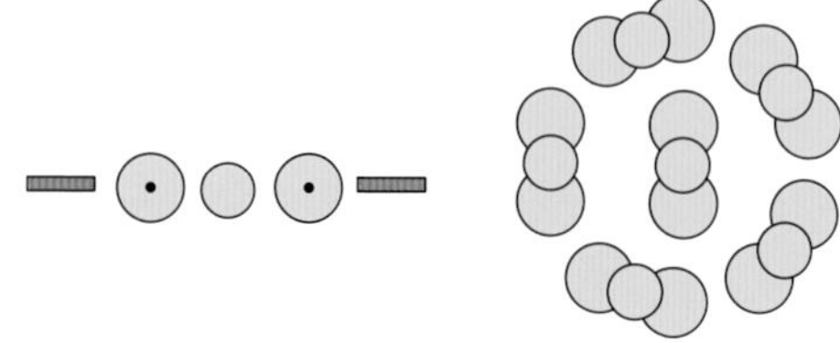

Bring the needle through, thread up the components above, in the order that they have been shown, drop them to the bottom of the thread and take the needle down close to where

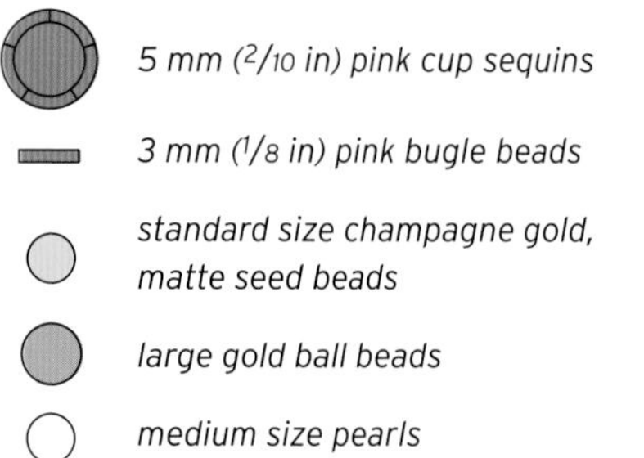

3 mm (1/8 in) gilt spangles

5 mm (2/10 in) gilt spangles

gilt no. 1 bright bullion

gilt façonée

no. 6 pink rough purl

no. 6 fuchsia rough purl

Figure 5

the needle came through. Support the thread with a mellor or tapestry needle as it is taken through the fabric.

To create a cluster, have one set of components in the centre and arrange five sets around this centre one.

Ornament C

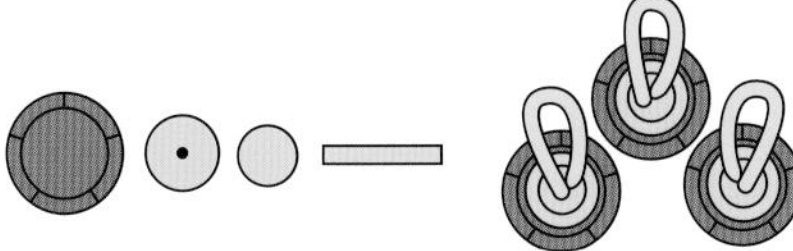

Cut the gilt no. 1 bright bullion into 7 mm (3/10 in) lengths.

Bring the needle through, thread up the components above, in the order that they have been shown, drop them to the bottom of the thread and take the needle down through the holes of the standard gold matte seed bead, 3 mm (1/8 in) spangle and pink cup sequin. Support the thread with a mellor or tapestry needle as it is taken through the fabric. Allow the bright bullion to curve over the mellor or tapestry needle.

This set of components is used in groups of three.

Ornament D

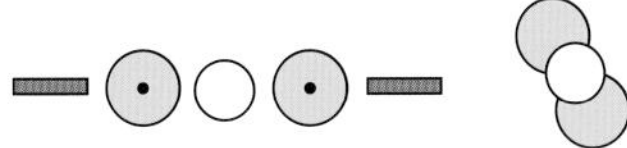

Bring the needle through, thread up the components above, in the order that they have been shown, drop them to the bottom of the thread and take the needle down close to where the needle came through. Support the thread with a mellor or tapestry needle as it is taken through the fabric.

This set of components is used singly.

Ornament E

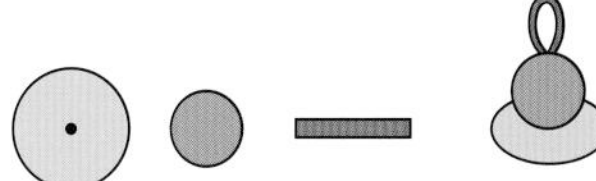

Cut an 8 mm (a fraction over 3/10 in) length of fuchsia rough purl.

Bring the needle through, thread up the components above, in the order that they have been shown, drop them to the bottom of the thread and take the needle down through the holes of the gold ball and 5 mm (2/10 in) spangle. Support the thread with a mellor or tapestry needle as it is taken through the fabric. Allow the fuchsia rough purl to curve over the mellor or tapestry needle.

This set of components is used singly.

Ornament F

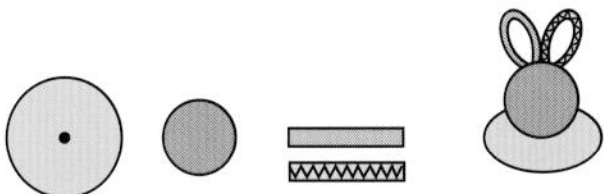

Cut the pink rough purl and the gilt façonnée purl into 8 mm (a fraction over 3/10 in) lengths.

Bring the needle through, thread up the components above, in the order that they have been shown, drop them to the bottom of the thread and take the needle down through the holes of the gold ball and 5 mm (2/10 in) spangle. Support the thread with a mellor or tapestry needle as it is taken through the fabric. Allow the pink rough purl to curve over the mellor or tapestry needle. Once the needle and thread have been taken through the components and fabric, pull the thread firmly from beneath to make the purl crinkle.

Bring the needle up through the holes of the 5 mm (2/10 in) spangle and gold ball. (If the spangle moves while you are trying to negotiate the hole, hold it in place with the mellor or tapestry needle.) Thread up the length of gilt façonnée and take the needle down through the holes of the gold ball and 5 mm ($^{2}/_{10}$ in) spangle. Support the thread with a mellor or tapestry needle as it is taken through the fabric. Allow the façonnée to curve over the mellor or tapestry needle. Pull the thread firmly from beneath to make the façonnée crinkle.

This set of components is used singly.

Ornament G

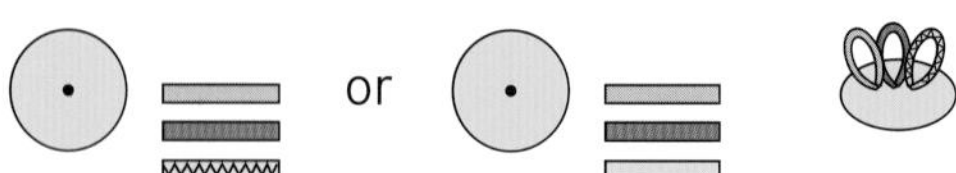

This ornament features pink rough purl and fuchsia rough purl. It also uses either gilt façonnée or gilt no. 1 bright bullion.

Cut the purls and bullions into 8 mm (a fraction over $^{3}/_{10}$ in) lengths.

Bring the needle through, thread up the two components above, in the order that they have been shown, drop them to the bottom of the thread and take the needle down through the hole of the 5 mm ($^{2}/_{10}$ in) spangle. Support the thread with a mellor or tapestry needle as it is taken through the fabric. Allow the bullion to curve over the mellor or tapestry needle. Once the needle and thread have been taken through the components and fabric, pull the thread firmly from beneath to make the bullion crinkle.

Bring the needle up through the hole of the 5 mm ($^{2}/_{10}$ in) spangle. Thread up a length of fuchsia rough purl and take the needle down through the hole of the 5 mm ($^{2}/_{10}$ in) spangle. Support the thread with a mellor or tapestry needle as it is taken through the fabric. Allow the purl to curve over the mellor or tapestry needle. Pull the thread firmly from beneath to make the purl crinkle. Repeat the same step for attaching the pink rough purl.

This set of components is used singly.

Ornament H

Cut an 8 mm (a fraction over $^{3}/_{10}$ in) length of façonnée purl.

Bring the needle through, thread up the two components above, in the order that they have been shown, drop them to the bottom of the thread and take the needle down through the hole of the 3 mm ($^{1}/_{8}$ in) spangle. Support the thread with a mellor or tapestry needle as it is

Figure 6
Placement of ornaments

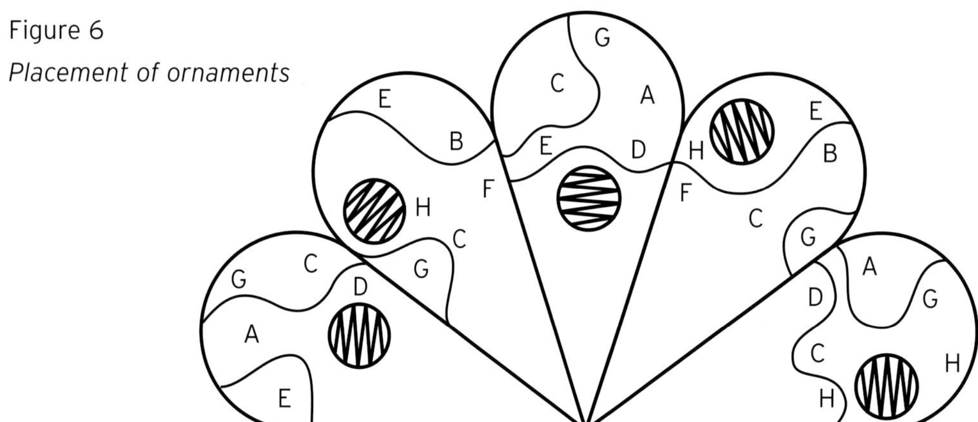

taken through the fabric. Allow the façonnée purl to curve over the mellor or tapestry needle.

This set of components is used singly.

Meandering lines

The meandering lines in the top half of each segment are overstretched lengths of gilt façonnée which have been couched with a single thread of Gutermann 968. These lines are taken around the ornaments in the top half of the segments of the fan as shown in Figure 6.

Purls and bullions in bottom half of each segment

In preparation for this work, cut the remainder of the purls and bullions that have been used for the ornaments, into a variety of lengths. The corners of the segments are dense with the smallest of the lengths of purls and bullions. Use the longer lengths and allow more space between the purls and bullions, as you work towards the ornaments in the top half of the segments. Allow one or two of these lengths to encroach into the area occupied by the ornaments.

Portrait of a Woman

This fashionable woman is wearing a coat that echoes a military uniform. Contemporary fashion designers constantly reference masculine attire for female costumes because it heightens a woman's femininity. Her severe dark purple coat is softened by richly textured cuffs and collar. Her curly hair is crowned with a magnificent, heavily encrusted Russian-style hat. A classical frame is the perfect foil for the woman's sumptuous costume.

EQUIPMENT AND MATERIALS

76 cm (30 in) slate frame or 30 cm (12 in) ring frame
calico to fit the frame
square of cream duchesse silk satin an appropriate size for the frame
10 cm (4 in) square dark purple duchesse silk satin
10 cm (4 in) square yellow felt
3 x A4 sheets 110 gsm tracing paper
Vliesofix, HeatnBond Lite or Bondaweb
orange dressmaker's carbon
Gutermann thread to match the cream silk
Gutermann thread to match the dark purple silk
Gutermann 968
Anchor stranded cottons, nos 403 (black), 381 (dark brown), 361 (beige), 22 (burgundy)
DMC stranded cotton 29 (red)
sizes 10 and 7 crewel needles and size 12 sharps needle
mellor or size 18 chenille needle

Figure 1 *How the parts come together*

METAL THREADS AND SPANGLES

20 cm (8 in) gilt no. 1 pearl purl
2.8 m (3 yd) no. 8 Japanese gold
4 m (4⅓ yd) gilt tambour thread
1 m (1⅛ yd) gilt no. 7 check thread
80 cm (32 in) gilt 1½ twist
1.6 m (1⅔yd) gilt no. 6 bright check
20 cm (8 in) gilt no. 8 bright check
80 cm (32 in) gilt no. 8 rough purl
15 cm (6 in) cardinal red no. 6 rough purl
15 cm (6 in) pink no. 6 rough purl
60 cm (24 in) mixture of brown no. 6 rough purls
1.2 m (1⅓yd) gilt narrow plate
2 grams of 3 mm gilt spangles
1 gram of 4 mm gilt spangles

METHOD

Cream silk background

This design is best transferred onto the silk after it has been stretched taut on the frame because of the long straight lines in the design. Refer to the instructions for dressing a slate frame in chapter 3. Trace the lines in Figure 2(a) onto tracing paper and then transfer the design onto the silk using orange dressmaker's carbon, with a book for support under the fabric in the frame.

Purple silk coat

Iron Vliesofix (HeatnBond Lite or Bondaweb) onto the wrong side of the purple silk square. Peel off the backing paper. Trace the lines in Figure 2(b) onto tracing paper and then transfer these design lines onto the right side of the purple silk, using orange dressmaker's carbon. Match the edges of the purple silk with the design lines for the coat on the cream silk. To initially hold the appliqué piece in place, work a few stab stitches around the edges of the appliqué. Then use minute stab stitches, 1 mm (1⁄20 in) apart, to appliqué the purple silk onto the cream silk background. When stab stitching, come up in the cream silk, and down into the purple silk.

Figure 2(a) *Tracing outline*

Felt padding

Trace the shapes in Figure 2(c) onto tracing paper and then transfer these design lines onto the square of yellow felt, using orange dressmaker's carbon. Press more heavily when tracing onto felt otherwise the orange carbon will not show on the yellow felt. Cut the shapes out of the felt. Use a single sewing thread to attach the felt shapes onto the silk. The hat has two layers of felt. The collars and cuffs have one layer of felt, plus the smaller shapes, that are attached on top. Each of the three decorative bands, on the front of the coat, has one layer of felt.

Facial features

Take one strand of dark brown Anchor stranded cotton and work the eyebrows, eyes and eyelids in split stitch. The iris of each eye is worked in satin stitch, using one strand of black Anchor stranded cotton. One strand of beige Anchor stranded cotton is used to define the nose and chin in split stitch. Use one strand of burgundy

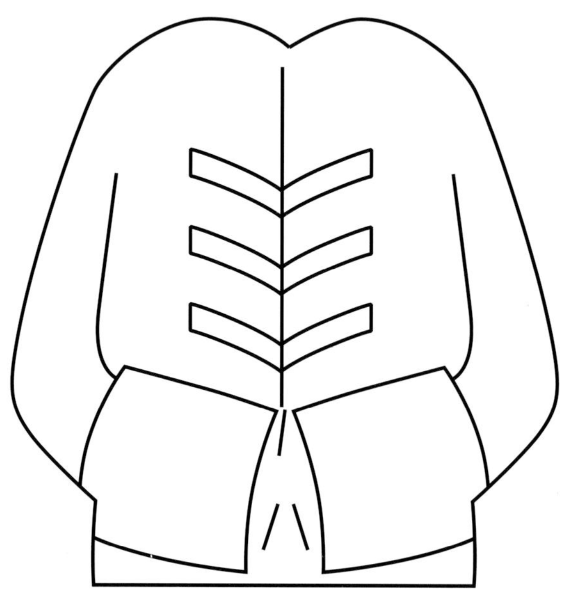

Figure 2(b) *Tracing for coat*

Figure 2(c) *Felt padding shapes*

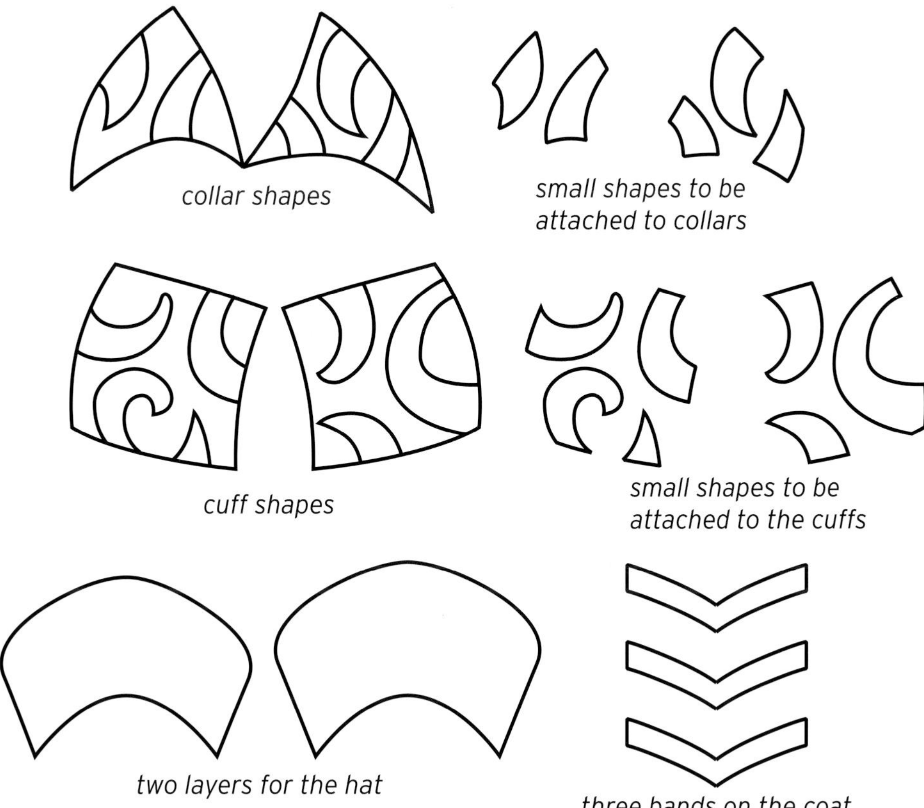

Anchor stranded cotton and work the top lip in satin stitch. Take one strand of burgundy and one strand of red and use them alternately to work the bottom lip in satin stitch.

Frame

The frame is worked in laid work. Refer to Figures 3(a), (b), (c), (d), (e) and (f). Place two threads of no. 8 Japanese gold across the bottom of the drawn rectangle for the frame. Leave tails, and working from right to left, couch over the two metal threads as one, every 4 mm (2/10 in), with Gutermann 968. Before rounding the corner, plunge the two tails at the start, to the back and couch the metal threads at the back of the work. To turn the two threads at the corner, couch each thread separately at a 45° angle. The outside thread is couched from the outside to the inside and the inside thread is couched from the inside to the outside.

When one row of laid work has been completed around the frame, turn the corner as shown in Figure 3(b). The couching stitches for the second row of laid work are to be placed in

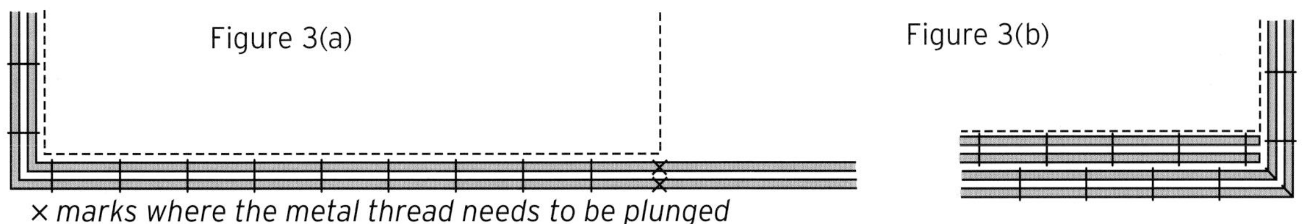

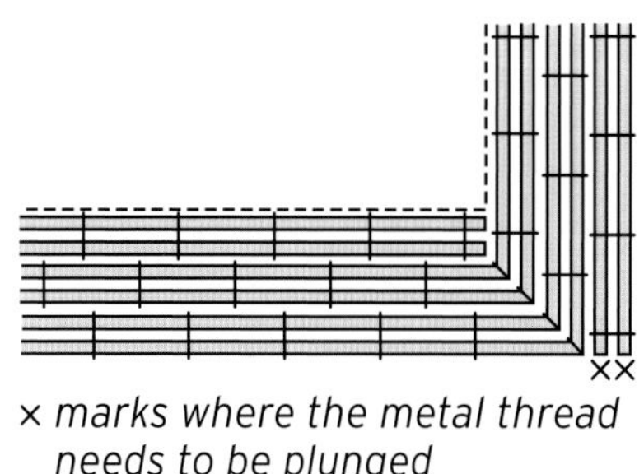

Figure 3(c)

between the couching stitches of the previous row. This will create a 'brick' pattern.

Work three rows of laid work around the frame. Finish according to Figure 3(c). The last couching stitch should be back at least 1.5mm (1⁄10 in) from where the tails will be plunged. Secure the last couching stitch by coming up along the edge of the metal threads and doing a minute stab stitch. Plunge the tails and couch them at the back of the work.

The zigzag pattern on top of the laid work has been done with gilt no. 7 check thread and gilt tambour thread. Lay the check thread across the bottom right-hand corner. Leave a tail for plunging. Using the gilt tambour thread in a size 7 crewel needle, come up at A and work a back stitch over the check thread. Come up at B with the tambour thread and back stitch over the check thread. Come up at C with the tambour thread. Hold the check thread across the laid work to C, and work a back stitch over the check thread at C. Repeat this across the bottom of the

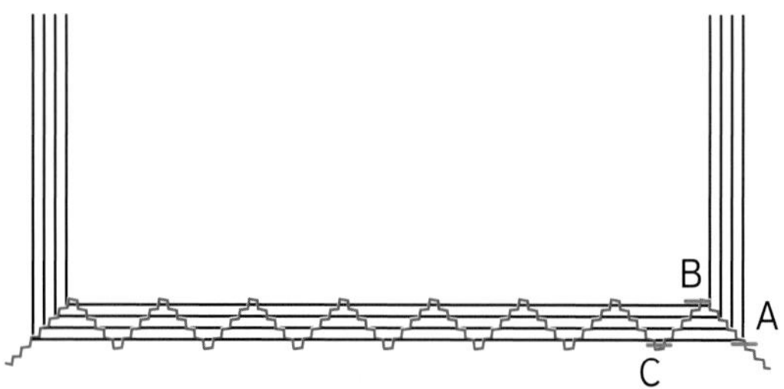

Figure 3(d)

frame and finish as shown in Figure 3(d). The tail at the end of this row needs to be plunged and couched at the back before proceeding any further.

Work the two sides of the frame as shown in Figure 3(e).

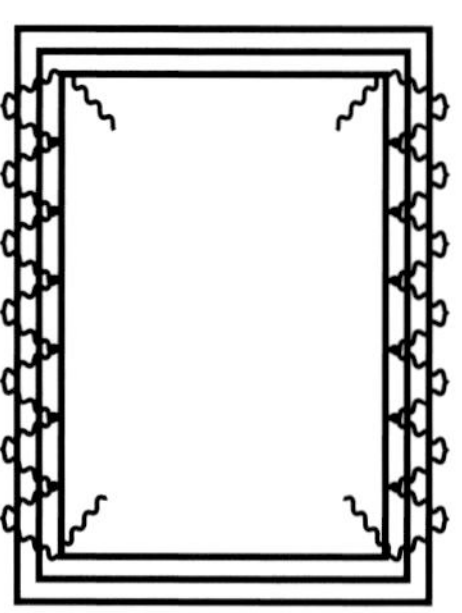

Figure 3(e)

Work the top of the frame as shown in Figure 3(f).

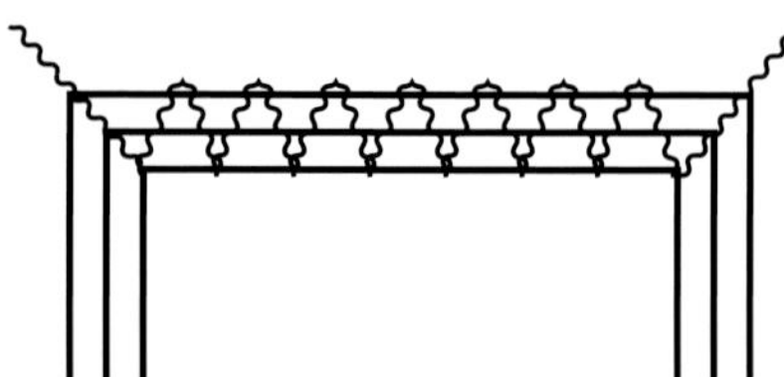

Figure 3(f)

Hat

Thread gilt tambour thread into a no. 7 crewel needle. Work continuous spirals of chain stitch on the right side of the hat. Build up a couple of layers of chain stitch and leave an irregular edge. Outline the hat with gilt 1½ twist before doing any other work on the hat.

On the left side of the hat, create a flower posy with 4 mm (2⁄10 in) gilt spangles and 4 mm (2⁄10 in) lengths of cardinal red no. 6 rough purl and gilt no. 8 bright check. For the centre spangle, bring the needle up through the fabric. Thread up a spangle and length of bright check (in that order). Drop both to the bottom of the doubled sewing thread, and then take the needle down through the hole of the spangle. The sewing thread needs to be supported by a mellor or chenille needle as it is pulled through the fabric. Also allow the cut purl to curve over the mellor or chenille needle. Come up through the hole of the spangle and thread up a length of the cardinal red no. 6 rough purl, and attach and loop in the same way as the gilt no. 8 bright check.

For the circle of spangles and loops of gilt no. 8 bright check and cardinal red no. 6 rough purl around the centre spangle, attach in the same manner as explained above, but overlap the spangles according to Figure 4. The black dots represent where the needle will go up and down through the holes of the spangles.

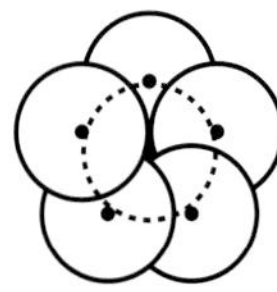

Figure 4

Cover the remaining yellow felt with tiny chips of gilt no. 6 bright check. Attach the chips in different directions to completely cover the felt. Scatter 3 mm (⅛ in) loops of cardinal red no. 6 rough purl and 3 mm (⅛ in) gilt spangles with 3 mm (⅛ in) loops of cardinal red no. 6 rough purl over the spirals of chain stitch.

Hair

To make the woman's curly hair, cut the brown no. 6 rough purls into 4 mm (²⁄₁₀ in) and 6 mm (¼ in) lengths. Mix the purls and loop them over one another, and in different directions. The longer lengths of purl are looped over the shorter lengths of purl.

Coat collar

Outline the collar with gilt 1½ twist. Cut the gilt no. 8 rough purl into 4 mm (²⁄₁₀ in) lengths. These are to be used for the rows of S-ing on the raised felt shapes on the felt padded collar. The instructions for S-ing are in chapter 3. Fill the areas in between the padded areas of S-ing with rows of 3 mm (⅛ in) lengths of gilt no. 6 bright check. Slightly loop the bright check purls by making the distance between where the needle comes up and is taken down, shorter than the length of the purl. Use 3 mm (⅛ in) lengths of gilt no. 8 bright check for the very confined spaces.

Decorative bands on the coat

The felt padded bands are covered with narrow plate work. The instructions for closed plate work are in chapter 3. Each band has to be worked in two sections. Leave enough space between the two sections to accommodate the gilt no. 1 pearl purl which will be couched down through the centre of the coat, after the plate work has been completed.

Flowers

Use 4 mm (²⁄₁₀ in) gilt spangles and 4 mm (²⁄₁₀ in) lengths of gilt no. 6 bright check for the six flowers on the coat. The flowers are done in the same way as the flower on the hat, minus the cardinal red no. 6 rough purls.

Coat cuffs

The cuffs are to be worked in exactly the same manner as the collars, using the same metal threads.

Coat outline

Once the cuffs have been done use gilt no. 1 pearl purl to outline the sleeves and the lower edges of the coat just under the cuffs.

Posy

Refer to Figure 5. Cut a 2 mm (1/10 in) and a 2.5 mm length of gilt no. 8 rough purl. Use these two purls to create a 'cross' for the centre of the flower. Surround the cross with a loop of gilt no. 6 bright check. Cut an 8 mm (4/10 in) length of bright check. Bring the needle and thread through the fabric, close to one side of the 'cross', and thread up the cut length of bright check. Drop it to the bottom of the sewing thread, and with a mellor or chenille needle, hold the bright check purl in a loop around the 'cross', while taking the needle down through the same hole. Come up again on the opposite side and very gently put in a couching stitch over the bright check purl. It should not be a visible couching stitch.

Cut five 6 mm (1/4 in) lengths of cardinal red no. 6 rough purl and loop them around the centre of the posy to represent petals. Cut seven 8 mm (4/10 in) lengths of pink no. 6 rough purl and loop them around the pink petals.

Cut three 12 mm (1/2 in) lengths of gilt no. 6 bright check and three 3 mm (1/8 in) lengths of pink no. 6 rough purl. The leaves of bright check are done in the same way as the circle of bright check in the centre of the flower, except that they have to be pulled into a leaf shape. Stitch a pink rough no. 6 purl length inside each bright check leaf.

Figure 5 *Posy*

Basket of Flowers

The flowers and leaves in this design have been stylised into simple geometric shapes, reminiscent of the Art Deco style. The combination of gold and silver threads and the variety of textures makes this embroidery appear like a piece of jewellery and the dark purple velvet ground only serves to heighten the effect.

EQUIPMENT AND MATERIALS

76 cm (30 in) slate frame or 36 cm (14 in) ring frame
calico to fit the frame
square of dark purple velvet an appropriate size for the frame
2 x A4 sheets 110 gsm tracing paper
1 gram pounce (and roll of felt to apply pounce)
1 tube yellow ochre watercolour paint
1 x 000 paint brush
orange dressmaker's carbon
15 cm (6 in) square yellow felt
1 skein yellow DMC soft cotton or yellow bumpf
Gutermann 968
Gutermann 800
2 grams of 2 mm (1⁄10 in) gilt spangles
1 packet gold Mill Hill petite glass beads 40557
size 12 sharps and size 10 crewel needles
mellor or size 18 chenille needle

METAL THREADS

70 cm (28 in) gilt super pearl purl
45 cm (18 in) gilt no. 1 pearl purl
10 cm (4 in) gilt no. 2 pearl purl
10 cm (4 in) silver-plated no. 2 pearl purl
4 m (4⅓ yd) no. 8 Japanese gold
70 cm (28 in) gilt 1 ½ twist
50 cm (20 in) gilt no. 7 check thread
50 cm (20 in) silver-plated no. 5 smooth passing
90 cm (1 yd) gilt no. 6 smooth purl
60 cm (24 in) gilt no. 6 bright check
30 cm (12 in) gilt no. 6 wire check
50 cm (20 in) silver-plated no. 6 bright check
30 cm (12 in) gilt broad plate

Figure 1 *Tracing outline*

METHOD

Dark purple velvet background

Mount the velvet square and the calico into a ring frame or sew the velvet square onto calico which has already been laced up on a square or slate frame. Refer to the instructions for dressing a slate frame in chapter 3.

Trace the lines in Figure 1 onto tracing paper. Use the prick-and-pounce method to transfer the design on to the velvet. Refer to the instructions for the prick-and-pounce method in chapter 3. The transferring of the design can be done after mounting the velvet onto the slate frame. Place books beneath the frame to support the fabric while pouncing and painting the design lines.

Further secure the velvet to the calico by pin stitching along the design lines, allowing approximately 3 cm (1¼ in) in between each pin-stitch. The pin stitches will eventually be hidden.

Felt padding

All elements of this design are padded with felt, with the exception of the ornamental grass lines. Trace the shapes in Figure 2(a) onto tracing paper. Some of the shapes have details which must also be traced and transferred onto the felt.

Three shapes in this design require more than one layer of padding. The centre flower has two layers. The layer with internal design lines is attached last. The two tulip-like flowers have two layers of felt padding on one side only—right side for the flower on the left and left side for the flower on the right. The smaller layer is attached first.

The shapes in Figure 2(a) are in numerical order. This is matched to the numerical order in Figure 2(b). Refer to Figure 2(b) when attaching the felt shape.

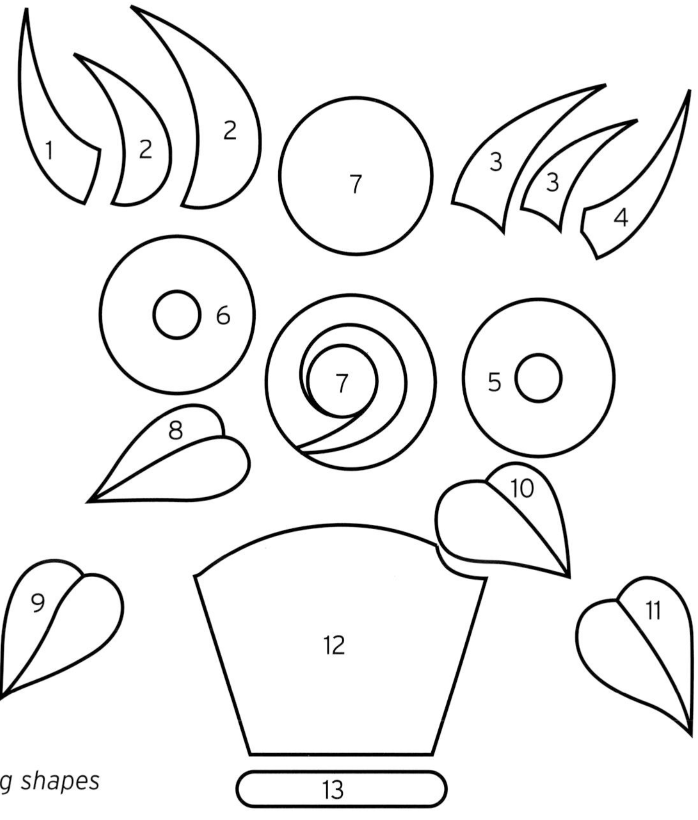

Figure 2(a) *Felt padding shapes*

Figure 2(b) *Order of attachment of shapes*

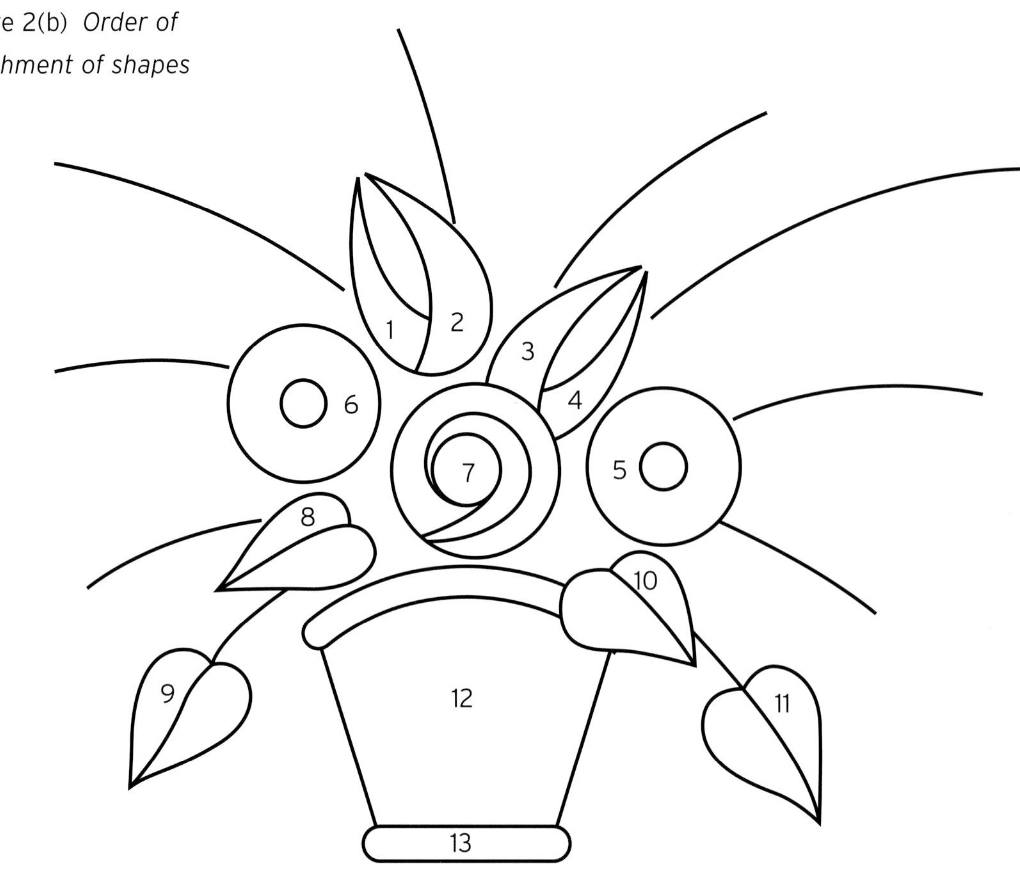

String padding

Prepare ten lengths of yellow bumpf or yellow DMC soft cotton to pad the rim of the basket. Refer to the instructions for horizontal cutwork over string padding in chapter 3.

The body of the basket requires rows of vertical string padding in preparation for creating a basket weave pattern. Three lengths of yellow bumpf or yellow DMC soft cotton are used for each row of string padding. Refer to the instructions for string padding and for the basket weave pattern in the raised laid work section in chapter 3.

Embroidery

The elements of the design to be embroidered are listed alphabetically in Figure 3 and are matched to the alphabetical order of work which follows.

A *Centre flower*. Outline the outside circle with gilt no. 2 pearl purl and work the design lines on the felt with gilt super pearl purl. Refer to Figure 4. The beginning and end of each internal design line is marked with an **X**. The centre of the flower is worked with horizontal rows of gilt no. 6 smooth purl. The outside scroll shape of the flower is filled with chips of gilt no. 6 bright check and the inside scroll with chips of gilt no. 6 wire check as shown in Figure 4.

B *Tulip-like flower on left*. The petals of the flower are worked with alternate lines of couched gilt no. 7 check thread and gilt no. 5 smooth passing. Fold each length of metal thread in half. Commence couching the folded end of each metal thread at the bottom of the petals. Leave tails of the metal threads at the other end to be plunged on the edge of the felt. Refer to

Figure 3

Figure 4

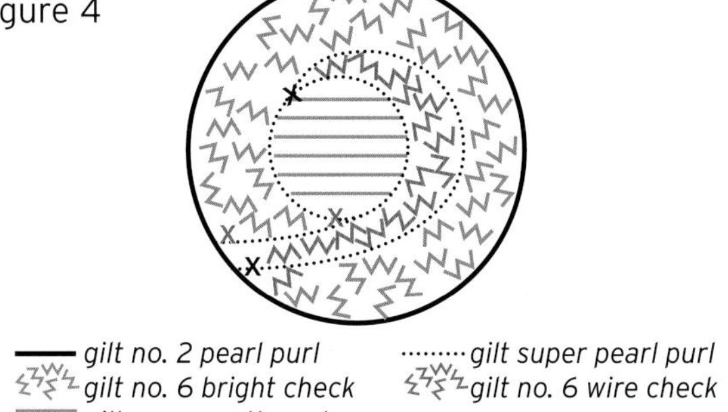

Figure 5. Once the laid work has been completed, outline the petals of the flower with gilt no. 1 pearl purl according to Figure 5. The beginning and end of the design line is marked with an **X**. The inside of the petals is filled with 5 mm (2/10 in) lengths of gilt no. 6 bright check. Allow a 3 mm (1/8 in) space between where the needle comes up and is taken down after picking up the purl. This will make the purl stand proud of the surface.

C *Tulip-like flower on right*. This flower is worked in the same manner as the tulip on the left; the only difference being in its outlining with gilt no. 1 pearl purl. Each petal is outlined separately.

Figure 5

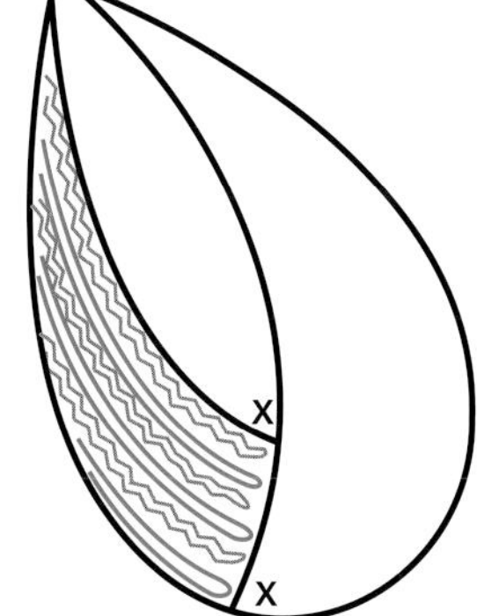

D The *two circular flowers* on either side of the centre flower are worked identically. Outline the small circle in the centre with gilt super pearl purl and fill the centre with chips of gilt no. 6 bright check.

A single thread of gilt 1½ twist is invisibly couched in a spiral around the outside of the flower's centre. Refer to the instructions for invisibly couching twist in chapter 3. Start couching on the outside edge of the circle, leaving a tail to be plunged. Leave a gap between the completed spiral and the centre of the flower to allow for a row of looped purls to be worked around the outside of the pearl purl outline. Plunge the tail at the end of the spiral before working the loops of gilt no. 6 smooth purl. Cut 5 mm (2⁄10 in) lengths of gilt no. 6 smooth purl for the loops.

Plunge the outside tail of twist and then outline the flower with overstretched silver no. 2 pearl purl.

E *Leaves*. Each of the four leaves is a variation of the other. Outline the leaves with gilt super pearl purl and then follow the legend in Figure 6 to work the cutwork, the chip work and the S-ing on the leaves. All leaves have one side that is worked with lengths of gilt no. 6 smooth purl. The lengths are worked diagonally across the felt. A 1 mm (1⁄20 in) space needs to be left between the cut work on one side of the leaf and the chip work on the other side to accommodate the row of S-ing, which is done after the two sides have been worked. Refer to the instructions for S-ing in chapter 3.

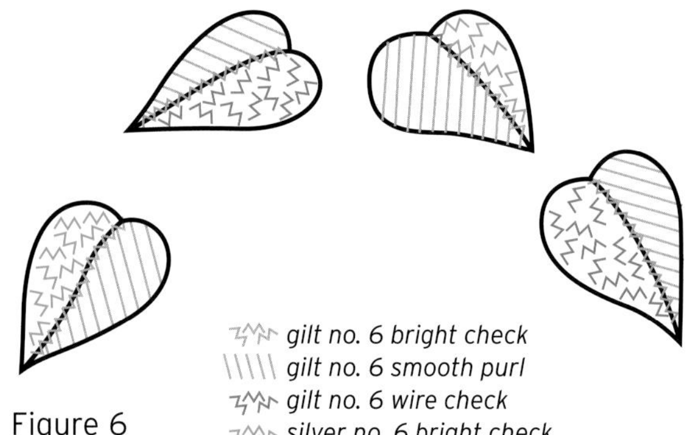

Figure 6

F *The body of the basket* is worked in a basket-weave pattern with no. 8 Japanese gold couched with Gutermann 968. Basket weave is a form of raised laid work. The instructions for this technique are in chapter 3. Use Technique 1 under flat laid work in chapter 3. This method was chosen because it gives a better definition to the curve of the basket at the top. Note that the sides of the basket are not outlined until the plate work for the base of the basket has been completed.

G The *rim of the basket* is worked with horizontal cutwork over string padding which is described in chapter 3. Gilt no. 6 bright check and silver no. 6 bright check are used alternately for the cutwork.

H The *base of the basket* is worked with closed plate work which is described in chapter 3. Use gilt broad plate and couch with Gutermann 968. When the plate work has been completed, outline the plate work and then the sides of the basket with gilt no. 1 pearl purl.

I The *ornamental grass stems* are worked with overstretched gilt super pearl purl. Couch every third groove with Gutermann 968. Work the seeds of the ornamental grass with 2 mm (1⁄10 in) spangles anchored with gold Mill Hill petite glass beads 40557. Vary the number and the spacing of spangles and beads from one grass stem to the next. Use a size 12 sharps needle for the spangles and beads.

Vine of Flowers

This design was inspired by the embroidery designs on eighteenth-century court costumes. The serpentine line, which is the foundation of this design, was considered by the 18th century English artist Hogarth to be the 'Line of Beauty'.

The design can be repeated to use on a costume. The area of design between the red markers on Figure 1 is the section to repeat. Note that this design needs to be worked on a slate frame or a 50 cm (20 in) quilter's frame.

EQUIPMENT AND MATERIALS

76 cm (30 in) slate frame or 50 cm (20 in) quilter's frame
55 x 70 cm (22 x 28 in) calico
45 cm (18 in) square cream duchesse silk satin
2 x A4 sheets 110 gsm tracing paper
orange dressmaker's carbon
10 cm (4 in) square yellow felt
Gutermann 968
2 grams of 5mm (2⁄10 in) gilt spangles
2 grams of 3 mm (1⁄8 in) gilt spangles
1 packet 2 mm (1⁄10 in) gilt spangles
1 packet gold Mill Hill petite glass beads 40557
size 12 sharps needle (for the no. 8 purls, 2 mm spangles and petite glass beads)
size 10 crewel needles
mellor or size 18 chenille needle

METAL THREADS

1.2 m (1⅓ yd) gilt extra fine pearl purl
70 cm (28 in) gilt super pearl purl
1 m (40 in) gilt medium rococo
4.5 m (4⅓ yd) gilt no. 7 check thread
2 m (2¼ yd) gilt 1½ twist
1.5 m (60 in) gilt no. 6 smooth purl
1.5 m (60 in) gilt no. 6 bright check
40 cm (16 in) gilt no. 8 smooth purl
20 cm (8 in) gilt no. 8 bright check

METHOD

Cream duchesse satin silk background

This design is best transferred onto the silk after it has been stretched taut on the frame because of the long serpentine lines in the design. Refer to the instructions for dressing a slate frame in the Preparation chapter. Trace the lines in Figure 1(a) onto tracing paper and then transfer the design onto the silk using orange dressmaker's carbon, with a book for support under the fabric in the frame.

Yellow felt padding

Trace the shapes in Figure 1(b) onto tracing paper. Transfer these shapes onto the yellow felt using the prick-and-pounce method, or orange dressmaker's carbon. The former technique is preferable because the shapes are repeated. The various flowers and stems in this design have been identified with capital letters in Figure 1(a).

You will require three sets of felt shapes for

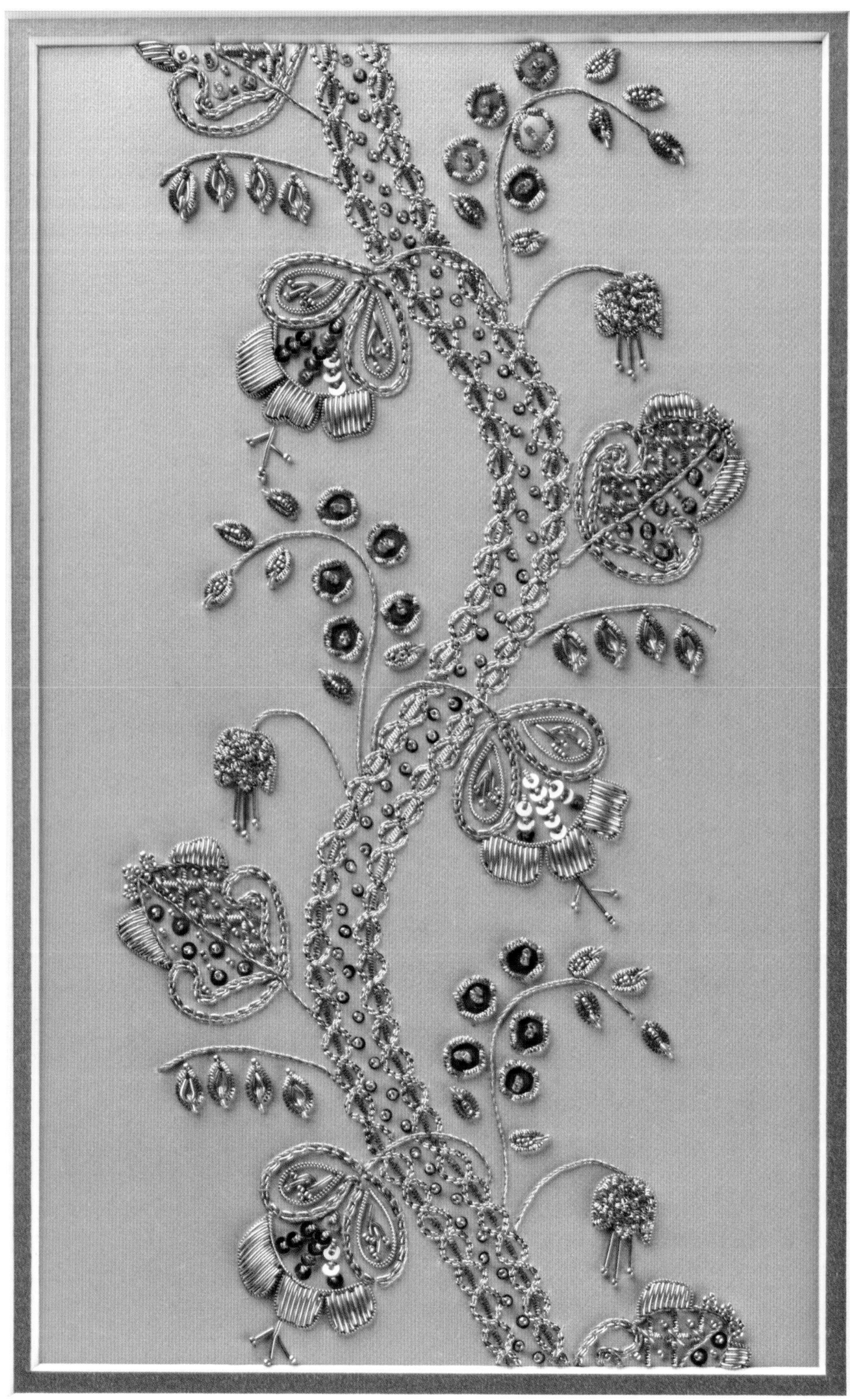

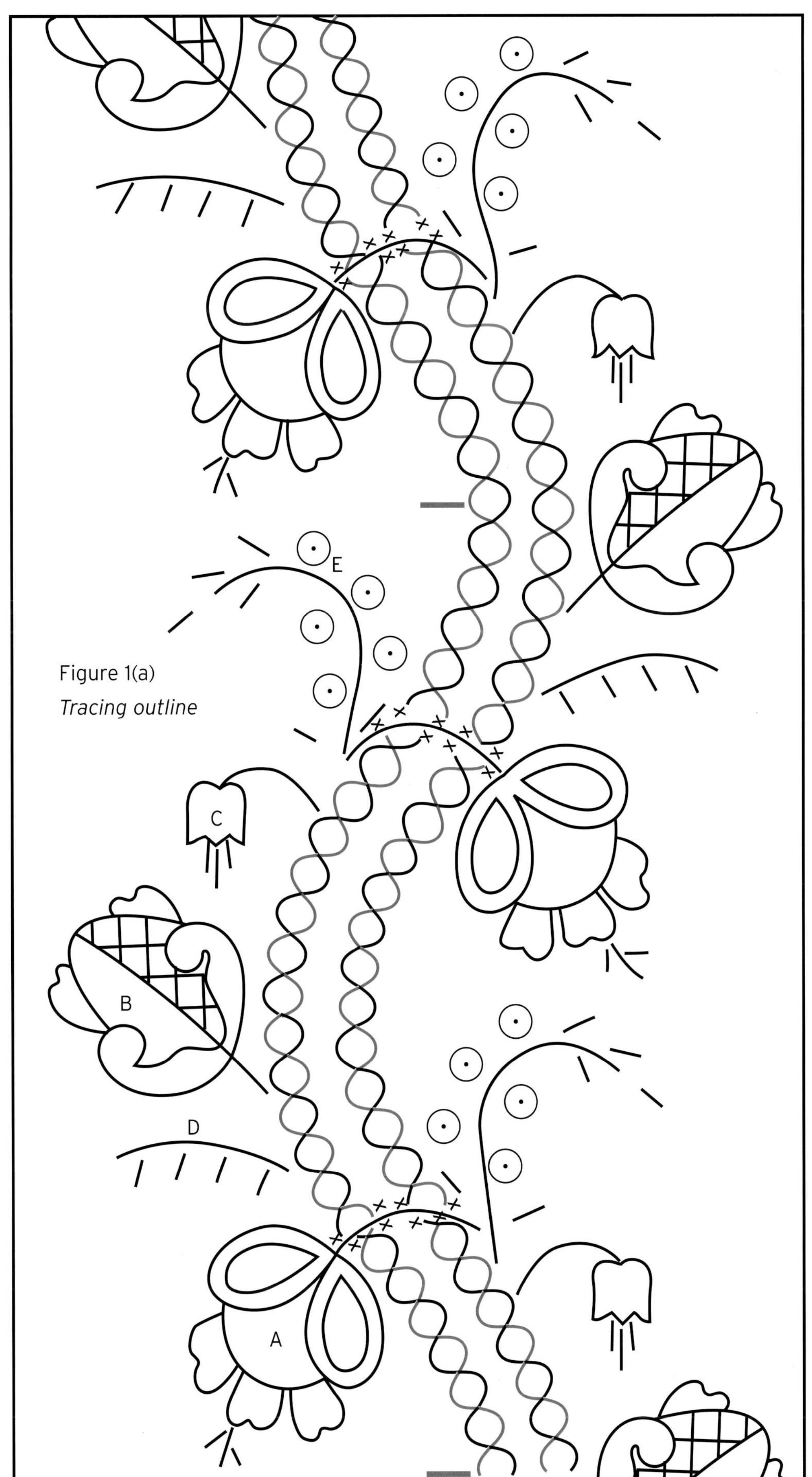

Figure 1(a)
Tracing outline

three small petals for flower A

two small petals for flower B

bell-shaped flower C

partial petal for flower B at top

petals for flower B at bottom

Figure 1(b)
Shapes for felt padding

flowers A and C, two complete sets for flower B and two partial sets that are different for flower B.

Cut the shapes out as you need them and attach them with minute stab stitches.

Serpentine line

The two rows of chains forming the serpentine line are each worked with two lines of doubled gilt no. 7 check thread couched with Gutermann 968. Note that in Figure 1(a), one line in the row is in red and the other is in black—work one line and then the other. When working the second line, couch across the two lines where they intersect. There are breaks in the lines to allow the stems of flower A to pass over the serpentine line. An **X** on the line in Figure 1(a) marks where there will be tails of the check threads to plunge through to the back of the work.

Fill the circular spaces created by the two lines intersecting with 3 mm (1/8 in) lengths of gilt no. 6 bright check.

The space between the two rows of chains is filled with 2 mm (1/10 in) spangles anchored with gold Mill Hill petite glass beads 40557 arranged in a zigzag movement.

Remaining embroidery

A *Flower A*. The order for working the various parts of the flower is represented alphabetically in lower case letters in Figure 2.

a. Outline shape inside the two large petals with gilt super pearl purl.

b. The large petals are outlined with couched gilt medium rococo (this is the inside thread) and gilt 1½ twist (the outside thread). The two threads

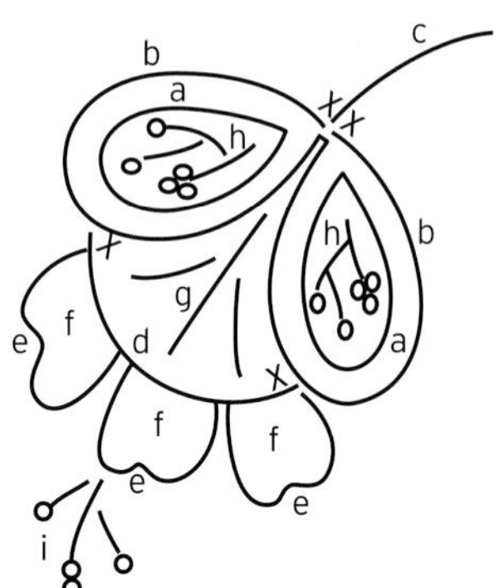

Figure 2

are couched as one. Couch across where the groove of the Gilt medium rococo occurs with Gutermann 968. The beginning and the end of the couching is marked with an X. Plunge the four tails through to the back of the work.

c. The stem is worked with invisibly couched gilt 1½ twist. (This is the stem that is carried across the serpentine line.) Refer to the instructions for invisibly couching twist in chapter 3.

d. Outline the centre of the flower with gilt super pearl purl. The beginning and the end of the pearl purl is marked with an X.

e. Outline the three small petals with gilt extra fine pearl purl.

f. The small petals are worked as cutwork over felt padding using gilt no. 6 smooth purl. Refer to the instructions for cutwork over felt padding in chapter 3.

g. The centre of the flower is filled with three rows of 3 mm (⅛ in) spangles and chips of gilt no. 8 bright check. There are five spangles and chips in the centre row and a row of three spangles and chips on either side of the centre row. Cut the bright check into 2 mm (1⁄10 in) chips.

Starting with the centre row and working from the small petals towards the large petals, bring the needle and double thread up through the fabric, pick up a spangle and a bright check chip, drop them to the bottom of the thread, and take the needle down on the top side of the spangle. Bring the needle up again, as close as possible to where the needle went down. Thread a spangle and bright check chip, drop them to the bottom of the thread, and take the needle down close to the spangle. Repeat this step for the remainder of the row. The spangles should be propped up by the bright check chips. Work the two shorter rows in the same way on either side of the centre row.

h. The design lines inside outline a are worked with cut lengths of gilt no. 8 smooth purl. A gold Mill Hill petite glass bead 40557 is attached at the end of two lengths and there are three beads attached to one length of smooth purl. Refer to Figure 2.

i. These little design lines are worked in the same manner as for h. Also refer to Figure 2.

B *Flower B.* The order for working the various parts of the flower is represented alphabetically in lower case letters in Figure 3.

Figure 3

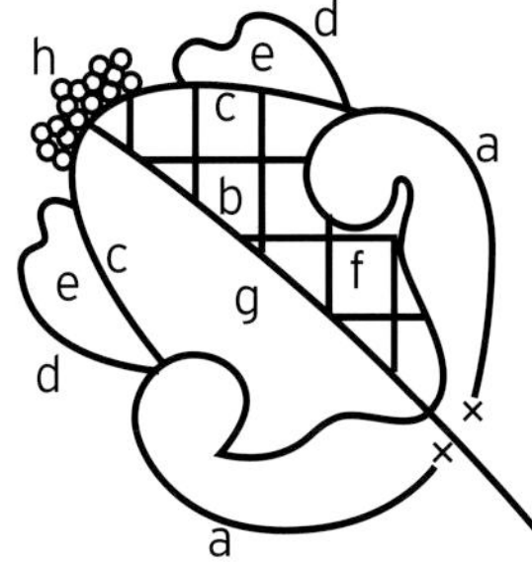

a. Outline these scroll-like leaves with couched gilt medium rococo (this is the inside thread) and gilt 1½ twist (the outside thread). The two threads are couched as one. Couch across where the groove of the gilt medium rococo occurs with Gutermann 968. The beginning and the end of the couching is marked with an X. Plunge the four tails through to the back of the work.

b. The stem of this flower runs up through the centre of the flower. Invisibly couch gilt 1½ twist for the stem.

c. Invisibly couch this outline with gilt 1½ twist

d. Outline the two small petals with gilt extra fine pearl purl.

e. The small petals are worked as cutwork over felt padding using gilt no. 6 smooth purl.

f. This half of the flower is filled with a trellis pattern. Figure 4 shows the three steps of working this trellis pattern. Use gilt no. 8 bright check for the trellis lines, 4 mm (²⁄₁₀ in) lengths of gilt no. 8 smooth purl to cross the intersections of the trellis and gold Mill Hill petite glass beads 40557 to decorate the spaces formed by the intersecting trellis lines.

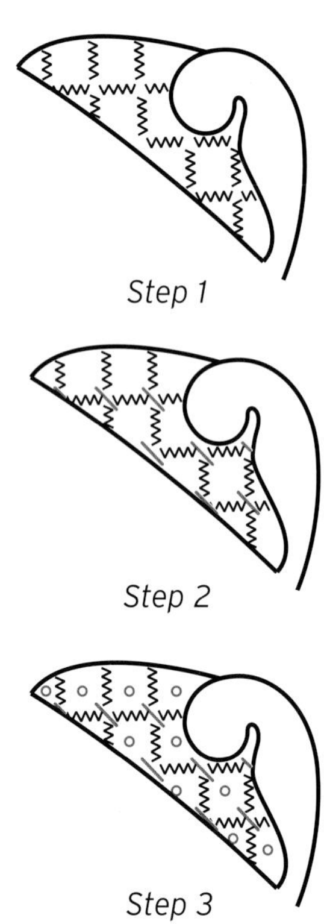

Figure 4

g. This half of the flower is filled with 3 mm (⅛ in) spangles anchored with gold Mill Hill petite glass beads 40557 arranged in a zigzag movement. Single Mill Hill petite glass beads 40557 are scattered between the spangles and beads.

h. The top of the flower is capped with three loops of gold Mill Hill petite glass beads 40557. Each loop has been formed with five beads on a doubled thread of Gutermann.

C *Flower C*. Outline the bell-shape flower with gilt extra fine pearl purl and fill in the flower with chips of gilt no. 6 bright check. The three stamens are worked with cut lengths of gilt no. 8 smooth purl. The centre stamen is slightly longer than the two on either side. Attach a gold Mill Hill petite glass bead 40557 at the end of each stamen. Invisibly couch gilt 1½ twist for the stem.

D *Spray of small flowers*. Invisibly couch gilt 1½ twist for the stem.

In preparation for working the four small flowers on the stem, cut four 12 mm (½ in) lengths of gilt no. 6 bright check, four 8 mm (⅜ in) lengths of gilt no. 6 smooth purl and 6 mm (a fraction over ²⁄₁₀ in) lengths of gilt no. 6 smooth purl.

Each flower is formed with a double chain stitch. To work these chain stitches, bring needle and doubled sewing thread through at the top (close to the stem) of the design line representing the flower. Thread up a length of gilt bright check, drop it to the bottom of the thread and take the needle down close to where the needle came up. Support the thread with a mellor or chenille needle as it is taken through. Allow the purl to curve around the mellor or chenille needle. Bring the needle through again on the inside of the chain to thread up the gilt smooth purl for the second chain. Once both chains have been formed, hold them down with

a mellor and bring the needle up on the inside of the two chains to thread up the smaller length of gilt smooth purl. Take the needle down on the outside of the two chains and support the thread as it is taken through the fabric. This smaller purl now holds both chains in place. Attach a gold Mill Hill petite glass bead 40557 at the point where the needle came up and went down to form the outside bright check chain.

E *Spray of small flowers*. Invisibly couch gilt 1½ twist for the stem.

Attach 5 mm (²⁄₁₀ in) spangles and loops of gilt no. 6 bright check on the five circles drawn along the stem. Cut 5 mm (²⁄₁₀ in) lengths of bright check for the loops. Cut five 4 mm (a fraction under ²⁄₁₀ in) lengths of gilt no. 6 bright check and attach them around the spangle. Do this for all five spangles.

The small straight lines along this stem represent chain stitches. Cut six 12 mm (½ in) lengths of gilt no. 6 bright check, and six 6 mm (a fraction over ²⁄₁₀ in) lengths of gilt no. 6 smooth purl. The bright check forms the chain and the smooth purl is taken across the bottom of the chain to hold it in place. Bring needle and doubled sewing thread up on the inside of the chain at one end, thread up three gold Mill Hill petite glass beads 40557 and take the needle through at the other end of the chain. The beads will stand proud within the chain.

Japanese Landscape

This design references the formally stylised and decorative Japanese designs. Balance and harmony pervades every aspect of Japanese culture, especially in design, and nature is a great source of inspiration to the Japanese designer, providing a wealth of motifs for their arts. Traditionally in goldwork, chipwork generally appears as accents, but this design employs it extensively to emphasise the two-dimensional and decorative quality of Japanese design. It is a contemporary use of chipwork and is combined with more traditional goldwork techniques, such as laid work, plate work, cutwork over string padding and S-ing.

EQUIPMENT AND MATERIALS

76 cm (30 in) slate frame or 36 cm (14 in) ring frame
calico to fit the frame
square of light moss green dupion silk an appropriate size for the frame
2 x A4 sheets 110 gsm tracing paper
orange dressmaker's carbon
18 x 15 cm (7 x 6 in) yellow felt
12 cm (5 in) square white felt
1 skein yellow DMC soft cotton or yellow bumpf
Gutermann 968
Gutermann 800
5 cm (2 in) square matte gold kid leather
1 packet gold Mill Hill petite glass beads 40557
size 12 sharps and size 10 crewel needles
mellor or size 18 chenille needle

GILT THREADS

1.75 m (70 in) gilt super pearl purl
80 cm (32 in) gilt no. 1 pearl purl
40 cm (16 in) gilt no. 3 pearl purl
60 cm (24 in) gilt no. 4 pearl purl
6 m (6⅝ yd) gilt no. 5 smooth passing
1.4 m (1½ yd) gilt no. 6 bright check
1 m (1¼yd) gilt no. 6 wire check
70 cm (28 in) gilt no. 6 smooth purl
1.5 m (1¾ yd) gilt no. 6 rough purl
50 cm (20 in) gilt fine rococo
50 cm (20 in) gilt no. 1 twist
65 cm (26 in) gilt and copper 3-ply twist
80 cm (32 in) gilt narrow plate

SILVER THREADS

25 cm (10 in) silver-plated super pearl purl
70 cm (28 in) silver-plated no. 6 bright check
90 cm (36 in) silver-plated no. 6 wire check
40 cm (16 in) silver-plated no. 6 rough purl

COPPER THREADS

60 cm (24 in) copper super pearl purl
25 cm (10 in) copper no. 1 pearl purl
1 m (1¼yd) copper no. 6 bright check
80 cm (32 in) copper no. 6 smooth purl

Figure 1 *Tracing outline*

Figure 2 *Yellow felt padding shapes*

METHOD

Moss green dupion silk background

This design is best transferred onto the linen after it has been stretched taut on the frame because of the long straight lines in the design. (Refer to the end of the instructions for dressing a slate frame in the Preparation chapter.) Trace the lines in Figure 1 onto tracing paper and then transfer the design onto the silk using orange dressmaker's carbon, with a book for support under the fabric in the frame.

Felt padding

All elements of this design are padded with felt or string padded, with the exception of the undulating horizon line running through the design. Trace the shapes in Figure 2 (yellow felt

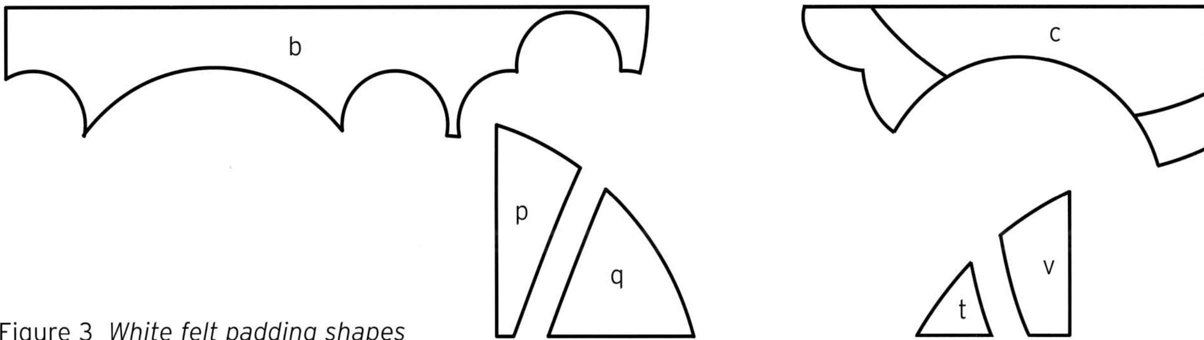

Figure 3 *White felt padding shapes*

shapes for padding) and Figure 3 (white felt shapes for padding) onto tracing paper. Details on shapes must also be traced and transferred onto the felt. Transfer these shapes onto the yellow and white felt using the prick-and-pounce method, or orange dressmaker's carbon. Both methods are described in chapter 3.

Most of the padded shapes require only one layer of felt. The exceptions are: a white felt shape is superimposed on top of the yellow felt cloud on the left side of the design, four small circles within the large circular flower on the left side of the design, have two layers of felt, and the small circle in the middle of the centre flower of the design, has four layers of felt. These shapes in Figures 2 and 3 are numbered. Number 1 indicates that this shape is to be attached first; then 2, 3 and 4.

The shapes in Figures 2 and 3 are in alphabetical order. This is matched to the alphabetical order in Figure 4. Refer to Figure 4 when attaching the felt shapes.

Figure 4 *Placement of felt shapes*

String padding

The four petals of the centre flower have string padding. Figure 5 shows the area of the petal which needs to be padded with yellow bumpf or yellow DMC soft cotton. The string padding needs to be within the borders of the shape to allow the cutwork to sit on the curved design line, and on the felt on the relatively straight side. Refer to Figure 5.

Start in the centre with eight strands of bumpf or DMC soft cotton. Couch the eight strands with a double thread of Gutermann 968. Continue to couch, first one side, and then the other. The space between the couching stitches is approximately 1 mm (1/20 in). Cut away two underneath strands after each couching stitch until there are two strands remaining. Couch the two strands, cut one strand, and couch the last strand. Finally, cut the last strand and place a small stitch perpendicularly across the last two couching stitches. These steps are demonstrated in Figure 5.

The circle around the centre flower is padded with ten strands of yellow bumpf or yellow DMC soft cotton. The string padding needs to be within the design lines of the circle to allow the cutwork to sit on the design lines.

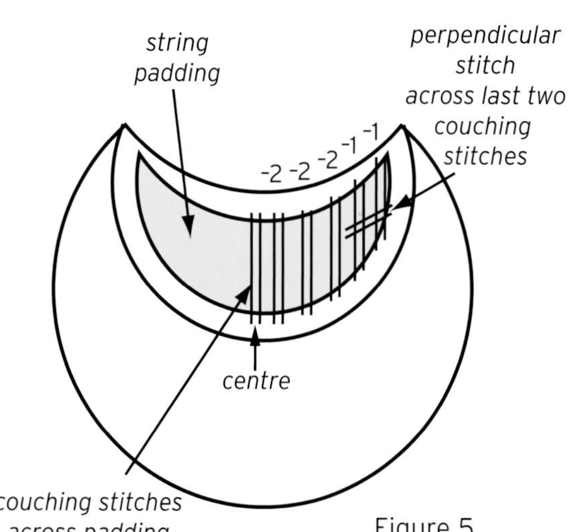

Figure 5

Couch the ten strands with a double thread of Gutermann 968. The space between the couching stitches is approximately 2 mm (1/10 in). Where the circle is broken by the felt padding for the large leaf shapes, shape the string padding by cutting across the ten strands as shown in Figure 6. Leave a 1 mm (1/20 in) space between the string padding and the felt padding to accommodate the eventual outlines of pearl purl, as shown in Figure 6.

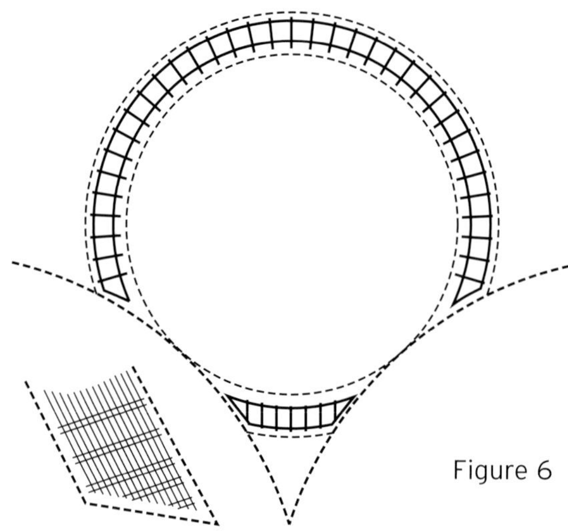
Figure 6

Embroidery

The elements of the design to be embroidered are listed alphabetically in Figure 7 and are matched to the alphabetical order of work which follows.

A *Frame*. Outline the design line for the frame of the design with overstretched gilt no. 3 pearl purl. Consistently couch every third groove with Gutermann 968.

B *Border of flower F*. Work the circular border of flower F from the outside to the inside with rows of metal threads. Outline the circle with gilt super pearl purl and follow it with gilt fine rococo, gilt no. 1 twist, gilt super pearl purl, gilt no. 1 twist, gilt fine rococo, and finally a circle of

Figure 7

gilt super pearl purl. Leave tails at the beginning and end of each circle of gilt fine rococo and gilt no. 1 twist to be plunged to the back of the work.

C *Border of flower G.* Work the circular border of this flower exactly the same as border B.

D *Left-side cloud.* Refer to Figure 8 for the colours of the super pearl purls to be used for the outline of the cloud shape and for the curved contours within the cloud shape.

The no. 1 area is filled with chips of silver no. 6 bright check across the top of the shape, merging into a mix of silver no. 6 bright check and silver no. 6 wire check chips through the middle of the shape, and finally chips of silver no. 6 wire check across the bottom of the shape. The no. 2 areas are filled in with chips of gilt no. 6 bright check and the no. 3 areas are filled with chips of copper no. 6 bright check.

E *Right-side cloud.* Refer to Figure 9 for the colours of the super pearl purls to be used for the outlines of this cloud shape. Fill no. 1 areas with chips of silver no. 6 bright check and fill no. 2 area with chips of silver no. 6 wire check.

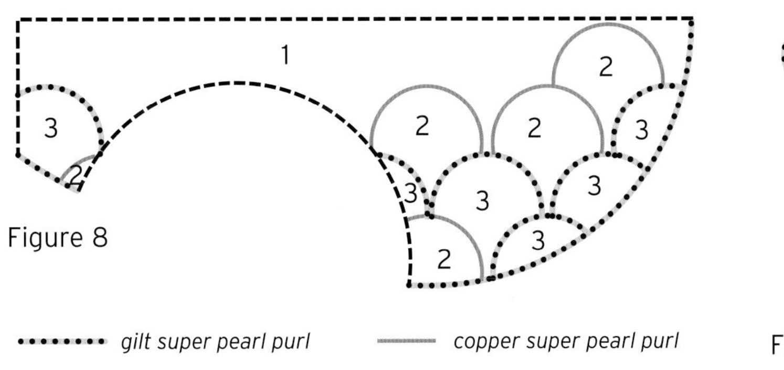

Figure 8

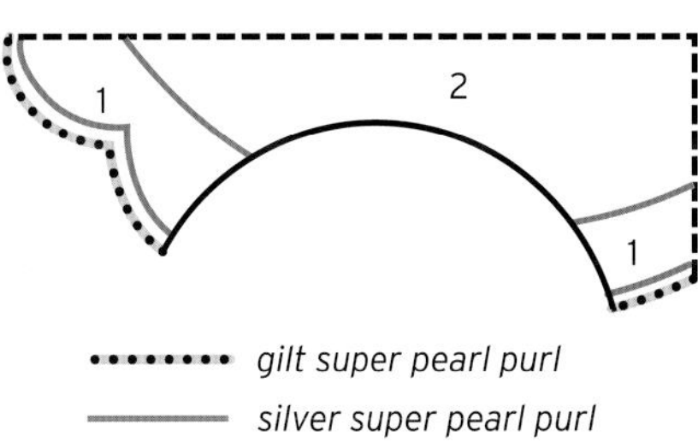

Figure 9

F The *four small circles* within the left-side flower. Refer to Figure 10 for the working of the four small circles inside border B. The circles are covered with cutwork over felt padding, which is described in chapter 3.

G *Right-side flower*. Refer to Figure 11 for the working of the shapes inside border C. The shapes are filled in with cutwork over felt padding or chip work.

H *Kid leather centre of main flower*. Trace the centre of this flower from Figure 1 onto tracing paper. Make the circle a fraction bigger than it is in Figure 1, to ensure that it will cover its felt padding. Transfer the shape onto gold kid leather using the pinpricking method described in chapter 3. Cut the shape out and attach it over the felt padding with small stab stitches. Outline the centre with gilt no. 3 pearl purl.

I *Four large petals of main flower*. Refer to Figure 12 for the working of the four large petals of the centre flower.

J The four *small triangular-shaped petals* of the centre flower are outlined with gilt super pearl purl and are then filled in with a mix of gilt no. 6 bright check chips and copper no. 6 bright check chips.

K The *stem of the flower on the left* is first worked in gilt narrow plate over the felt padding, and then the left side of the plate work is outlined with a row of S-ing using gilt no. 6 bright check. Refer to the instructions for closed plate work and S-ing in chapter 3.

L The *stem of the flower on the right* is worked in gilt narrow plate only.

Figure 10

gilt super pearl purl
loops of gilt no. 6 bright check
gilt no. 6 smooth purl
gilt no. 6 rough purl
silver no. 6 rough purl
copper super pearl purl
loops of copper no. 6 bright check
copper no. 6 smooth purl

Figure 11

gilt super pearl purl
gilt no. 6 wire check chips
gilt no. 6 rough purl
silver no. 6 rough purl
copper super pearl purl
copper no. 6 bright check

Figure 12

outline of gilt super pearl purl
cutwork with gilt no. 6 smooth purl over the felt padding
cutwork with gilt no. 6 bright check over the string padding

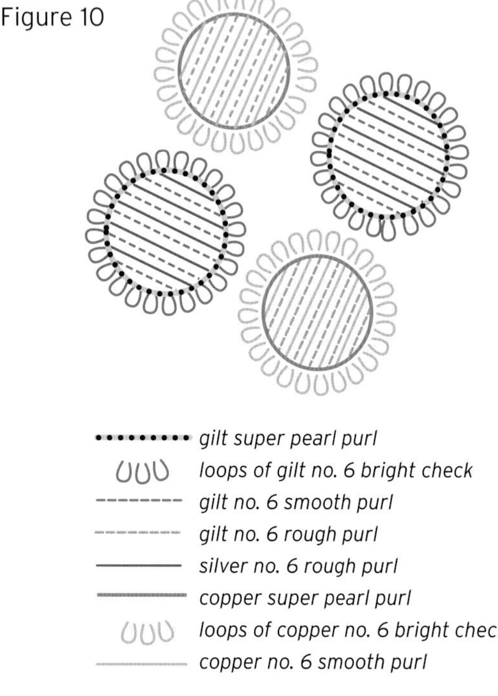

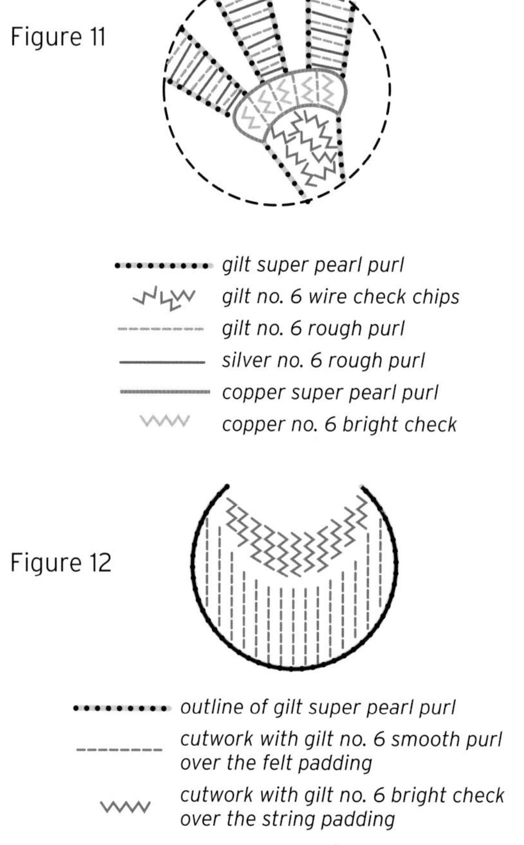

M The *four large leaves* are to be worked in the following order:

Work the laid work border on the two lower leaves. The border consists of six rows of couched gilt no. 5 smooth passing. Refer to the instructions for couching a leaf shape in chapter 3. This will explain how to turn the corners, but the laid work for the lower leaves is not continuous, as it is for the top leaves. Use Gutermann 968 to couch the metal threads. Allow a space of 4 mm (2/10 in) between the couching stitches for the laid work. Create a brick pattern with the couching stitches. Plunge the tails at the beginning and the end of each row after the six rows of laid work for each lower leaf have been completed.

Work the laid work on the two top leaves. Leave a 1 mm space on the bottom edge of the top leaves to accommodate the outline of gilt no. 1 pearl purl. The laid work for these leaves is a continuous row of two threads of gilt smooth passing couched with Gutermann 968. Refer to the instructions for couching a leaf shape in chapter 3. Create a brick pattern with the couching stitches. Finish the laid work so that there is a narrow space running through a part of the centre to make it easier to work a row of S-ing through the centre of these leaves. Plunge the tails at the beginning and the end of the laid work.

Work a row of S-ing, using gilt no. 6 bright check, through the centre of each top leaf.

Outline the top leaves with gilt no. 1 pearl purl.

Outline the bottom leaves with gilt super pearl purl.

The space within the borders of the lower leaves is outlined with two rows of super pearl purl. Use gilt super pearl purl against the gilt smooth passing laid work and copper super pearl purl on the inside of this outline. Lay alternate cut lengths of gilt no. 6 wire check and copper no. 6 smooth purl across the felt within this space.

N *Circular border*. Cover the string padding around the centre flower with cutwork using gilt no. 6 rough purl and gilt no. 6 wire check. Lay two lengths of gilt no. 6 rough purl beside each other followed by a length of gilt no. 6 wire check. Repeat this pattern around the entire circle. Lay the purls perpendicularly over the string padding.

O The *silver hillocks* are scattered with gold Mill Hill petite glass beads 40557 surrounded by loops of silver no. 6 bright check. In preparation for this work cut 8 mm (4/10 in) lengths of silver bright check. Use a double thread of Gutermann 800. Bring the needle through the fabric, close to the bead. Thread the cut length of silver bright check. Drop it to the bottom of the sewing thread, and with a mellor or a chenille needle hold the silver bright check purl in a loop around the bead, while taking the needle back down through the same hole. Come up again on the opposite side, and very gently put in a couching stitch over the silver bright check purl. It should not be a visible couching stitch. Fill the spaces around the beads and loops of silver bright check with chips of silver no. 6 wire check.

P The *copper hillocks*. Outline these small hillocks with copper super pearl purl and then fill in with chips of copper no. 6 bright check.

Q The *top row of the horizon* is worked with copper no. 1 pearl purl followed by a row of gilt no. 1 pearl purl, and finally a row of copper super pearl purl.

R The *stretch of land in the distance* is outlined at the top with a row of copper no. 1 pearl purl, followed by a row of gilt no. 1 pearl purl. A row of copper super pearl purl outlines the bottom contour of the land. Working from right to left, fill in the shape with chips of copper no. 6 bright check, followed by a mix of copper and gilt no. 6 bright check chips, and finally chips of gilt no. 6 bright check.

S *Second outline of frame*. Surround the existing frame of overstretched gilt no. 3 pearl purl with a row of gilt and copper 3-ply twist. Plunge the tails of the twist to the back of the work.

T *Third outline of frame*. Finally, complete the rectangular frame of the design with a row of gilt no. 4 pearl purl.

Byzantine Angel

Angels in Byzantine art are arrayed in very decorative garments. There is an abundance of pattern and ornament in Byzantine art, and hence, in this design, there is a profusion of patterns to be worked with coloured purls, spangles, beads and ribbled plate. The Byzantines also have a great love for gold and rich colours which carry meaning in their art. By giving the angel an architectural frame, this design takes on the appearance of an icon.

EQUIPMENT AND MATERIALS

76 cm (30 in) slate frame or 45 cm (18 in) quilter's frame
calico to fit the frame
square of gold yellow duchesse silk satin an appropriate size for the frame
orange dressmaker's carbon
3 x A4 sheets 110 gsm tracing paper
Vliesofix, HeatnBond Lite or Bondaweb
5 cm (2 in) square white silk
15 cm (6 in) square yellow felt
1 skein yellow DMC soft cotton or yellow bumpf
10 cm (4 in) purple velvet ribbon 3.5 cm (1½ in) wide
18 cm (7 in) burgundy velvet ribbon 3.5 cm (1½ in) wide
5 cm (2 in) brown velvet ribbon 3.5 cm (1½ in) wide
5 cm (2 in) square shiny gilt kid leather
5 cm (2 in) square matte gilt kid leather
2 grams of 2 mm (1⁄10 in) gilt spangles
2 grams of 3 mm (1⁄8 in) gilt spangles
1 packet gold Mill Hill petite glass beads 40557
1 packet dark pink Mill Hill petite glass beads 42012
3 x 4 mm (2⁄10 in) filigree gold cup sequins
DMC stranded cotton, purple 327
Gutermann 968
Gutermann 800
Gutermann sewing thread to match purple velvet
Gutermann sewing thread to match burgundy velvet
Gutermann sewing thread to match brown velvet
size 12 sharps and sizes 10 and 7 crewel needles
mellor or size 18 chenille needle

METAL THREADS

1.5 m (60 in) gilt super pearl purl
70 cm (28 in) gilt no. 1 pearl purl
15 cm (6 in) gilt no. 3 pearl purl
15 cm (6 in) gilt no. 4 pearl purl
9 m (10 yd) no. 8 Japanese gold
1 m (40 in) gilt broad plate
25 cm (10 in) gilt narrow plate
65 cm (26 in) gilt 1½ twist
75 cm (30 in) gilt no. 7 check thread
12 cm (5 in) gilt milliary
1.5 m (60 in) gilt tambour thread
50 cm (20 in) gilt no. 6 bright check
1.5 m (60 in) gilt no. 6 wire check
10 cm (4 in) bright violet no. 6 wire check
1.5 m (60 in) wine no. 6 wire check
30 cm (12 in) pink no. 6 rough purl
45 cm (18 in) purple no. 6 rough purl

Figure 1 *Tracing outline*

METHOD

Gold silk background

This design is best transferred onto the silk after it has been stretched taut on the frame because of the long straight lines in the design. Refer to the instructions for dressing a slate frame in chapter 3. Trace the lines in Figure 1 onto tracing paper and then transfer the design onto the silk using orange dressmaker's carbon, with a book for support under the fabric in the frame.

Yellow felt padding

Trace the shapes in Figure 2(a) onto tracing paper. Some of the shapes have details which must also be traced and transferred onto the felt. Transfer these shapes onto the yellow felt using the prick-and-pounce method, or orange dressmaker's carbon. The former technique for transferring the design is preferable because of the inner details on several pieces. All the padded shapes require only one layer of felt.

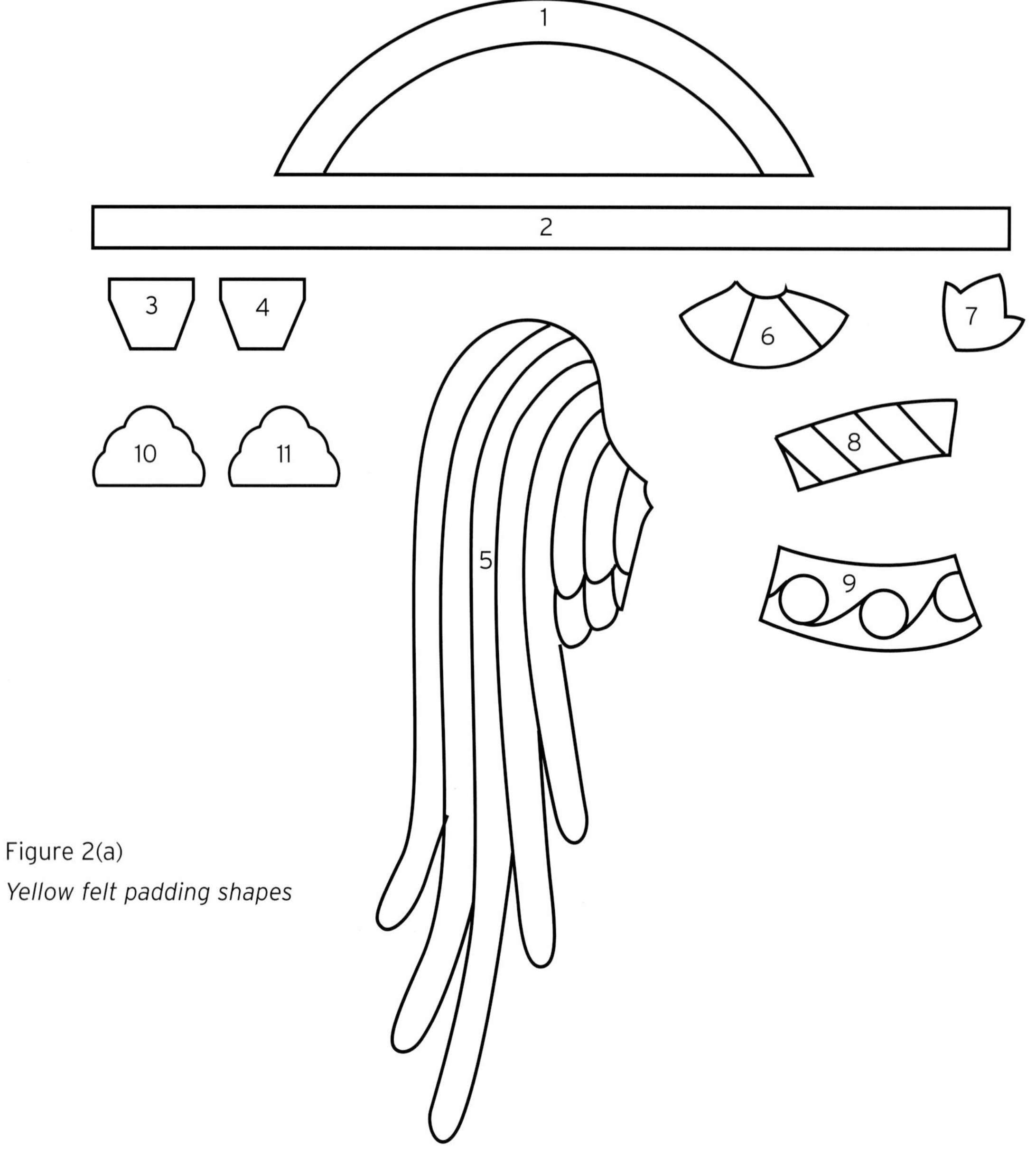

Figure 2(a)
Yellow felt padding shapes

White silk

Trace the shape and the features of the face in Figure 2(b) onto tracing paper. Iron Vliesofix (HeatnBond Lite or Bondaweb) onto the wrong side of the white silk square. Peel off the backing paper. Place and weight the tracing paper on the right side of the white silk square. Slip a sheet of orange dressmaker's carbon in between the tracing paper and the silk, and trace the design lines onto the silk. Carefully cut the shape out of the silk.

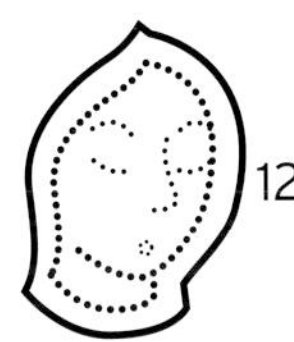

.... this line represents the design for the face; the white silk appliqué is to extend beyond the outline of the face so that the brown velvet appliqué will overlap the silk—trace these lines

——— this line is the line to trace and cut

Figure 2(b) *Design and tracing lines for face*

Burgundy velvet ribbon

Place the Vliesofix, paper side up, over Figure 2(c) and trace the shapes onto the Vliesofix. Iron the Vliesofix on the wrong side of the burgundy velvet ribbon. Carefully cut out the four shapes. Peel the paper off the velvet shapes.

Purple velvet ribbon

Place the Vliesofix, paper side up, over Figure 2(d) and trace the shapes onto the Vliesofix. These shapes are drawn in reverse because the 'border' shape for the angel's skirt is not symmetrical. Iron the Vliesofix on the wrong side of the purple velvet ribbon. Carefully cut out the three shapes. Peel the paper off the velvet shapes.

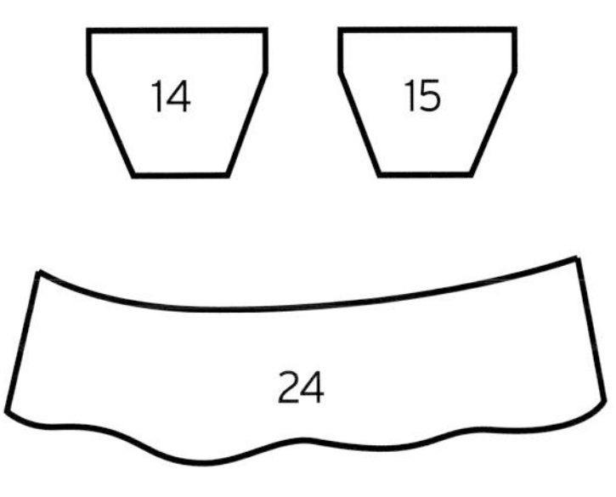

Note: these shapes have been drawn in reverse

Figure 2(d) *Shapes for purple velvet ribbon*

Brown velvet ribbon

Place the Vliesofix, paper side up, over Figure 2(e) and trace the shape onto the Vliesofix. This shape has been drawn in reverse. Iron the Vliesofix on the wrong side of the brown velvet ribbon. Carefully cut out the shape. Peel the paper off the velvet shapes.

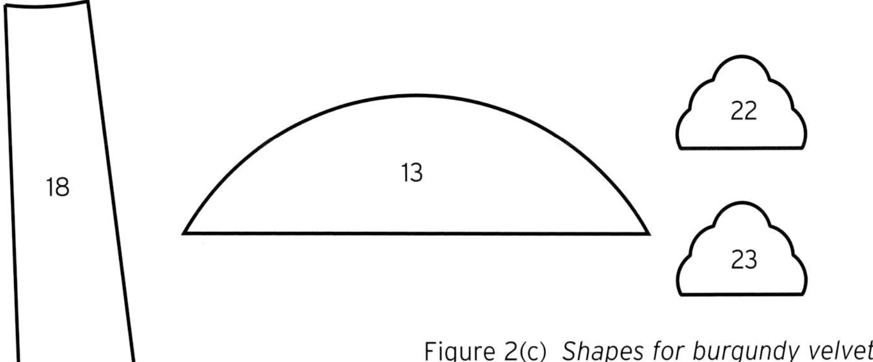

Figure 2(c) *Shapes for burgundy velvet ribbon*

Note: this shape has been drawn in reverse

Figure 2(e) *Shape for brown velvet ribbon*

Kid leather

Trace the shapes in Figure 2(f) onto tracing paper. Place the tracing paper over the kid leather and prick the outlines onto the leather. Cut out the kid leather shapes.

shiny gilt kid leather

matte gilt kid leather

Figure 2(f) *Tracing shapes for kid leather*

Appliqué and padding work

All appliqué and felt pieces are numbered. Refer to Figure 3 for the order of felt padding and appliquéing. The numbers of the shapes in the list of attachments match up to the numbers in Figure 3. Use minute stab stitches to attach appliqué pieces and felt padding. When stab stitching, come up in the silk background, and down into the appliqué or felt. Refer to the instructions for cutting and attaching kid leather in chapter 3. Use Gutermann 968 for the yellow felt and kid leather pieces and matching sewing threads for the appliqué pieces.

- Attach shape 1—the felt semi-circle above the columns
- Attach shape 2—the felt pediment above the columns
- Attach shapes 3 and 4—the felt capitals for the two columns
- Attach shape 5—the felt angel's wing
- Attach shape 6—the felt neck ornament
- Attach shape 7—the felt flower
- Attach shape 8—the felt breast ornament
- Attach shape 9—the felt band at the bottom of the angel's top
- Attach shapes 10 and 11—the felt bases of the two columns
- Attach shape 12—the white silk face and neck
- Attach shape 13—the burgundy velvet semi-circle
- Attach shapes 14 and 15—the purple velvet capitals
- Attach shape 16—the brown velvet hair (it will slightly overlap the white silk face)
- Attach shape 17—the kid leather cross on the orb
- Attach shape 18—the burgundy velvet centre panel on the skirt
- Attach shapes 19, 20 and 21—the kid leather circles on the velvet panel on the over-skirt
- Attach shapes 22 and 23—the burgundy velvet bases of the columns

Figure 3 *Order of felt padding and appliqué*

- Attach shape 24—the purple velvet border on the hem of the skirt
- Attach shapes 25 and 26—the kid leather boots

String padding for columns

Couch eight strands of bumpf or yellow DMC soft cotton down the full length of the columns in between the capitals and bases of the two columns.

Embroidery

The elements of the design to be embroidered are listed alphabetically in Figure 4 and are matched to the alphabetical order of work which follows.

A The *border of the semi-circular arch* is worked as laid work over felt padding, using Technique 2, which is described in chapter 3. Use no. 8 Japanese gold and couch with Gutermann 968.

Figure 4 *Embroidery elements identified alphabetically*

B The *burgundy velvet semi-circular arch* is covered with a trellis pattern which is worked with gilt tambour thread. Thread the gilt tambour up into a size 7 crewel needle. The intersections of the trellis pattern are anchored with 2 mm (1⁄10 in) lengths of gilt no. 6 bright check. Each diamond created by the trellis pattern is filled with a 2 mm (1⁄10 in) gilt spangle anchored with a gold petite bead (40557). Using a double thread of Gutermann 968, thread up a spangle first, then the bead. Drop both to the bottom of the thread and take the needle down through the hole of the spangle, supporting the thread with a mellor or chenille needle as the thread is drawn through the fabric. Refer to Figure 5 (a), (b), (c) and (d) to work this pattern.

(a)

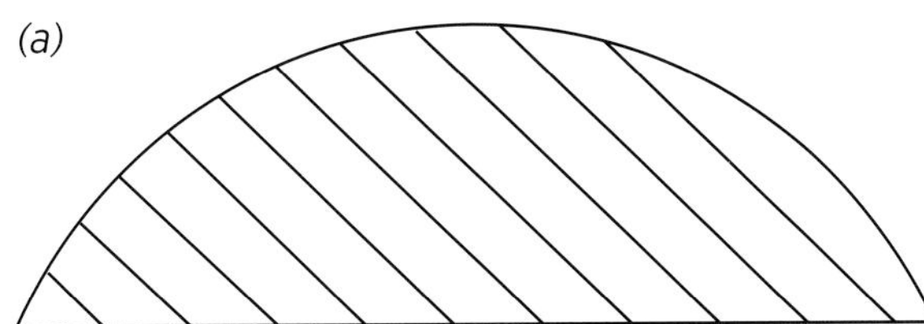

(b)

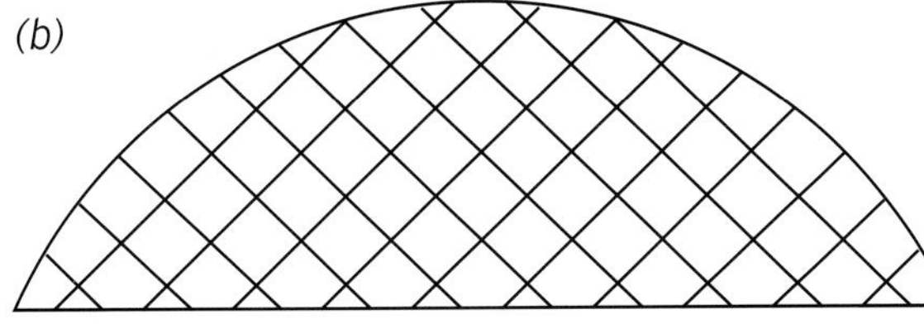

(c)

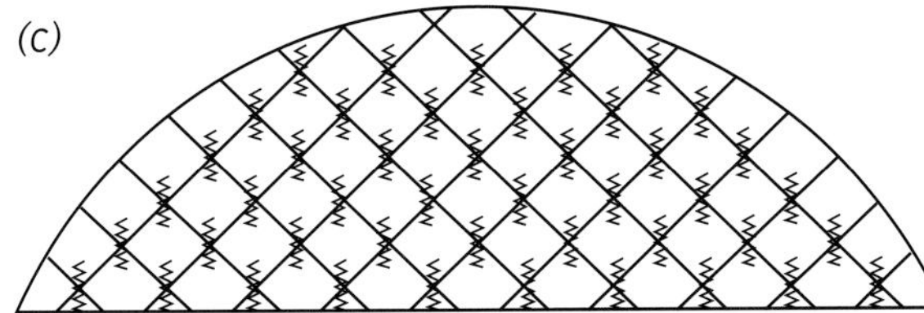

(d)

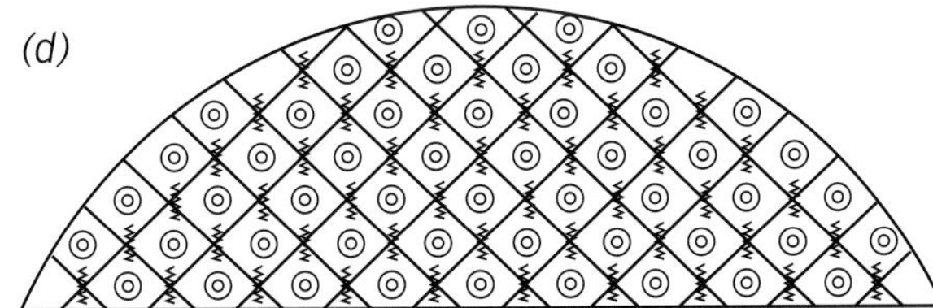

Figure 5

C The *entablature* is worked as closed plate work, using gilt broad plate. Work from left to right over the felt padding. Refer to the instructions for closed plate work in chapter 3.

D *Outline the plate work* with gilt no. 1 pearl purl. Also outline both sides of the laid work border of the semi-circular arch with gilt no. 1 pearl purl.

E *Outline the capitals* of both columns with gilt no. 1 pearl purl.

F The *columns* are worked as vertical cutwork over string padding. Refer to the instructions for vertical cutwork over string padding in chapter 3, but note that the instructions are written for the traditional direction of vertical cutwork, which will be appropriate for the column on the right side. The cutwork on the left-side column is facing the opposite direction, as shown in Figure 6. Work the column on the left side at this stage, and work the column on the right side after you have outlined the angel's boots (X).

Figure 6

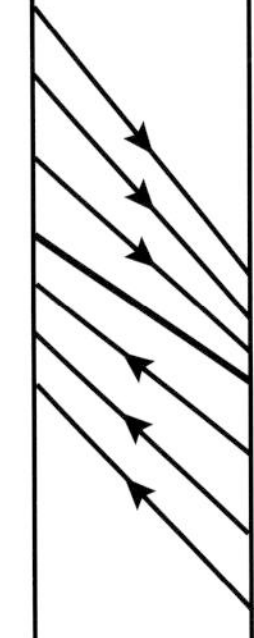

G *Angel's face and hair*. Outline both the angel's white silk face and brown velvet hair with gilt super pearl purl according to the design lines in Figure 7. Work the eyebrows, the nose and closed eyelids with gilt super pearl purl (the angel's left eyebrow and nose form a continuous contour line). The angel's mouth is a gold Mill Hill petite bead 40557.

Figure 7

H *Halo*. Outline the angel's halo with overstretched gilt no. 4 pearl purl. Stretch a 6 cm (2½ in) length of gilt no. 6 bright check to 15 cm (6 in). Couch two rows of the overstretched bright check around the inside of the halo with Gutermann 968.

I The *angel's wing* is quite complex. For this reason it is to be worked according to an alphabetical and numerical order. The feathers are represented with letters in lower case, a to k, and the outlines of the feathers are represented numerically 1 to 11. The beginning and the end of the outline for each feather is marked with an **X** in Figure 8.

Work feathers a to e as laid work, using Technique 1 which is described in chapter 3. Each laid-worked feather is worked across, from left to right. Technique 1 requires tails to be left at the beginning and end of each couched row. Plunge the tails at the completion of each feather. No. 8 Japanese gold is used for the laid work of these feathers and Gutermann 968 for the couching.

Work feathers **f** to **k** as chipwork.

Follow this order for working the angel's wing. Also refer to Figure 8.

a. Work this feather with three complete rows of couched Japanese gold. Start the laid work on the felt.

b. Leave a very fine gap between the laid work for feather a, and the laid work for feather b (only on the yellow felt), to accommodate outline 1 (in super pearl purl). This feather has two complete rows of couched Japanese gold, followed by a third row that begins as two threads of Japanese gold, but is reduced to a single thread, from where feather b meets feather c. Refer to Figure 8.

c, d and e. These feathers are worked in the same manner as feather b.

1. Outline with gilt super pearl purl from **X** to **X** (see Figure 8). The outline for feather a continues around the top of the wing and ends at the outline of the angel's brown velvet hair. The pearl purl for this outline is couched on the silk background, up against the edge of the felt.

2. Outline with gilt super pearl purl from **X** to **X** (see Figure 8).

3–5. Work these outlines in the same manner as outline 2.

6–11. These are the outlines for the smaller feathers. As these feathers are filled with chip work, they need to be outlined first with gilt super pearl purl. Refer to Figure 8.

f. This feather is filled in with chips of gilt no. 6 bright check.

g. This feather is filled in with chips of gilt no. 6 wire check.

h. This feather is filled in with chips of gilt no. 6 wire check.

i. This feather is filled in with chips of gilt no. 6 bright check.

j. This feather is filled in with chips of gilt no. 6 bright check. Do not fill in this feather, however, until the angel's arm has been outlined.

k. This feather is filled in with chips of gilt no. 6 wire check. Do not fill in this feather, however, until the angel's arm has been outlined.

Figure 8

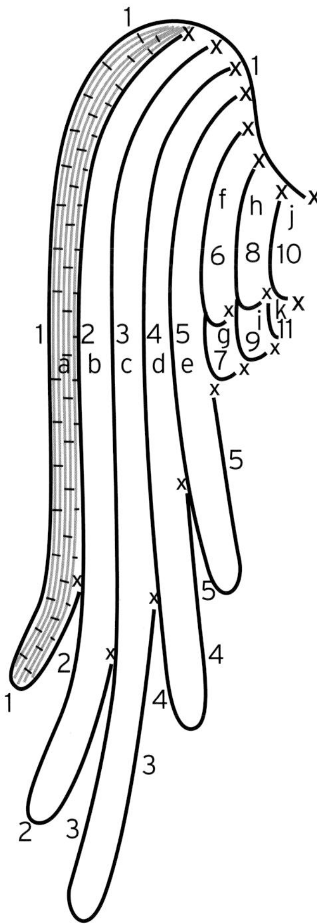

J The angel's *neck ornament*. Outline the shape and the divisions of the shape with gilt super pearl purl according to the design lines in Figure 9. The centre compartment is filled with chips of gilt no. 6 wire check, the left compartment with chips of wine no. 6 wire check and the right compartment with chips of bright violet no. 6 wire check.

Figure 9 *Neck ornament*

K The angel's *breast ornament* is worked as laid work, using technique 2 as described in chapter 3. Use no. 8 Japanese gold for the laid work and one strand of DMC stranded cotton purple 327 to create the diagonal lines across the breast ornament and Gutermann 968 for the couching stitches in between the diagonal lines. Couch twice with purple stranded cotton on the diagonal line, keeping the two stitches close together, and couch once with Gutermann 968 in the centre of the space between two diagonals. Plunge the four tails on completion of the laid work.

L *Angel's top*. In preparation for outlining the angel's top, take an 18 cm (7 in) length of gilt no. 1 pearl purl and stretch it to 30 cm (12 in). Wrap every groove of the overstretched pearl purl with two strands of DMC stranded cotton purple 327. Run the stranded cotton through beeswax before winding it around the pearl purl. Outline the angel's top according to Figure 10. The beginning and the end of each line of pearl purl is indicated with an **X**. (Note that the angel's left side and arm are not outlined at this stage. The maniple over the left arm needs to be worked before outlining the arm. The bottom of the angel's top is not outlined until the angel's right hand and orb are completed.) Couch every groove of the overstretched and wrapped pearl purl with one strand of DMC stranded cotton purple 327.

Figure 10

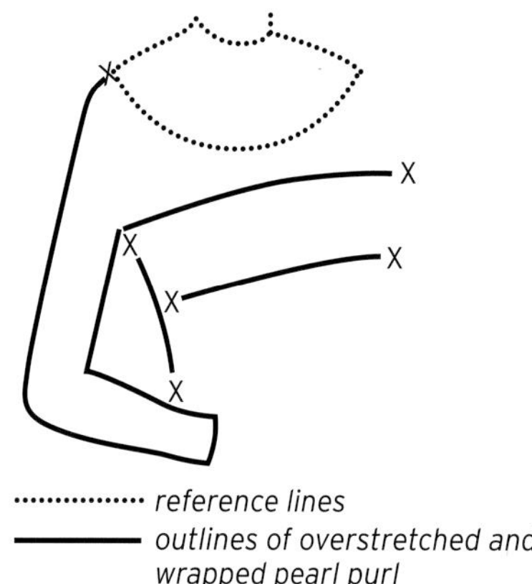

M The angel's *right hand* is worked with gilt super pearl purl. Follow the design lines in Figure 11. The pearl purl will need to be carefully manipulated with tweezers.

Figure 11

N The *orb* held in the angel's right hand is outlined with gilt no. 1 pearl purl. The kid leather cross on the orb is outlined with gilt super pearl purl.

O The *maniple* over the angel's left arm. Couch gilt 1½ twist and gilt no. 7 check thread together for the outlines of the maniple. Use Gutermann 968 for the couching stitches and regularly space the couching stitches 3 mm (⅛ in) apart. Follow the design lines in Figure 12. The beginning and the end of each line of couched gilt 1½ twist and gilt no. 7 check thread is indicated with an **X**. Leave tails at the beginning and end to plunge. Finally, work a line of vertical S-ing down the length of the maniple, using purple no. 6 rough purl. The instructions for S-ing are in chapter 3.

P Complete the *outlining of the angel's top* on the left side with overstretched and wrapped pearl purl, following the design lines in Figure 13.

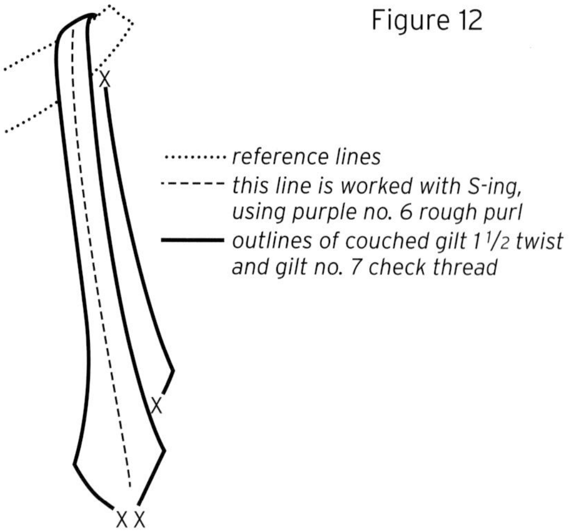

Figure 12

reference lines
this line is worked with S-ing, using purple no. 6 rough purl
outlines of couched gilt 1 1/2 twist and gilt no. 7 check thread

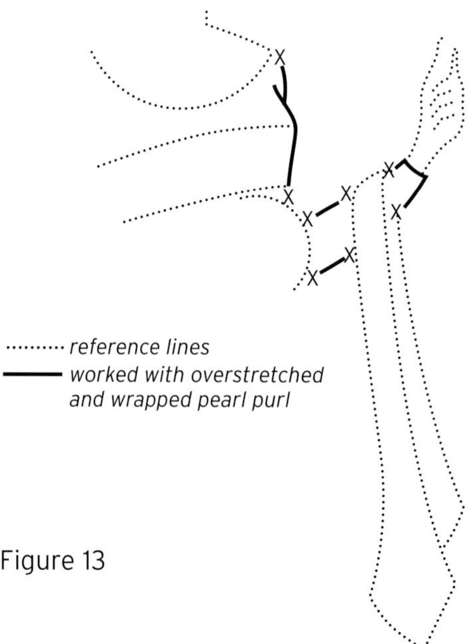

Figure 13

Figure 14

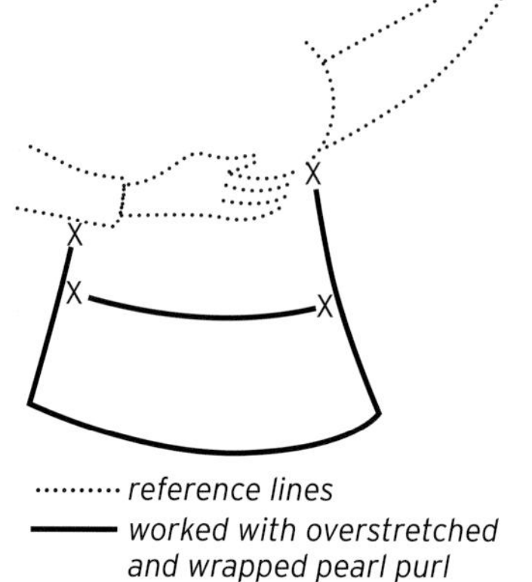

Q Outline the *remaining design lines* for the angel's top with the overstretched and wrapped gilt no. 1 pearl purl, as shown in Figure 14.

R The *pattern* on the angel's top between the two bands is worked with pink no. 6 rough purl and purple no. 6 rough purl. Alternate between the two colours.

S The *angel's left hand* is worked with gilt super pearl purl. Follow the design lines in Figure 15. The pearl purl will need to be carefully manipulated with tweezers.

Figure 15

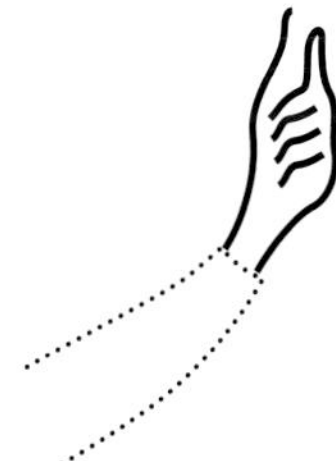

T The *lily* is outlined with gilt super pearl purl. The lily is filled in with chips of bright violet no. 6 wire check. The stem is worked with gilt no. 7 check thread. The stem is worked in two sections. The upper section of the stem begin beneath the lily and runs between the angel's thumb and forefinger, and the lower section starts beneath the closed fingers and runs across the pearl purl outlining the angel's hand. There will be four tails to plunge to the back of the work.

U The *hem-line border* of the angel's top. The lines of three waves forming circles within the border are worked with gilt super pearl purl. The centre circle is filled with chips of bright violet no. 6 wire check, and the circles on either side are filled with wine no. 6 wire check. The area above the circles is filled in with chips of gilt no. 6 bright check, and the area below the circles is filled with chips of gilt no. 6 wire check.

V The *angel's overskirt* is to be worked in the following order:

- Outline the skirt with ribbled (crinkled) gilt broad plate. As plate cannot be turned at a corner, outline the two sides first, and then outline the bottom of the skirt, taking the plate over the burgundy velvet panel. Couch every groove of the ribbled broad plate with Gutermann 968.
- Couch ribbled gilt narrow plate along the vertical design line running between the two rows of rectangles on the over-skirt.
- Outline both sides of the burgundy velvet panel with gilt milliary. Couch the milliary with Gutermann 968 in every second or third groove.
- The small rectangles on the overskirt are filled in with vertical cutwork, using alternate lengths of pink no. 6 rough purl and purple no. 6 rough purl. Note that the overskirt on the angel's left side requires two lengths of the two coloured purls in three narrow rectangles on that side.
- The top and bottom of the pink and purple rectangles on both sides of the overskirt are edged with rows of 2 mm (1/10 in) spangles with Mill Hill petite glass beads 40557. Bring needle and doubled Gutermann 968 through the fabric and thread up a spangle and bead. Allow both to drop to the bottom of the thread, and return the needle through the hole of the spangle, supporting the thread with a mellor or chenille needle as it is taken through the fabric.

- Outline the kid leather circles on the velvet panel with overstretched gilt no. 1 pearl purl.
- Attach a 4 mm (²⁄₁₀ in) filigree gold cup sequin and a Mill Hill petite glass bead 40557 in the centre of each kid leather circle. These are attached in the same way as the spangles and beads.

W The *angel's underskirt* is outlined with couched gilt 1½ twist and gilt no. 7 check thread in the same way as for the outlines of the maniple. Use Gutermann 968 for the couching stitches and regularly space the couching stitches 3 mm (⅛ in) apart. Follow the design lines in Figure 16. The beginning and the end of each line of couched gilt 1½ twist and gilt no. 7 check thread is indicated with an X. Leave tails at the beginning and end to plunge. Work a row of 3 mm (⅛ in) spangles with Mill Hill petite glass beads 42012. The purple velvet border of the underskirt features a cluster of 3 mm (⅛ in) spangles with Mill Hill petite glass beads 42012. See the instructions for spangles and loops of purl in chapter 3, and change the loops of purl to beads.

Figure 16

X The *angel's boots* are outlined with gilt super pearl purl.

Y *Bases of columns*. Note: both columns should now have been worked. Refer to Figure 17 for the design lines that are to be worked with gilt no. 1 pearl purl. The beginning and end of each line is marked with an X.

Figure 17

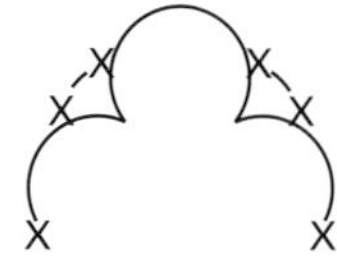

Z The *base of the design* is finished with two rows of overstretched gilt no. 3 pearl purl. Couch every second groove with Gutermann 968.

Cornucopia

This design was inspired by a fragment of an early 17th century Spanish or French valance which is in the Victoria & Albert Museum, London. The velvet fragment was embellished with satin appliqués, purls and couched metal threads and silk gimps, all sumptuous materials superbly suited to represent such a luscious subject as the 'horn of plenty'.

The appliqués in this design are also in satin silk and were matched to the colours used on the valance. The use of no. 4 Japanese gold, coloured gimps to match the silk appliqués and glittery gilt bright check purls in this design are a close match to the materials used on the seventeenth-century valance.

The style and subject is characteristic of Baroque art and design. The flowers and leaves are in the realm of the fantastic.

This design has been envisaged as a motif to be repeated, perhaps on a cushion cover. To use it otherwise, would require modifications to the design. Figures 1(a) and 1(b) demonstrate how the motif can be repeated. Note that this design needs to be worked on a slate frame or a 50 cm (20 in) quilter's frame.

EQUIPMENT AND MATERIALS

76 cm (30 in) slate frame or 50 cm (20 in) quilter's frame
55 x 70 cm (22 x 28 in) piece of calico
45 cm (18 in) square of dark purple silk velvet
18 cm (7 in) square golden yellow duchesse silk satin
18 cm (7 in) square light blue duchesse silk satin
10 cm (4 in) square dark pink silk ribbon
1.5 m (60 in) light blue gimp
1.75 m (70 in) golden yellow gimp
50 cm (20 in) dark pink gimp
5 cm (2 in) square yellow felt
4 x A4 sheets 110 gsm tracing paper
Vliesofix, HeatnBond Lite or Bondaweb
orange dressmaker's carbon
1 gram pounce (and roll of felt to apply pounce)
1 tube yellow ochre watercolour paint
1 x 000 paintbrush
Gutermann threads to match the silk fabrics and the gimps
Gutermann 968
size 12 sharps and sizes 10 and 9 crewel needles
mellor or size 18 chenille needle

METAL THREADS AND SPANGLES

1 hank no. 4 Japanese gold
1.5 m (60 in) gilt no. 8 bright check
70 cm (28 in) gilt no. 8 smooth purl
65 cm (26 in) gilt super pearl purl
90 cm (35 in) gilt no. 1 pearl purl
1 packet 4 mm (2/10 in) gilt spangles

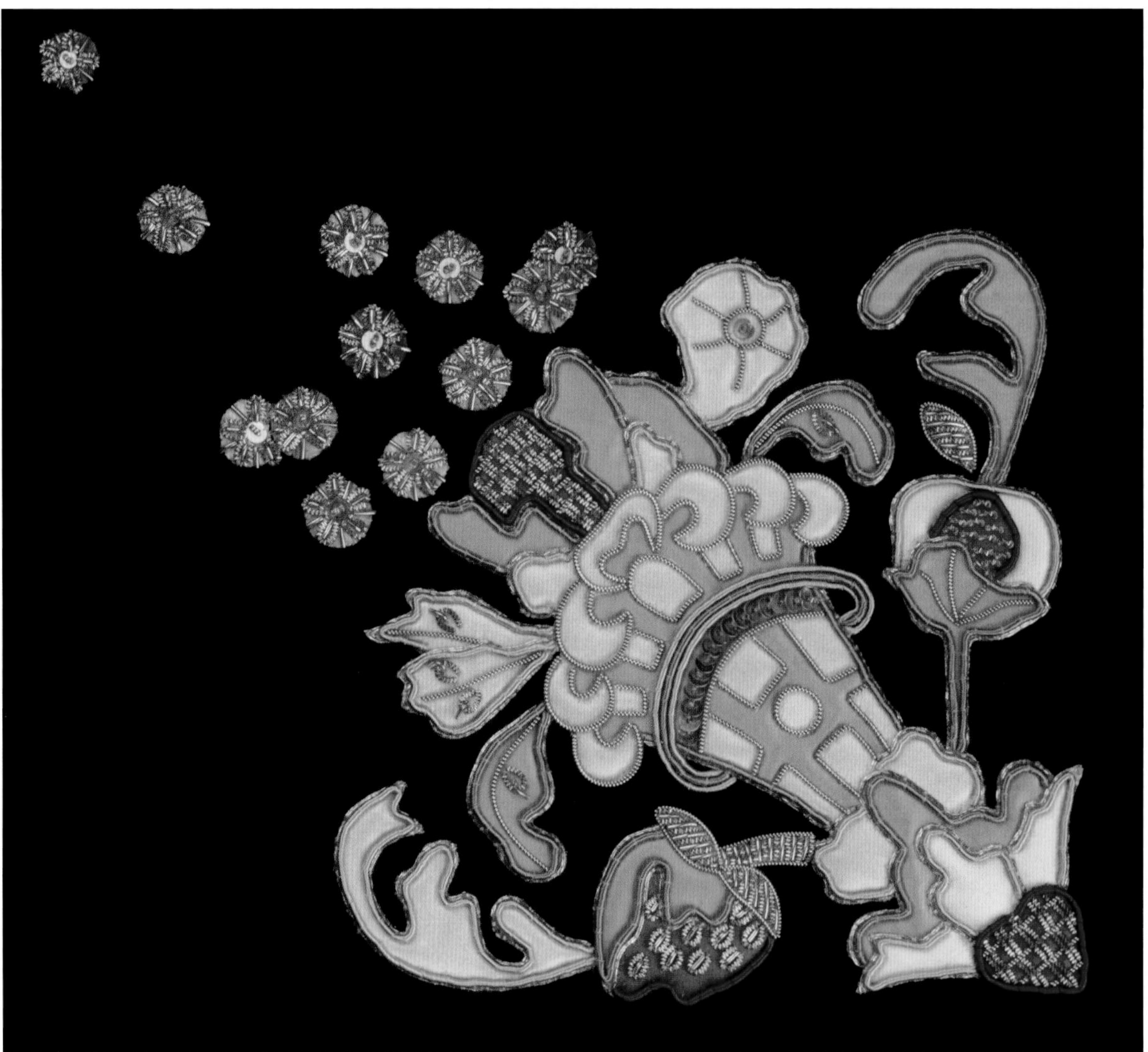

Note that the quantities specified here for the appliqués, the threads and spangles are for one repeat of this design. Double or quadruple the measurements and amounts if the design is to be repeated twice or four times.

METHOD

Dark purple velvet background

Refer to the instructions for dressing a slate frame in chapter 3. Mount the calico onto the frame. Threads will need to be drawn on all four sides of the calico because the 45 cm (18 in) square of velvet has to be centred on the calico. The width of the calico is 55 cm (22 in). Draw a thread 5 cm (2 in) in from the edge of the calico (not from the edge of the webbing) on the two laced sides.

Measure the length of the calico between the rollers. Deduct 45 cm (18 in) from this measurement. Divide the balance and this will be the measurement you need to take to draw threads along the roller sides of the frame.

Match the edges of the velvet square to the four drawn-thread lines on the calico. Pin and stitch the velvet onto the calico. Refer again to the instructions for dressing a slate frame in chapter 3. Once the velvet is stitched onto the

Figure 1(a)

Figure 1(b)

calico, tighten the frame so that the fabric is as taut as a drum.

It is important to find the centre of the velvet and to divide it into quadrants before transferring the motifs onto the velvet. First, find the exact centre on all four sides of the calico. Place pins perpendicularly to mark the centres. Refer to Figure 3. Wind sewing thread around one pin and take the thread to the pin on the opposite side and wind the thread around that pin. Repeat this for the remaining two sides. Ensure that the threads are taut. The intersection of the two threads marks the centre of the velvet and the velvet is now divided into quadrants by the two threads. Stitch 2 or 3 back stitches in the centre of the velvet. This marks the position for the no. 1 dark pink circle which is the absolute centre for all the repeated motifs. The no. 2 circle needs to be in the same relationship to the centre no. 1 circle for all repeats.

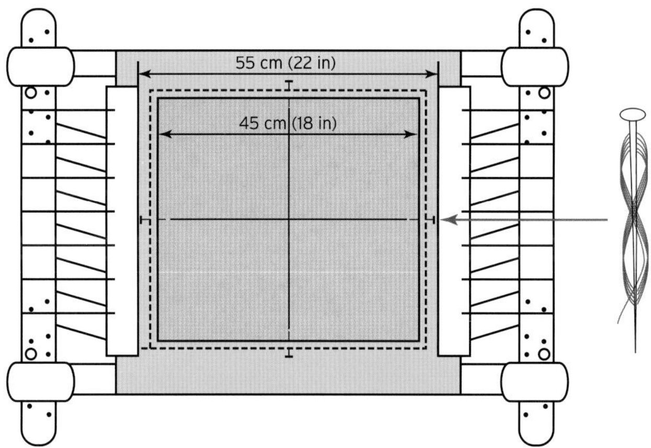

Figure 3 *Finding the centre of the velvet*

The Cornucopia design is actually a motif which needs to be repeated. Refer to Figures 1(a) and 1(b) to see the two design options for repeating the motif. To work Figure 1(a), trace Figure 2 onto tracing paper. This tracing can only be used for repeating the motif in the bottom right and top left quadrants. To work Figure 1(b), reverse Figure 2 for the motifs in the top right and bottom left quadrants.

Use the prick-and-pounce method to transfer the motif onto the velvet. Refer to the

Figure 2 *Tracing outline*

instructions for the prick-and-pounce method in chapter 3. Place books beneath the frame to support the fabric while pouncing and painting the design lines. Transfer the motif into the bottom right quadrant first. Once the pouncing and painting has been completed, remove the threads.

Further secure the velvet to the calico by pin stitching along the design lines, allowing approximately 3 cm (1¼ in) in between each pin-stitch. The pin-stitches will eventually be hidden.

Golden yellow duchesse silk satin

Trace the shapes and design lines in Figure 4 onto tracing paper. Iron Vliesofix (HeatnBond Lite or Bondaweb) onto the wrong side of the silk square. Peel off the backing paper. Place and weight the tracing paper on the right side of the silk. Slip a sheet of orange dressmaker's carbon in between the tracing paper and the silk, and trace the design lines onto the silk. Carefully cut the shapes out of the silk.

Figure 4 *Shapes and design lines for golden yellow duchesse silk satin*

Light blue duchesse silk satin

Trace the shapes and design lines in Figure 5 onto tracing paper. Iron Vliesofix onto the wrong side of the silk square. Peel off the backing paper. Place and weight the tracing paper on the right side of the silk. Slip a sheet of orange dressmaker's carbon in between the tracing paper and the silk, and trace the design lines onto the silk. Carefully cut the shapes out of the silk.

Dark pink silk ribbon

Trace the shapes and design lines in Figure 6 onto tracing paper. Iron Vliesofix onto the wrong side of the silk square. Peel off the backing paper. Place and weight the tracing paper on the right side of the silk. Slip a sheet of orange dressmaker's carbon in between the tracing paper and the silk, and trace the design lines onto the silk. Carefully cut the shapes out of the silk.

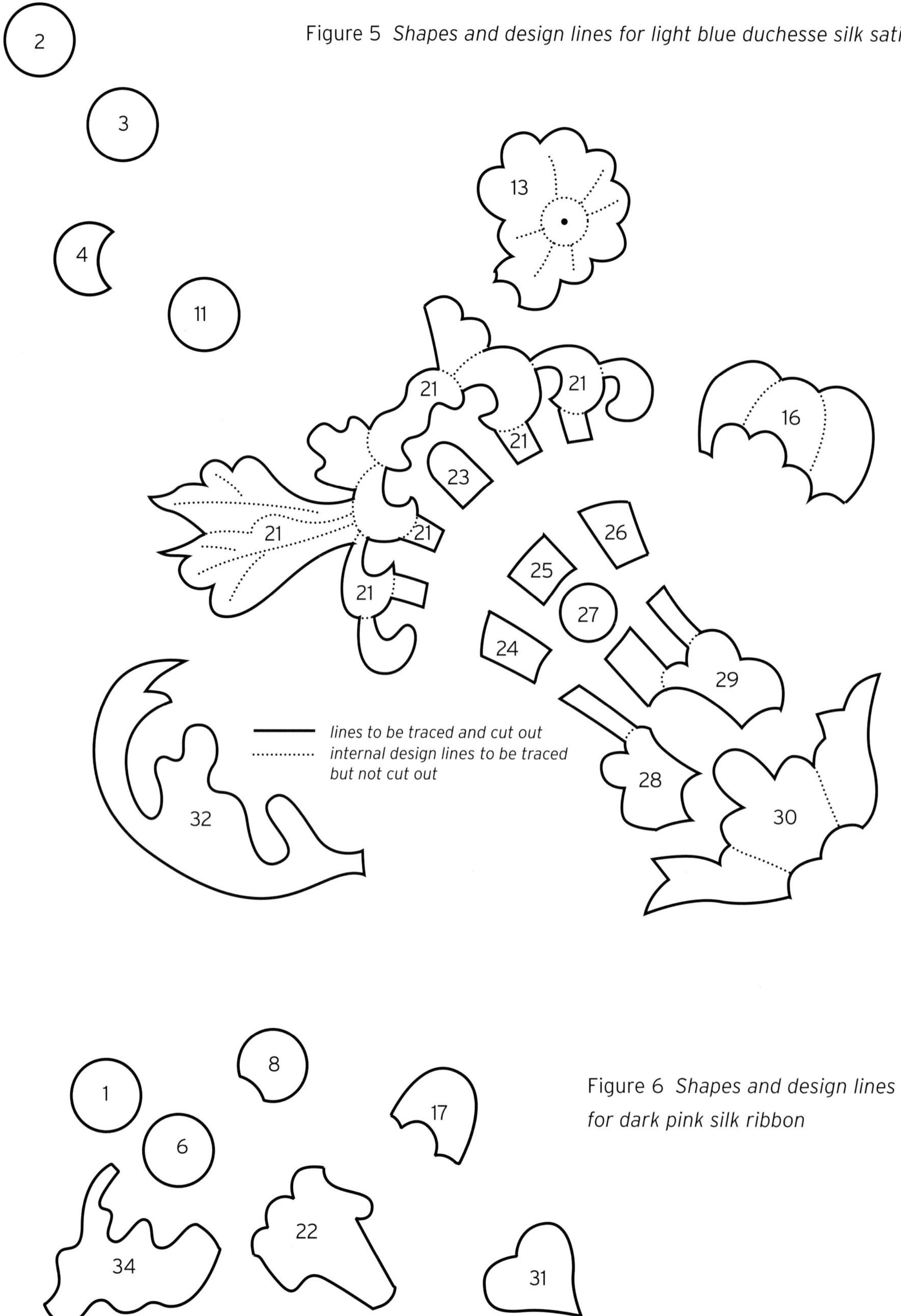

Figure 5 *Shapes and design lines for light blue duchesse silk satin*

Figure 6 *Shapes and design lines for dark pink silk ribbon*

Yellow felt shapes

Trace the shapes in Figure 7 onto tracing paper. Place and weight the tracing paper onto the yellow felt. Slip a sheet of orange dressmaker's carbon between the tracing paper and felt and firmly trace the design lines onto the felt. Cut the shapes out.

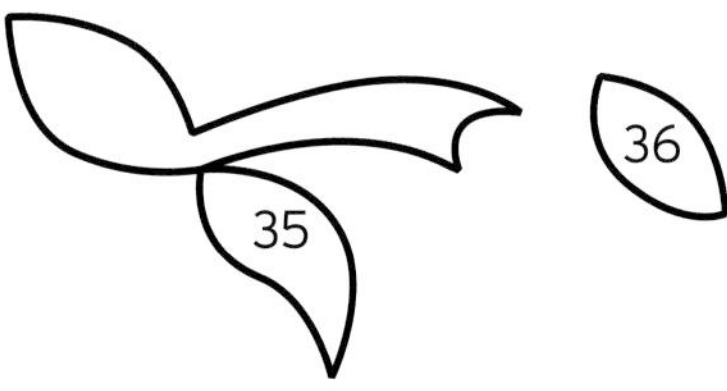

Figure 7 *Tracing shapes for yellow felt*

Appliqué and padding work

All appliqué and felt shapes are numbered. The numbers on the shapes are matched to the numerical order of work for the felt padding and appliquéing in Figure 8. Note that no. 20 is the cornucopia shape, which has been extended at the bottom to sit beneath no. 30 and the heart shape, no. 31. To initially hold the appliqué pieces in place, work a few stab stitches around the edges of the appliqués. Then use minute stab stitches, 1 mm (1/20 in) apart, to attach appliqué pieces and felt padding to the velvet. When stab stitching, come up in the velvet background, and down into the silk appliqué or felt. Use Gutermann 968 for the yellow felt pieces and matching sewing threads for the appliqué pieces.

Couching no. 4 Japanese gold and gimps

The motif is divided into four sections as represented in Figure 9(a), (b), (c) and (d). Each section is numbered which indicates the order of working the sections. There is also a legend with each section to indicate the order of couching.

The golden yellow and light blue shapes are outlined with no. 4 Japanese gold and gimp in a matching colour to the silk. Two Japanese gold threads are couched first as an outline on the edge of the silk. Leave tails at the beginning and end of each outline to plunge through to the back

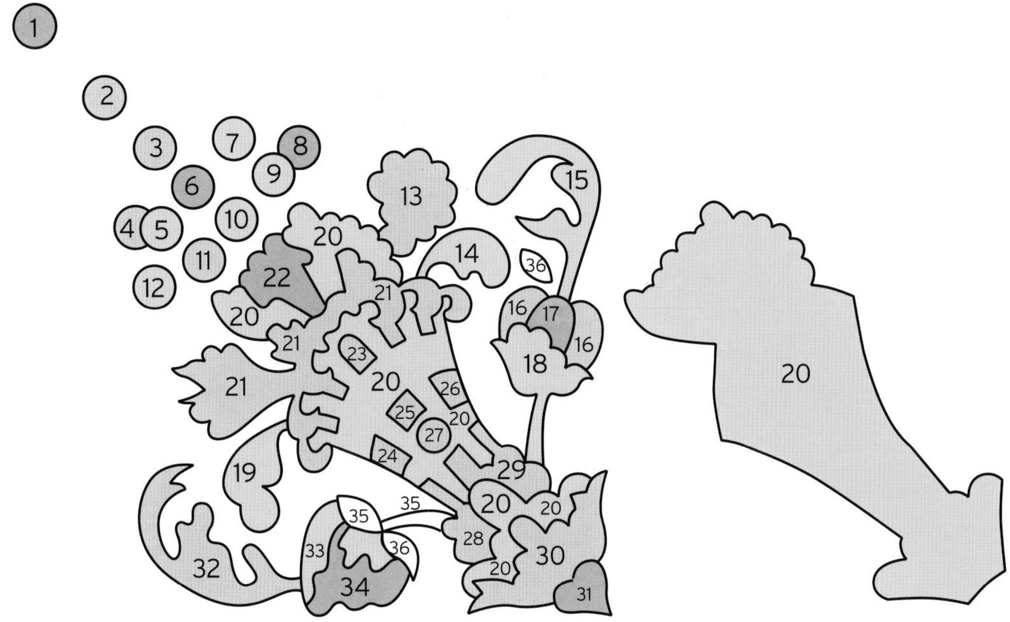

Figure 8 *Order of work for felt padding and appliqué*

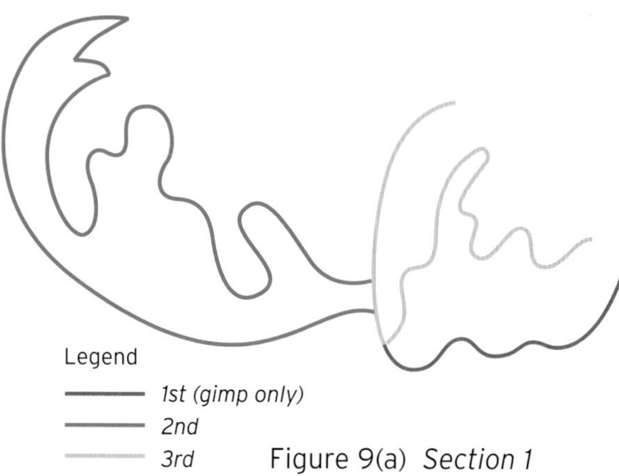

Figure 9(a) *Section 1*

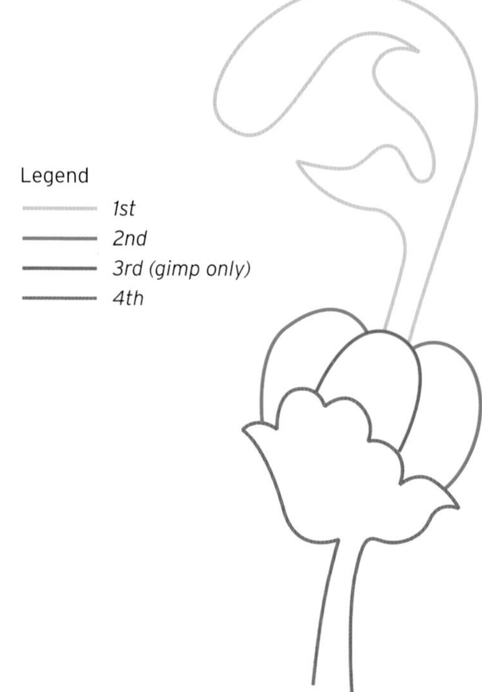

Figure 9(b) *Section 2*

of the work. To create a pattern on the metal thread outlines, do two couching stitches close together, using a Gutermann sewing thread which matches the silk shape that is being outlined, and repeat these two stitches every 3 mm (⅛ in) along the outline. Plunge each Japanese gold tail to the back of the work before commencing the gimp outline.

Figure 9(c) *Section 3*

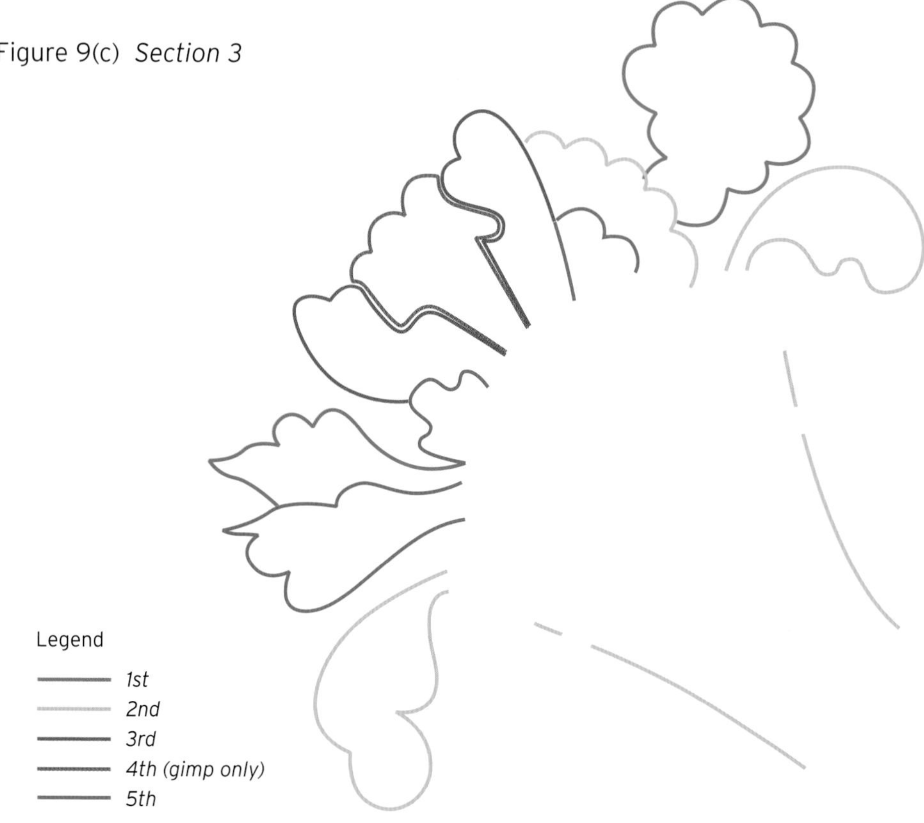

Figure 9(d) *Section 4*

The colour of the gimp, and the sewing thread for couching the gimp, is matched to the colour of the silk shape that is being outlined. The gimp follows the inside of the Japanese gold outline. Leave tails at the beginning and end of the outline. Couch the gimp and allow a space interval of 4 mm (2/10 in) between couching stitches. Plunge the tails at the completion of the outline. The tails of gimp require a large hole to take them through to the back of the work. Use an awl or stiletto to make the holes.

The dark pink silk shapes are only outlined with a matching gimp.

Pearl purl outlines on cornucopia

Refer to Figure 10. The beginning and the end of each outline of pearl purl is marked with an **X** on Figure 10.

Remaining embroidery

The elements of the motif to be further embroidered are listed alphabetically in Figure 11 and are matched to the alphabetical order of work which follows.

A *Medallions*. Attach a 4 mm (2/10 in) spangle and a 3 mm (1/8 in) loop of gilt no. 8 bright check in the centre of each medallion. Refer to spangles and loops of purl in chapter 3.

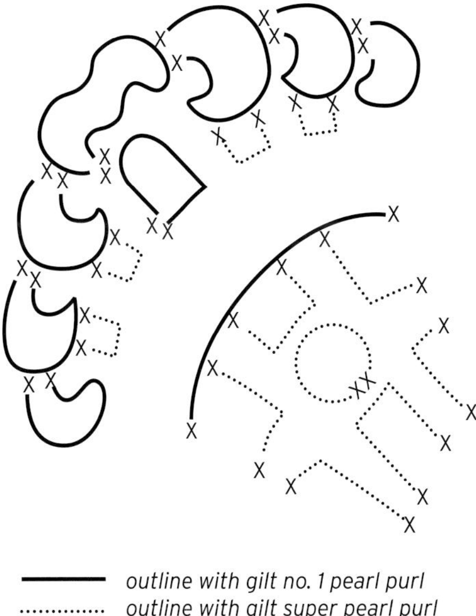

Figure 10

Cut five 9 mm (3/8 in) lengths of gilt no. 8 bright check and ten 3 mm (1/8 in) lengths of gilt no. 8 smooth purl. Organise and work five chain stitches of bright check around the spangle as shown in Figure 12.

Create each chain stitch by bringing the needle and thread through the fabric, close to the spangle, and thread up the cut length of bright check. Drop it to the bottom of the sewing thread, and with a mellor or chenille needle, hold the bright check purl in a loop, while taking the needle down through the same hole. Come up again on the opposite side and very gently put in a couching stitch over the bright check purl. It should not be a visible couching stitch. Fill the chain with a length of 3 mm (1/8 in) gilt no. 8 smooth purl. This length will stand proud within the chain. Stitch a 3 mm (1/8 in) spoke of gilt no. 8 smooth purl in between each chain.

B The *dark pink shape* is filled with burden stitch. Couch seven horizontal rows of gilt super pearl purl across the shape, allowing a regular space of

Figure 11 *Alphabetical order of working remaining embroidery*

Figure 12

3 mm (⅛ in) between each row. Cut 5 mm (²⁄₁₀ in) lengths of gilt no. 8 bright check. These lengths will be laid in pairs across one row of pearl purl. Allow a space between the rows of purls so that the dark pink silk will be seen. Refer to Figure 13 for the arrangement of the purls.

C The *three leaves* (one blue and two golden yellow) have a centre vein which is worked with gilt super pearl purl. Work one chain stitch on one side of the vein for each leaf. A 9 mm (⅜ in) length of gilt no. 8 bright check forms the loop of the chain stitch and a 5 mm (²⁄₁₀ in) length of gilt no. 8 smooth purl is used to hold the loop in

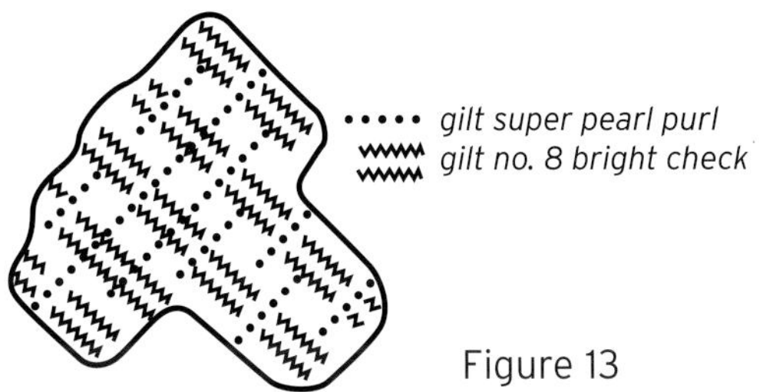

Figure 13

place. Work the loop of the chain stitch as described for the chain stitches on the medallions. Once the loop has been formed, hold it down with a mellor, bring needle and thread through on the inside of the loop, thread up the smooth purl and take the needle down on the outside, 1 mm (1⁄20 in) away from the loop.

D The l*ight blue leaf* is worked the same way as the (C) leaves. However, it has a chain stitch on both sides of the centre vein.

E *Light blue silk shape*. The design lines on the cloud-like, light blue silk shape are worked with gilt super pearl purl. Attach a 4 mm (2⁄10 in) spangle and a 4 mm (2⁄10 in) loop of gilt no. 8 bright check in the centre of the pearl purl circle on this shape.

F The single *cutwork leaf* is outlined with gilt super pearl purl and the felt padding is covered with cut lengths of gilt no. 8 bright check and gilt no. 8 smooth purl. Lay the purls alternately and at a 45° angle as shown in Figure 14.

Figure 14

G This *dark pink silk shape* is decorated with horizontal rows of loops of gilt no. 8 bright check. Cut the bright check into 9 mm (3⁄8 in) lengths. Allow a 2 mm (1⁄10 in) space between where the needle comes up and where it is taken down after being threaded with the purl. There is no space between the loops in the row, but allow a space between the rows so that the dark pink silk can be seen.

H *Golden yellow shape*. The design lines on this shape are worked with gilt super pearl purl.

I *Cutwork stem and leaves*. Outline the leaves with gilt super pearl purl according to the design line in Figure 15. The beginning and the end of the pearl purl is marked with an **X**. Outline the two sides of the stem with gilt super pearl purl. The felt padding for the leaves and the stem is covered with cut lengths of gilt no. 8 bright check and gilt no. 8 smooth purl. Lay the purls alternately and at a 45° angle for the leaves as shown in Figure 15. The cutwork on the stem sits perpendicularly across the padding.

Figure 15

J *Dark pink silk shape*. This shape is evenly scattered with chain stitches worked with the same threads and in exactly the same way as the chain stitches on the medallions.

K *Design lines on cornucopia*. For these three design lines, couch two rows of light blue gimp on either side of a row of golden yellow gimp.

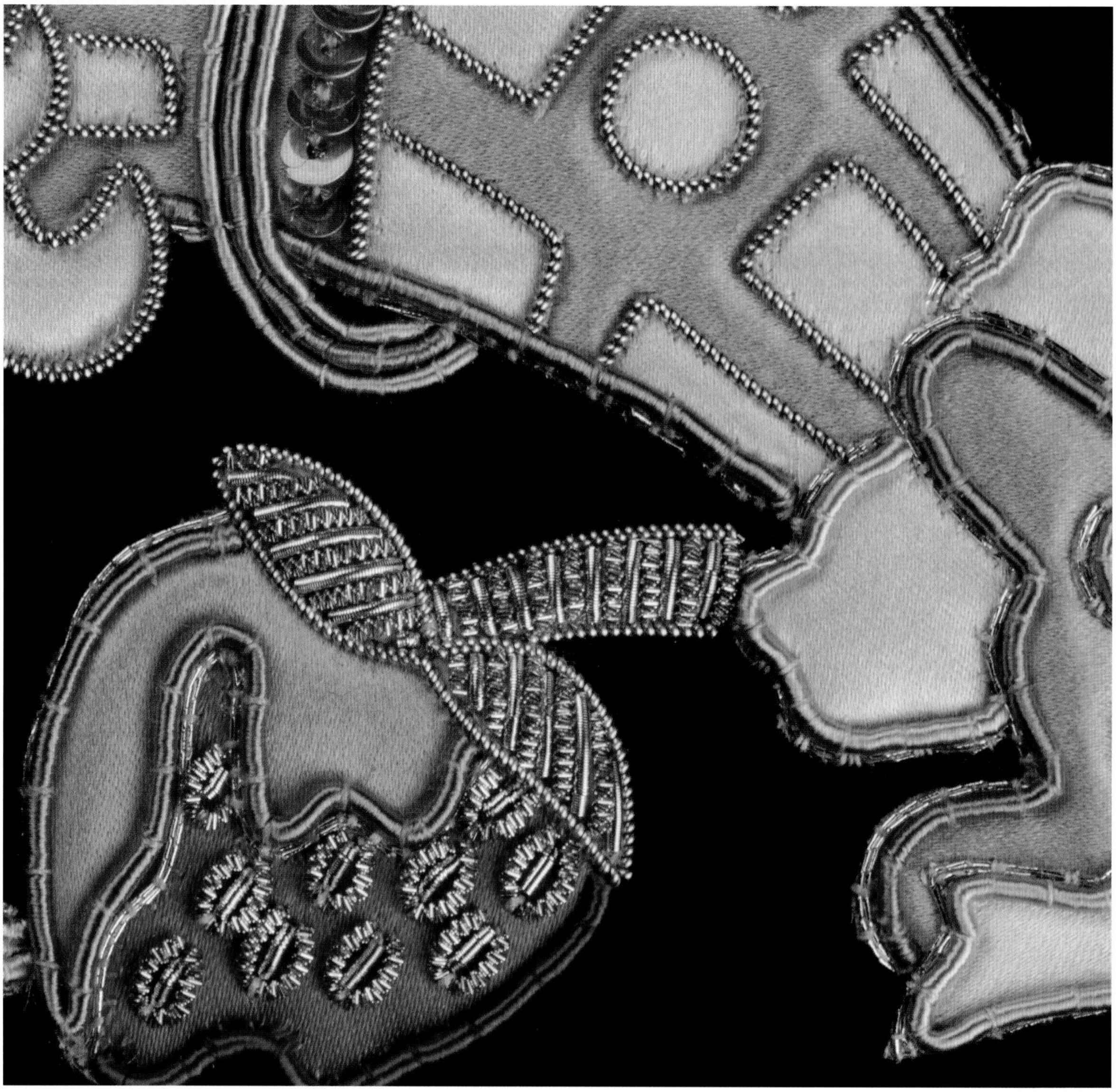

L *Decorative band*. Work a row of 4 mm (2/10 in) spangles and gilt no. 8 bright check chips along the decorative band on the cornucopia. Cut the bright check into 2 mm (1/10 in) chips. Working from left to right, bring the needle and double thread up through the fabric, pick up a spangle and a bright check chip, drop them to the bottom of the thread, and take the needle down on the right side of the spangle. Bring the needle up again, as close as possible to where the needle went down. Thread a spangle and bright check chip, drop them to the bottom of the thread, and take the needle down close to the spangle. Repeat this step for the remainder of the row. The spangles should be propped up by the bright check chips.

M The *dark pink silk heart* is worked in burden stitch in exactly the same way as the dark pink silk shape B. Refer to Figure 16.

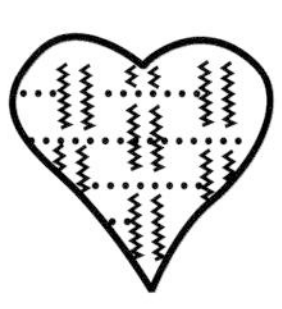

Figure 16

Memories of Russia

This design is representative of the heavily embroidered peasant costumes that I saw in Moscow museums. Gold embroidery was used extensively on Russian peasant costumes and was not restricted to ecclesiastical and court costumes, as in Western Europe. The architectural frame around the design is a reference to the classical architecture of St Petersburg.

Surface stitching is a feature of this design. Elizabethan and Stuart embroideries carried a great variety of surface stitches worked in silk and metal threads. Surface stitches became obsolete in metal thread embroidery by the end of the 17th century but were revived again, mainly by Margaret Nicholson, in the latter part of the 20th century. I have further enriched and embellished this work with silk velvet ribbon appliqués, purls, beads and crystals to convey the Russian love of jewels and bright colour.

EQUIPMENT AND MATERIALS

76 cm (30 in) slate frame or 45 cm (18 in) quilter's frame
calico to fit the frame
square of cream dress linen an appropriate size for the frame
15 cm (6 in) square yellow felt
yellow DMC soft cotton or yellow bumpf
3x A4 sheets 110 gsm tracing paper
Vliesofix, HeatnBond Lite or Bondaweb
orange dressmaker's carbon
blue dressmaker's carbon
10 cm (4 in) square white silk
15 x 8 cm (6 x 3 in) blue duchesse satin silk
12 cm (5 in) dark pink velvet ribbon, 5 cm (2 in) wide
10 cm (4 in) dark purple velvet ribbon, 7.5 cm (3in) wide
10 cm (4 in) square pink kid leather
burgundy and pink Nymo thread for crystals and beads
130 denier black silk thread
1 skein Anchor stranded cotton burgundy 70
Gutermann threads to match appliqué pieces
Gutermann 968
size 12 sharps and sizes 10 and 7 crewel needles
size 24 tapestry needle
mellor or size 18 chenille needle

METAL THREADS

2.5 m (3 yd) gilt super pearl purl
1.75 m (2 yd) gilt no. 1 pearl purl
12 cm (5 in) gilt milliary
6.25 m (7 yd) gilt no. 1 twist
6.25 m (7 yd) gilt no. 5 check thread
2 m (2⅛ yd) gilt tambour thread
4 m (4⅓ yd) no. 8 Japanese gold
4 m (4⅓ yd) no. 20 black and gold couching thread
1.5 m (1⅝ yd) no. 20 pink couching thread
1.5 m (1⅝ yd) purple 3-ply twist
1.5 m (1⅝ yd) burgundy 3-ply twist

30 cm (12 in) gilt no. 6 bright check
1 m (40 in) gilt no. 8 bright check
1.5 m (1⅝ yd) gilt no. 8 rough purl
30 cm (12 in) gilt no. 8 wire check
80 cm (32 in) gilt no. 8 smooth purl
10 cm (4 in) pink no. 6 rough purl
6 cm (3 in) black no. 6 rough purl

SPANGLES, BEADS AND CRYSTALS

1 gram packet 2 mm gilt spangles
2 gram packet 3 mm gilt spangles
1 gram packet 4 mm gilt spangles
2 x 1 cm pink Swarovski crystals with flat backs
20 x 6 mm Swarovski square volcano crystals
14 pink Swarovski bicone crystals
14 dark pink Swarovski bicone crystals
1 packet Mill Hill petite glass beads pink 42024
1 packet Mill Hill petite glass beads dark pink 42012

METHOD

Cream linen dress background

This design is best transferred onto the linen after it has been stretched taut on the frame because of the long straight lines in the design. (Refer to the end of the instructions for dressing a slate frame in chapter 3.) Trace the design lines in Figure 1 onto tracing paper. Omit design lines representing the folds on the curtain, the facial features, folds on the shawl and the interior lines of the raised arm and hand.

Insert a book beneath the frame to provide support as you trace the design. Place the tracing paper on top of the cream linen. Ensure that all straight lines of the design are on the weft and the warp of the linen. Weight the tracing paper at the top and slip a piece of orange dressmaker's carbon in between the tracing paper and linen. It would now be advisable to also add a weight to one side to prevent any movement. Using a ball-point pen, with considerable pressure, trace the design onto the linen. Use a ruler for all the straight lines.

White silk

Trace the shapes and design lines in Figure 2(a) onto tracing paper. Iron Vliesofix (HeatnBond Lite or Bondaweb) onto the wrong side of the white silk square. Peel off the backing paper. Place and weight the tracing paper on the right side of the white silk. Slip a sheet of orange dressmaker's carbon in between the tracing paper and the silk, and trace the design lines onto the silk. Carefully cut the three shapes out of the silk.

Dark purple velvet ribbon

Place the Vliesofix, paper side up, over Figure 2(b) and trace the shapes onto the Vliesofix. Iron the Vliesofix on the wrong side of the dark purple velvet ribbon. Carefully cut out the four shapes. Peel the backing paper off the velvet shapes.

Dark pink velvet ribbon

Place the Vliesofix, paper side up, over Figure 2(c) and trace the shapes onto the Vliesofix. Iron the Vliesofix on the wrong side of the dark pink velvet ribbon. Carefully cut out the three shapes. Peel the backing paper off the velvet shapes.

Blue duchesse satin silk

Trace the shape and design lines in Figure 2(d) onto tracing paper. Iron Vliesofix onto the wrong side of the blue silk. Peel the backing paper off. Place and weight the tracing paper on the right side of the blue silk. Slip a sheet of orange dressmaker's carbon between the tracing paper and the silk, and firmly trace the design lines onto the silk. Cut this shape out.

Figure 1 *Tracing outline for linen background*

Yellow felt padding

Trace the shapes in Figure 2(e) onto tracing paper. Place and weight the tracing paper onto the yellow felt. Slip a sheet of blue dressmaker's carbon between the tracing paper and the felt and firmly trace the design lines onto the felt. Cut the shapes out. The blue lines from the carbon are on the wrong side of the felt because the shapes in Figure 2(e) have been drawn in reverse.

Pink kid leather

Trace the shapes in Figure 2(f) onto tracing paper. Place the tracing paper over the pink kid leather and prick the outlines onto the leather. Cut out the kid leather shapes.

Appliqué and padding work

All appliqué and felt shapes are numbered. Refer to Figure 3 for the order of felt padding and appliquéing. The numbers of the shapes in the list

Figure 2(a) *Tracing shapes and design lines for the cream silk; do not trace the dotted design lines*

Note: These shapes have been drawn in reverse

Figure 2(b) *Tracing lines for the dark purple velvet ribbon*

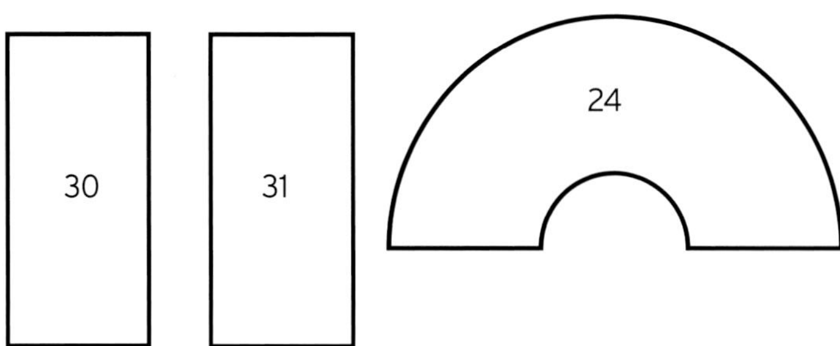

Figure 2(c) *Tracing lines for the dark pink velvet ribbon*

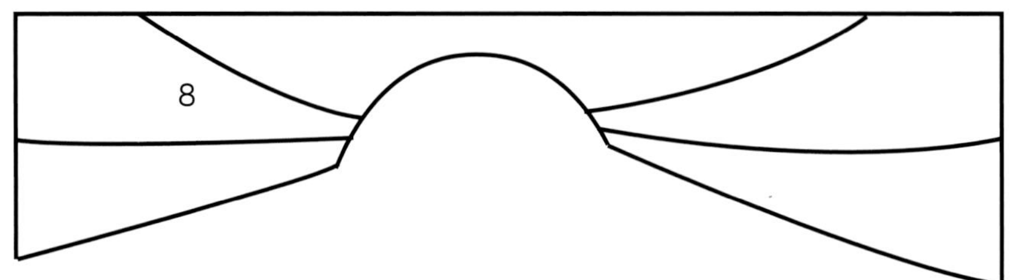

Figure 2(d) *Tracing shape and design lines for the blue silk*

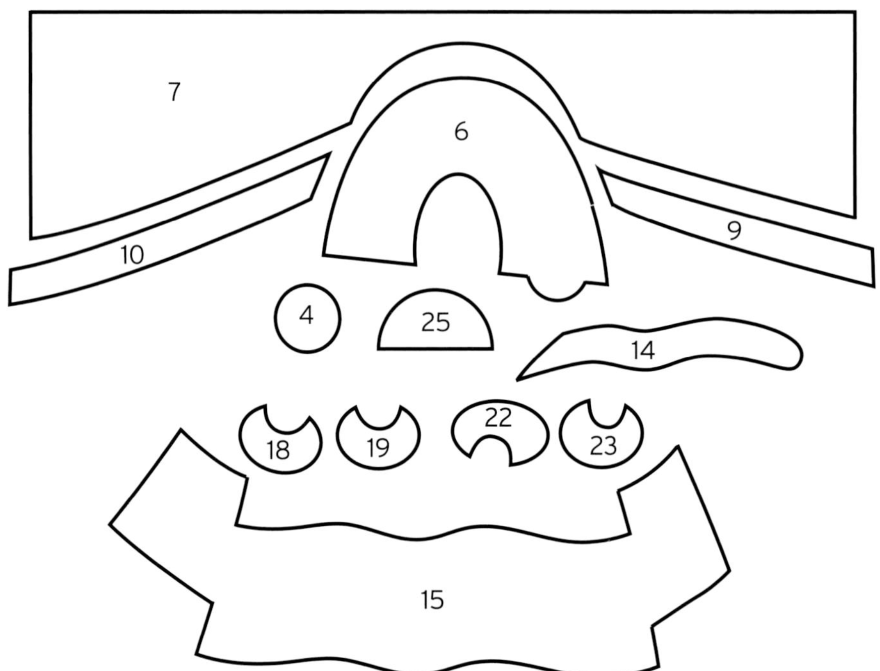

Note: These shapes are reversed so the blue lines from the dressmaker's carbon will be on the back of the felt

Figure 2(e) *Tracing shapes for the yellow felt*

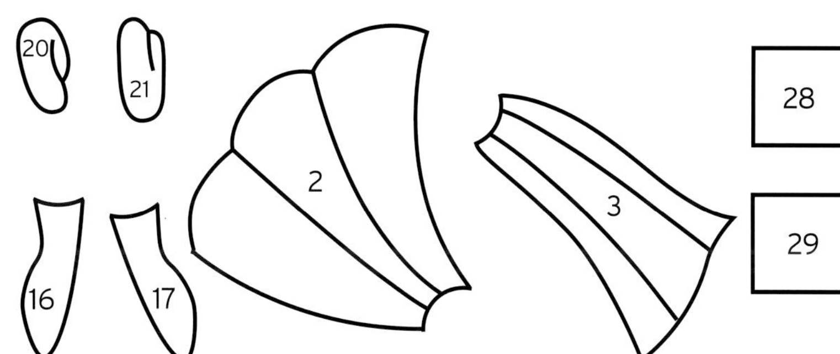

Figure 2(f) *Tracing shapes for the pink kid leather*

of attachments match up to the numbers in Figure 3. To initially hold the appliqué pieces in place, put in a few stab stitches around the edges of the appliqués. Then use minute stab stitches, 1 mm (1/20 in) apart, to attach appliqué pieces and felt padding. When stab stitching, come up in the linen background, and down into the appliqué or felt. Refer to the instructions for cutting and attaching kid leather in chapter 3. Use Gutermann 968 for the yellow felt pieces and matching sewing threads for the appliqué pieces.

- Attach shape 1—the white silk shape
- Match shapes 2 and 3 (the two pink kid leather shapes) to their outlines on the white silk shape and attach.
- Attach shape 4 (the felt circle on the shawl) first and then shape 5 (the dark purple velvet circle)
- Attach shape 6 (the felt shape for the woman's hat)
- Attach shape 7 (the felt shape for the duchesse satin blue silk curtain).
- Attach shape 8 (the duchesse satin blue silk curtain)
- Attach shapes 9 and 10 (the 2 felt shapes for the fringe of the curtain)
- Attach shapes 11 and 12 (the 2 white silk stockings)
- Attach shape 13 (the dark purple velvet skirt)
- Attach shape 14 (felt padding which forms the border on the woman's jacket)
- Attach shape 15 (the felt border of the skirt)
- Attach shapes 16 and 17 (pink kid leather boots)
- Attach shapes 18 and 19 (felt tops of boots)
- Attach shapes 20 and 21 (pink kid leather mittens)
- Attach shapes 22 and 23 (felt cuffs for mittens)
- Attach shape 24 (dark pink velvet semi-circle in the pediment)
- Attach shape 25 (the felt semi-circle within the dark pink velvet semi-circle)
- Attach shapes 26 and 27 (the dark purple velvet shapes on both sides of the pediment)
- Attach shapes 28 and 29 (the identical pink kid leather capitals of the columns)
- Attach shapes 30 and 31 (the identical dark pink velvet bases of the columns)

Figure 3 *Order of application for felt padding and appliqué*

Surface stitchery

The areas to be surfaced stitched are marked alphabetically in Figure 4 and are matched to the alphabetical order of work for the embroidery.

a. Scatter whipped wheels and woven wheels on the background material around the top half of the figure. Slightly vary the sizes. It is also possible to do half whipped wheels up against the woman's jacket. Use gilt tambour thread in a no. 7 crewel needle and refer to Figure 5 for instructions.

Figure 4 *Alphabetical order of work for surface stitchery*

b. A row of German interlacing. Use gilt no. 1 twist for the herringbone in a no. 18 chenille needle. Use no. 20 black and gold couching thread for the interlacing. Change from a chenille needle to a No. 24 tapestry needle once through the fabric. Refer to Figure 6 for instructions. Turn the embroidery around 180° to work this stitch.

c. The pink flowers are raised cross stitches. Use no. 20 pink couching thread in a no. 18 chenille needle to do the cross and change over to a no. 24 tapestry needle to work the stitches around the arms of the cross. Refer to Figure 7 for instructions.

d. The pattern on the jacket is created with raised closed herringbone. Use no. 20 black and gold couching thread in a no. 18 chenille needle and refer to Figure 8 for instructions.

e. The pattern on the floor is created with Maltese cross interlacing stitch. Use no. 20 black and gold couching thread for the grid in a no. 18 chenille needle and gilt no. 1 twist in a no. 24 tapestry needle for the interlacing and refer to Figure 9 for instructions.

f. A row of raised chain band. Use gilt no. 1 twist in a no. 18 chenille needle for the bars and change to a no. 24 tapestry needle for the chain stitch worked on the bars. Refer to Figure 10 for instructions.

g. A row of Portuguese band. Use gilt no. 1 twist in a no. 18 chenille needle for the bars and change over to a no. 24 tapestry needle for the stem stitch worked over the bars. Refer to Figure 11 for instructions.

Whipped and woven wheels

Whipped wheels require an even number of spokes. For this design, and working into the centre, stitch eight radiating spokes around the circle. Once the spokes have been worked, bring the thread up to the centre between two spokes and change over to a tapestry needle. To whip the spokes, do a back stitch over every spoke as you spiral out from the centre.

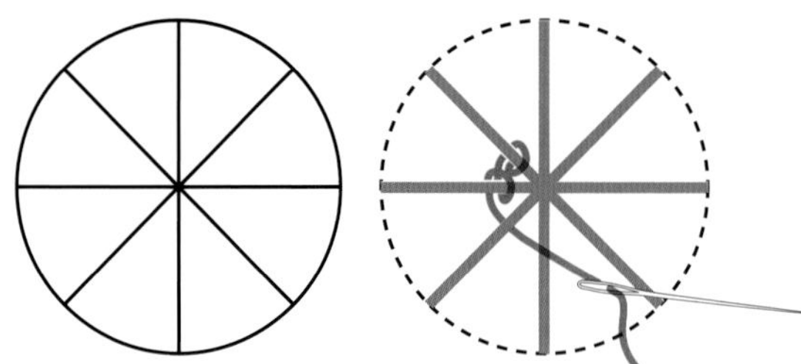

Figure 5(a) Whipped wheel

Woven wheels require an uneven number of spokes. For this design, and working into the centre, stitch seven radiating spokes around the circle. Once the spokes have been worked, bring the thread up to the centre between two spokes, and change over to a tapestry needle. Proceed to weave over one spoke and under the next. Repeat this under and over step as you spiral out towards the edge of the circle.

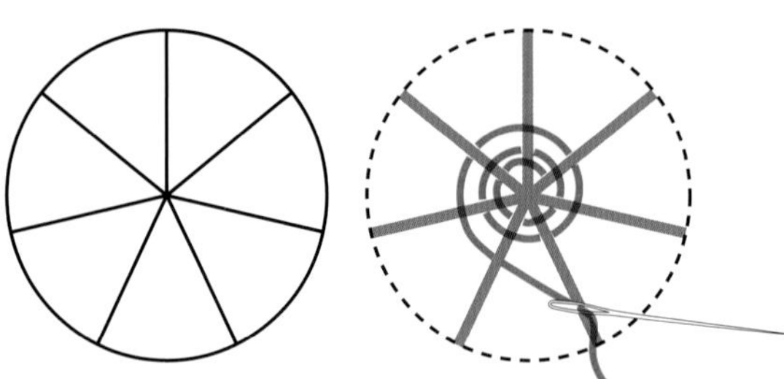

Figure 5(b) Woven wheel

German interlacing

Work a row of basic herringbone. In preparation for German interlacing, however, the needle is passed under the thread, instead of over it, as is usual for this stitch.

Come up at A and change over to a tapestry needle for the interlacing. Notice that the lacing thread is alternately passing under and over the herringbone stitches and itself.

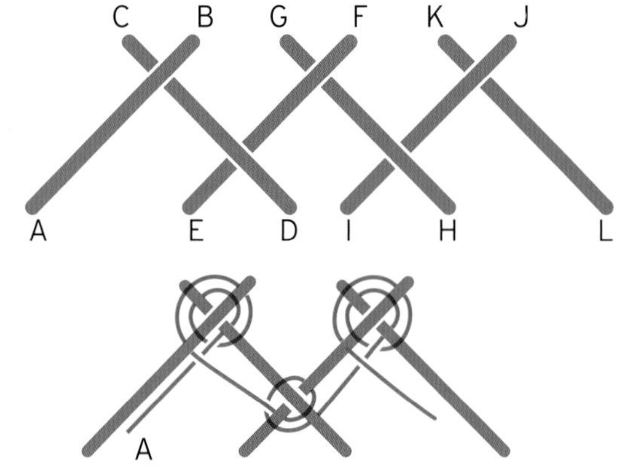

Figure 6 German interlacing

Raised cross stitch

Make a horizontal stitch from A to B, and a vertical stitch from C to D, to form a cross. Bring the needle up at E, which will be just under, and to the right, of the centre of the cross.

Change to the tapestry needle. Circle the thread anti-clockwise from E. Pass the needle under B without picking up the fabric. Pull the needle

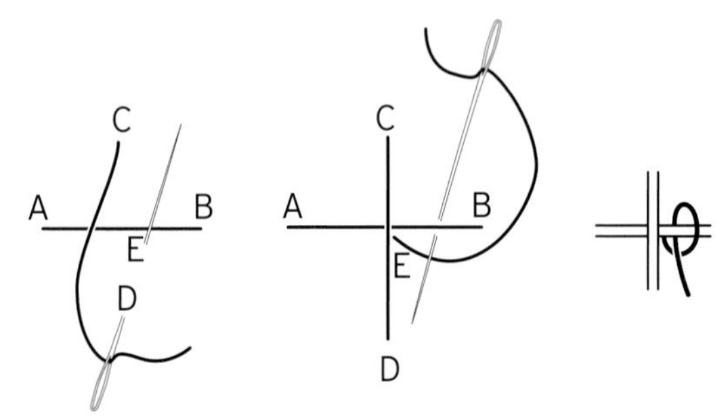

through to create a snug loop around the B arm of the cross. Push it over to the centre.

Still anti-clockwise, circle the thread, and pass the needle under C, and make another snug loop around the C arm of the cross. Continue working this way (anti-clockwise) around and around the arms of the cross until they have been completely covered.

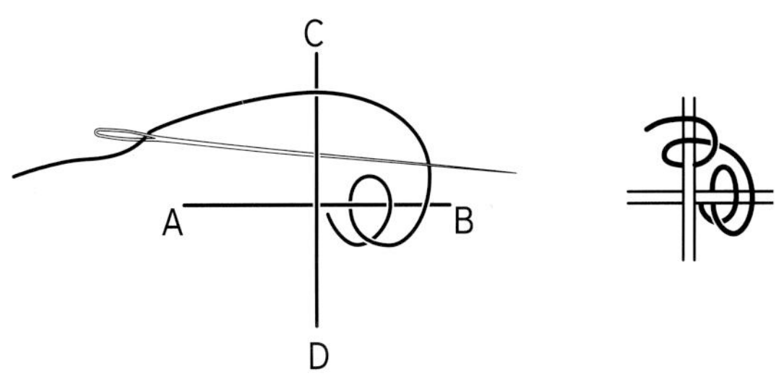

Figure 7 Raised cross stitch

Raised closed herringbone

Come up at A and go down at B to create a small vertical stitch that is about 2 mm (1⁄10 in) in length. Come up at C, which will be about 4 mm (2⁄10 in) below, and slightly left of the small vertical AB stitch. Pass the needle under the AB stitch from right to left without picking up the fabric. Go down at D, which is slightly right of C, and come up at E, which is just above C.

Pass the needle under AB again from right to left, and go down in the fabric at F and come up at G. Keep repeating this last step until AB has been covered. For this design, repeat this small diamond shape in a drop repeat pattern over the entire jacket.

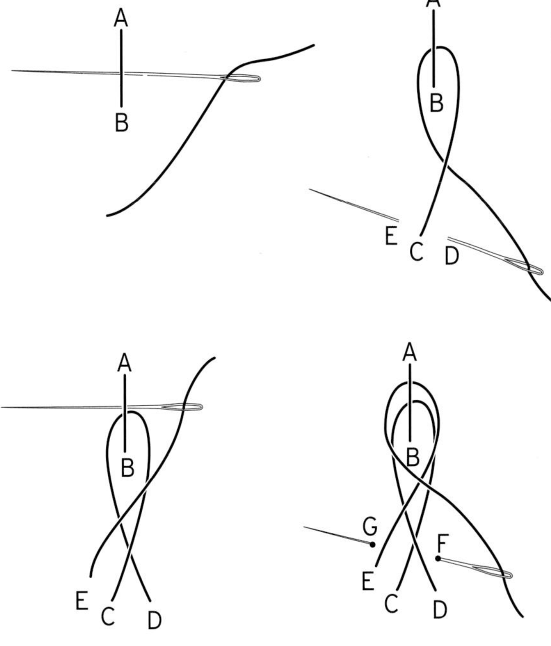

Figure 8 Raised closed herringbone

Maltese cross interlacing stitch

Work a grid for the first stage of this stitch.

Notice that on completion, the threads are alternating between passing under and over each other. It is important that you do not have two 'unders' or two 'overs' beside each other, either vertically or horizontally. If you do, you will find that in the second stage of this stitch, the interlacing thread will not remain looped around the intersection of a vertical and a horizontal.

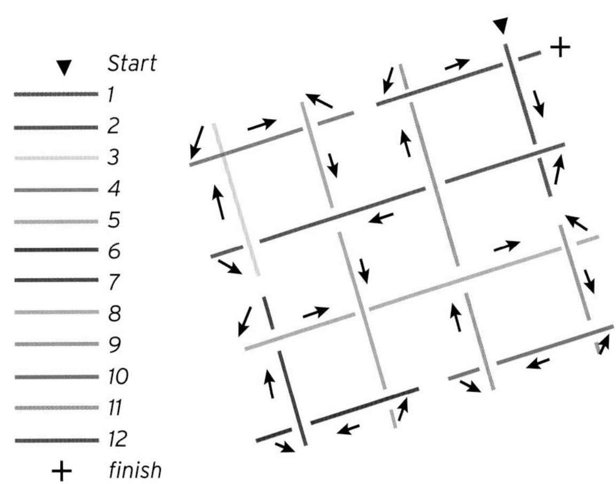

The second stage is the interlacing. X marks where the thread comes up to begin quarter 1 and where the thread will go down on the completion of quarter 4.

The interlacing thread has to pass under and over whatever thread it comes up to, whether it is a bar of the grid, or it is crossing over itself. There must not be two 'overs' or two 'unders' beside each other when lacing the bars.

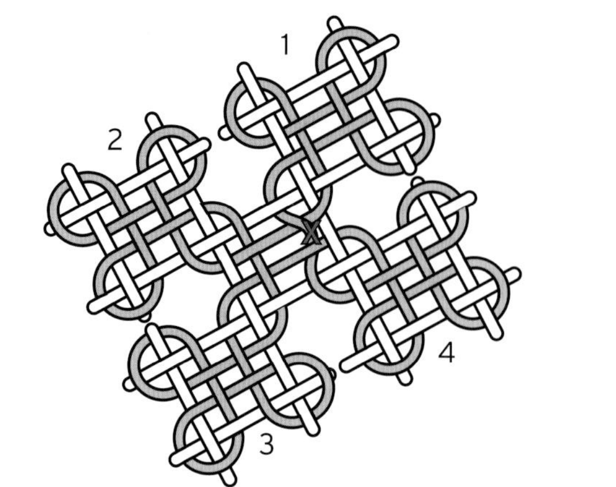

Figure 9 Maltese cross interlacing stitch

Raised chain band

Fill the long shape with 7 mm (3⁄8 in) horizontal bars. Keep a regular space of 3 mm (1⁄8 in) between the bars. Stitch in the alphabetical order, as shown above, to avoid overloading the back of the work with stitching.

Come up at A in the centre, above the top horizontal bar. Change to a tapestry needle. Pass the needle and thread up and under the first bar to the left of A.

Hold the thread down in a loop with your finger, and pass the needle down and under the bar, to the right of A. Pull the needle and thread completely through and over the loop of thread held with your finger, to make a chain.

Pass the needle and thread under and to the left of the next bar.

Hold the thread down in a loop with your finger, and pass the needle down to the right, and under the second bar. Pull the needle and thread completely through and over the loop of thread held with your finger, to make a second chain. Repeat Steps 4 and 5 down the ladder of bar stitches.

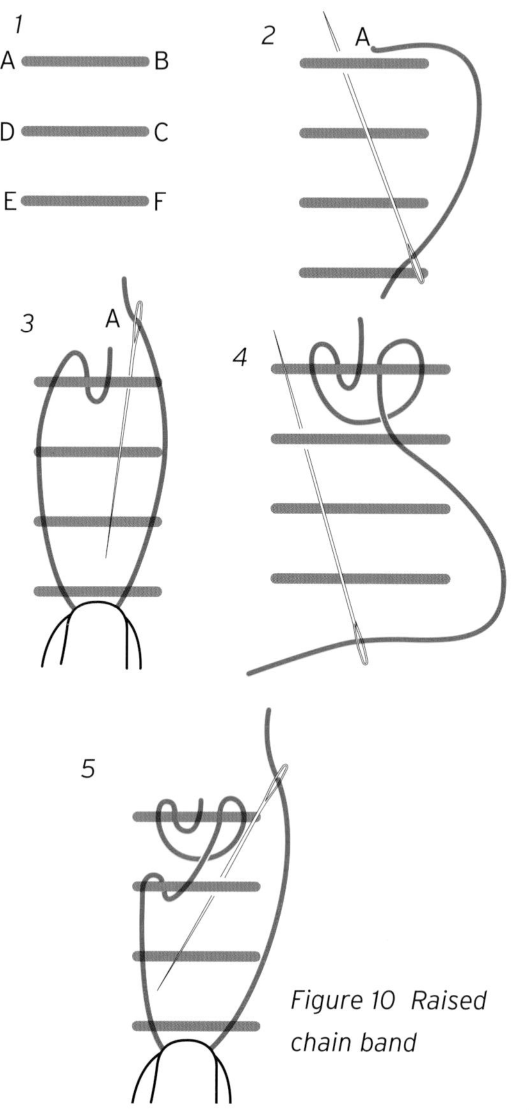

Figure 10 Raised chain band

Portuguese band

Fill the shape with 8 mm (4⁄10 in) horizontal bars. For this design, keep a regular space of 3 mm (1⁄8 in) between the bars. Stitch in the alphabetical order as shown to avoid overloading the back of the work with stitching.

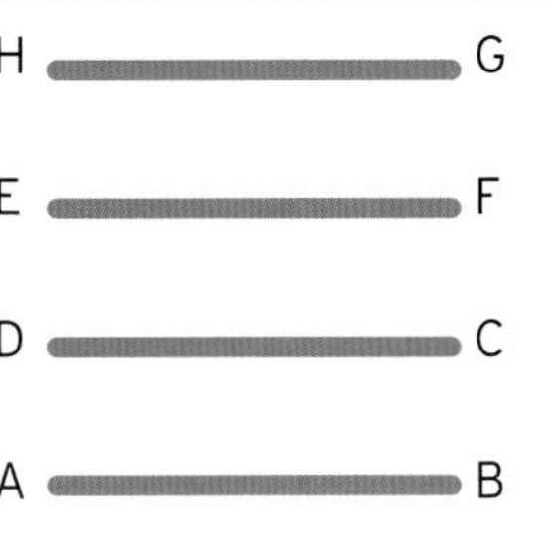

To begin the vertical rows of stem stitch over the bars, come up at 1 which is just slightly left of the centre of the bar. (The illustration is demonstrating the left-hand side rows of stem stitch.) Note that the left-hand side rows need to be worked separately to the right-hand side bars in order to create the V-shaped space running up through the centre of the band. Circle the thread over bars AB and CD. Slide the needle under both bars.

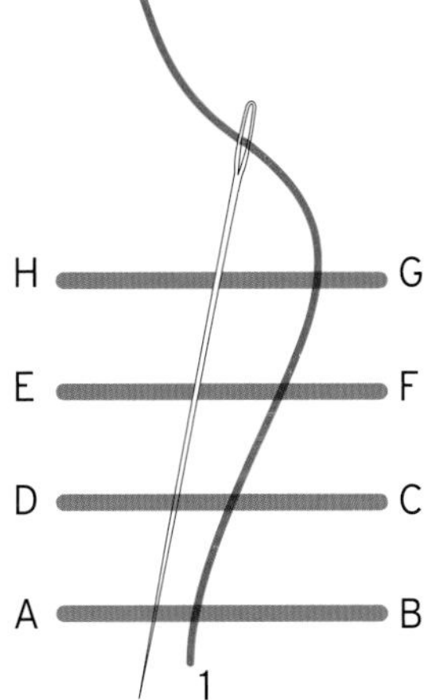

Circle the thread over bars AB and CD again, but this time, only pass the needle under bar CD and then circle the thread over bars CD and EF. Slide the needle under these two bars.

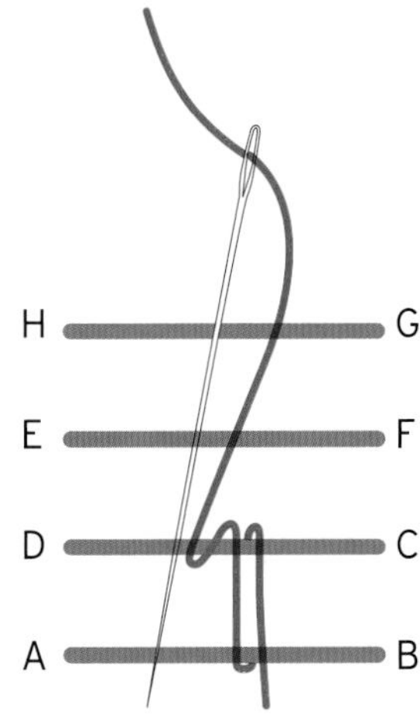

Circle the thread over bars CD and EF again, but this time, only slide the needle under the EF bar and then circle the thread over bars EF and GH. Repeat the above steps up the ladder of bars. Work in reverse for the right side rows.

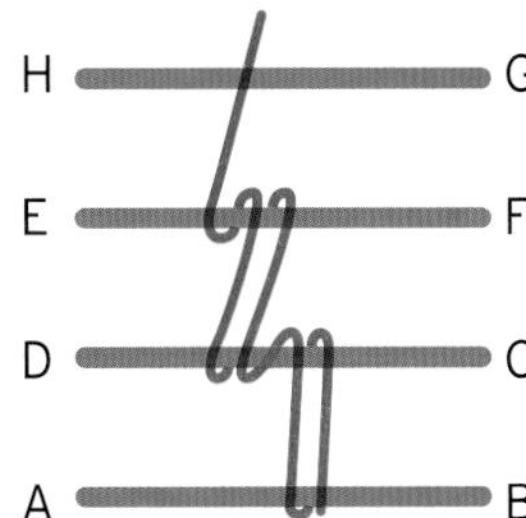

Figure 11 Portuguese band

Embroidery

The elements of the design to be embroidered are listed alphabetically in Figure 12 and matched to the alphabetical order of work which follows.

A The *laid work on the pediment* is comprised of four rows of couched no. 8 Japanese gold. The couching stitches (Gutermann 968) are 4 mm (2⁄10 in) apart and are 'bricked'. Fold four separate lengths of no. 8 Japanese gold in half. To reduce the number of tails to plunge, alternate between the turned ends and tails at the beginning and end of the rows. Plunge the tails separately.

Figure 12 *Alphabetical order of work*

B The *small semi-circle*, inside the larger velvet semi-circle in the pediment, is filled with rows of 2 mm (1⁄10 in) gilt spangles. Attach the spangles with a single thread of Gutermann 968. The bottom row is done first. Working from left to right, bring the needle up in the fabric, thread up a spangle, and drop the spangle to the bottom of the thread. Take the thread across the spangle at a 45° angle, as shown in Figure 13. Take the needle down, and bring the needle up again, as close as possible to the previous spangle. Thread up another spangle and attach it in the same way as the first. Repeat this last step across the bottom of the semi-circle. For the next row above (and for all succeeding rows), return to the left, and bring the needle up immediately above the spangle below. Repeat the same steps as for the first row.

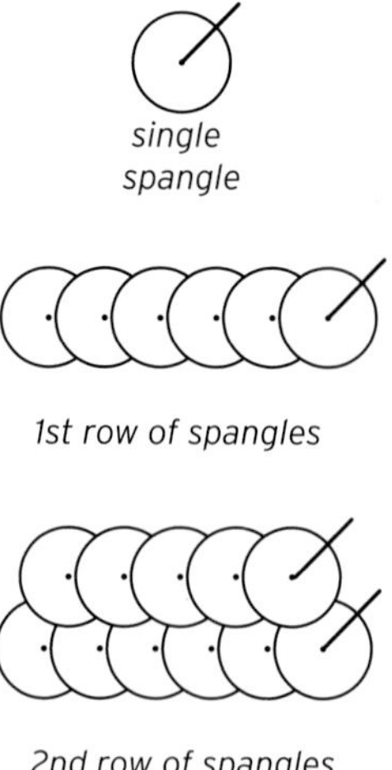

Figure 13 *The black dots represent where the thread comes up to attach a spangle*